HIGH PERFORMANCE

When Britain Ruled the Roads

PETER GRIMSDALE

**SIMON &
SCHUSTER**

London · New York · Sydney · Toronto · New Delhi

A CBS COMPANY

First published in Great Britain by Simon & Schuster UK Ltd, 2019
A CBS COMPANY

1 3 5 7 9 10 8 6 4 2

Simon & Schuster UK Ltd
1st Floor
222 Gray's Inn Road
London WC1X 8HB

www.simonandschuster.co.uk
www.simonandschuster.com.au
www.simonandschuster.co.in

Simon & Schuster Australia, Sydney
Simon & Schuster India, New Delhi

A CIP catalogue record for this book
is available from the British Library

Hardback ISBN: 978-1-4711-6845-1
Trade Paperback ISBN: 978-1-4711-6846-8
eBook ISBN: 978-1-4711-6847-5

Typeset in Sabon by M Rules
Printed and bound by CPI Group (UK) Ltd, Croydon, CR0 4YY

MIX
Paper from
responsible sources
FSC
www.fsc.org   FSC® C020471

OPER 1000 1275 **S'TYPES**

GB

For Jason

CONTENTS

INTRODUCTION

On the evening of 26 January 1964, upwards of 20 million view-
ers sat down to watch the nation's most popular show, ATV's
Sunday Night at the London Palladium. Bruce Forsyth was the
host, flanked by the glamorous, high-kicking Tiller Girls on a
vast, revolving stage. There, three months before, the Beatles
had made their first national TV appearance and Beatlemania
was born. If you were on the show, you had hit the big time. The
guest stars that January night were Kathy Kirby, whose single
'Let Me Go, Lover' had just made the Top Ten, comic-magician
Tommy Cooper and a very small red-and-white car flanked by
two nervous-looking young men in dark suits.

As the duo blinked into the lights, the orchestra struck up
'Rule, Britannia!' and the audience broke into applause to cele-
brate a most unlikely and peculiarly British triumph. The car was
a Mini Cooper, which just a few days before had achieved the
unthinkable: first place in the Monte Carlo Rally.

Paddy Hopkirk, the winning driver, and his navigator Henry
Liddon, were still trying to take it all in. In Hopkirk's pocket were
two telegrams. One was from 10 Downing Street and the other
from Ringo Starr, who said: 'It's nice to be number one, isn't it?'
But who, Hopkirk wondered, *was really the star tonight – him,
or the car?*

The Monte Carlo Rally sounds like a lot of fun. In reality, it's a brutal test of man and machine, played out across Europe in timed stages on ice-glazed mountain roads with multiple hairpin bends, much of it taking place at night.

That year, Ford of America shipped over no fewer than eight 4.7-litre, 300-horsepower Falcon Sprints to blast the opposition clean off the road. A handicap system went some way to evening out the odds between the massive American V8s and the Monte regulars – Mercedes, Citroëns and Lancias – but none of these could match the outright grunt of the Falcons. Beside them, the British Motor Corporation's (BMC) diminutive 1-litre Mini Coopers looked like no-hopers. But as Hopkirk and Liddon roared away from their starting line in Minsk under the glare of Kalashnikov-toting Russian guards for the dash across the Continent, they were not feeling quite as pessimistic as their rivals assumed they would be.

It may have had a fraction of the Falcons' raw power under its bonnet, but round the hairpin bends and up the sheer slopes of the Col de Turini in the Alpes-Maritime, the Mini came into its own. Its revolutionary, sideways-mounted engine and gearbox, front-wheel drive and all-round independent rubber suspension gave it giant-killing grip and agility. And deploying counter-intuitive techniques like left-foot braking – slowing the rear wheels while keeping the accelerator pressed to the floor – added to its apparent ability to defy the laws of physics.

Hopkirk gave it his all, finished the final timed stage, made the descent into Monte Carlo and went to bed. When French journalist Bernard Cahier knocked on his hotel-room door at 4am to tell him he had won, the British driver thought he was having a laugh.

The Mini was never envisaged as a racer. It was supposed to be an economy car, conceived after the Suez Crisis prompted a brief return of petrol rationing. Its winning ways were all down to the chance encounter, eighteen years before, of two of twentieth-century Britain's most iconoclastic engineers: a cerebral former child-refugee from Smyrna, Alec Issigonis, and John Cooper, a no-nonsense garage owner's son from Surbiton. Their first meeting, at a speed trial on Brighton's seafront in 1946, was the automotive equivalent of Keith Richards's and Mick Jagger's seismic first encounter on the platform at Dartford Station. After that, in motoring as in music, nothing would ever be the same.

The Mini Cooper's rise to international stardom is the closest thing Britain's car makers have to a creation myth, and like all the best creation myths, it makes no sense. How did an exercise in functional utilitarianism become both a track star and *the* must-have accessory for Swinging London's beautiful people – from Peter Sellers to Twiggy to Princess Margaret?

In 1964, the Mini was not the only British car to be catapulted into international stardom. For their third James Bond movie, *Goldfinger,* producers Harry Saltzman and Cubby Broccoli persuaded a little-known sports-car builder, Aston Martin, to loan them its latest development prototype. Production designer Ken Adam added a bulletproof shield, Browning machine guns, tyre shredders, revolving number plates and an ejector seat. For the Paris premiere, Sean Connery drove the Aston down the Champs-Élysées escorted by a praetorian guard of sixty gold-painted women, after which the car itself embarked on a world tour to plug the movie. *Goldfinger* recouped its $3 million budget in two weeks, broke box-office records worldwide and made the DB5 a global automotive star.

British cars and British drivers had a golden year in 1964. Lotus and BRM dominated Formula 1 – driven by Jim Clark and Graham Hill. British cars – Lotus, BRM and Brabham – won seven out of ten Grands Prix; Rover's revolutionary 2000 became the first European Car of the Year, the automotive Palme d'Or; Jaguar's new E-Type 4.2 out-glammed Ferrari for less than half the price; and Donald Campbell took his Bluebird up to 403 mph to become the fastest man on earth. All over the world, on road and track, Britain's cars were now the ones to beat, the climax of a twenty-year period of exceptional design and engineering achievement.

What made this all the more remarkable was that before the Second World War it had been quite a different story. In the '20s and '30s, Britain's car makers were deeply conservative and almost wilfully risk-averse, technically far behind America, France, Italy and Germany. Not since 1924 had a British machine won a Grand Prix.

And yet, by the 1960s, the British not only dominated Formula 1, they had overturned the rules of racing-car design, just as Issigonis's Mini revolutionised the thinking behind everyday road cars worldwide. A new generation of racers had emerged, led by Stirling Moss, Britain's first truly professional driver, and the Scottish prodigy Jim Clark, the first to have home-grown machinery with which to challenge the opposition – and win. And when indignant French, Italian and American officials tried to disqualify them, the ensuing furore merely added to the plucky Brits' reputation for ingenuity.

But to anyone with a good memory of the last decades of the twentieth century, these claims might come as a surprise. Why? Because the twenty years of stellar achievement after 1945 were almost completely obliterated by what came next – a perfect storm of strikes, oil crises, foreign competition and the rampant inflation of the 1970s that laid waste to Britain's car industry.

That gloomy saga of decline and fall, of militant workers, blinkered bosses and meddling politicians, still resonates. A slow-motion pile-up was played out through tabloid headlines and news footage of static production lines, grey men trudging into Downing Street for yet more deadlocked talks and strikers warming themselves round braziers outside factory gates. Forty years on, these are the images still seared onto the collective memory.

But you won't find any of those grey faces here. The heroes of this story were on a different trajectory. They were determined individualists, like Jaguar founder William Lyons dreaming up the XK engine while on fire-watching duty during the Coventry Blitz; the gifted, roguish Colin Chapman bunking off university lectures to flog the dodgy motors that funded his first Lotus. Alex Issigonis, the charming but stubborn genius behind the Morris Minor and Mini, who mixed with royals and lived with his mum; the playfully iconoclastic John Cooper, who revolutionised racing-car engineering using the remains of a pair of crashed Fiats; and the cerebral mathematician Malcolm Sayer, who used a slide rule to calculate the aerodynamic curves of his E-Type, which now graces New York's Museum of Modern Art.

So what was it about these plucky innovators? The *garagisti*, as Enzo Ferrari disparagingly dubbed them. What drove them? On the face of it, they seem to have had little in common. Among them were refugees, aristocrats, mechanics, artists, musicians and borderline criminals. In many ways they resembled the disparate and relentlessly ingenious serial escapers from German POW camps immortalised in *The Great Escape* (1963), whose obstinate determination and creative ingenuity might not have flowered in less testing circumstances. Indeed, Jaguar driver Tony Rolt was one of the brains behind the legendary Colditz Cock glider.

The lives of these designers and drivers were all profoundly shaped by the war, but also the years immediately after VE Day, when Britain's economic crisis threatened its very survival. Severely rationed, forced to seek out new markets to help save post-war Britain from bankruptcy, they thrived on adversity, using it as a further excuse to break long-established rules. But for the 1947 winter, the worst of that century, the Land Rover might never have come into existence; without the dollar crisis that almost sank Britain, America might never have fallen in love with the British sports car.

Many of the names of these mostly taciturn men have been forgotten. They were inclined to shun the limelight. Confronted with their achievements, they might look faintly embarrassed. So history somehow blinked and missed them. As the industry self-destructed in the '70s, many of its best and brightest retired, embittered and disillusioned, from the automotive stage. For the rest of the century it looked as if their legacy had vanished altogether.

But remarkably, in the twenty-first century, Mini and Jaguar, Bentley and Rolls-Royce, Aston Martin, Lotus and Land Rover, saved from oblivion, survive and thrive. Globally recognised as blue-chip brands, they sell in over 100 countries. And even when Britain's car manufacturers were imploding in the 1970s, the racing-car builders who had started out in lean-tos, stable blocks and draughty airfield Nissen huts survived unscathed to become a standalone £10-billion business. Today, when American, Japanese or German automotive giants want to go racing in Formula 1, they still have to start in what the *Wall Street Journal* has dubbed 'Gasoline Valley' – deep in the Home Counties, around the old aerodromes which were once home to the men and machines who fought the Battle of Britain.

Which is where this story begins.

THE FIRE-WATCHERS

In the early morning of 15 November 1940, William Lyons set off from his home in Leamington Spa for the 19-mile drive to the SS Cars factory in Foleshill, on the outskirts of Coventry. As he drove through the still-dark and deserted streets, he prepared himself for the worst.

That night, the Luftwaffe had launched Operation Mondscheinsonate (Moonlight Sonata), the systematic destruction of the city's industrial heart. For over ten hours, more than 400 bombers, wave after wave of them, pounded the city. The death toll would come to 568. Thankfully, a further 33,000 who had taken refuge in air-raid shelters survived the firestorm.

After the all-clear sounded, people streamed out of the ruined city, pushing belongings in prams, some just wandering, dazed, with nothing left but the clothes they stood up in. When Jean Taylor emerged from her shelter, she found an unrecognisable wasteland, devastation on a scale not seen in Britain since the Great Fire of London. 'I saw a dog running down the street with a child's arm in its mouth. There were lines of bodies stretched out on blankets. A poor fireman was watching helplessly while the buildings were still burning.'

As Lyons headed for his factory, the skyline was still aglow and shrouded in smoke. Triumph, Riley, Rover, Daimler, Morris and Armstrong Siddeley had been hit, along with the Alfred Herbert machine-tool works. A further nine aircraft factories were in flames.

Lyons pulled into Swallow Road and braced himself for what was ahead. 'As I stepped out of my car at the gates, I met a little man who we used to employ as a works barber. Where he had been I do not know, but he touched his cap and said: "A bit sharp this morning, sir."'

Spurred on by this spirited greeting, Lyons resolved to focus on the future and prepare for peace – however far off that might be. Like the rest of Coventry's car factories, his had been conscripted into Britain's war machine; first with a contract to repair Whitley bombers, then making parts for Spitfires, Lancasters and Mosquitoes. He'd also had a War Office order for ten thousand motorcycle sidecars, which was where he had started his manufacturing life some twenty years earlier.

Born in Blackpool in 1901, Lyons was a comparative latecomer to Britain's motor industry. His father, a musician who had come to Blackpool from Ireland, ran a piano-repair shop, the Music and Pianoforte Warehouse. But the young Lyons did not share his passion. He was smitten not by the seaside resort's thriving music halls, but by what was happening on the streets outside. Cars and motorcycles were where he found excitement. Not a good student, he was warned by his headmaster that he would 'never get anywhere messing about with engines'. Luckily for the British motor industry, Lyons failed to heed this advice.

He bought his first motorcycle from an older schoolmate, a 1911 Triumph that he rebuilt to a design he'd seen nowhere but inside his own head. When the Walmsley family moved in up the street, Lyon's eye was caught by their son's homemade motorcycle sidecar – a stylish, streamlined device of polished bare aluminium in an ash wood frame. William Walmsley, a war veteran nine years Lyons's senior, had learned the basics of bodywork by helping build wagons in his father's coal-merchant yard. The shape was reminiscent of the Zeppelin airships that were creating such excitement in the 1920s.

Lyons was smitten. The streamlined shape might have had some aerodynamic value, but what excited him was how an otherwise mundane, functional, passenger-carrying device had some visual excitement. It was an object of desire. He had to have one – but that was not all, as he explained in his own unpublished memoir: 'I became absorbed in the idea that the commercial prospects of the sidecar were very good and suggested to Walmsley that I would be willing to go into partnership with him to manufacture it in quantity.' But Walmsley said he was happy to lead a life of leisure and make the odd sidecar as a hobby. Lyons, however, despite his comparative youth, would not take no for an answer. Walmsley's parents, already concerned about how their war veteran son was going to get on in life, lent their support. Lyons got his way and, with a £1,000 overdraft guaranteed by their fathers, the Swallow Sidecar Company came into being in the summer of 1922. Officially it was founded on 4 September, once Lyons reached the age of twenty-one.

His hunch had been right. Within four years Swallow was selling over 100 units a month. But for him, the sidecars were just a stepping stone to greater things.

For the first half of the twentieth century, the process of car building involved two quite separate businesses: the manufacturers, who made the chassis and the moving parts, and the body builders. A common sight on Coventry streets in the '20s were convoys of chassis piloted by balaclava-clad drivers perched on no more than a soapbox en route to the coachbuilders, as they were still called, most of which dated back to the era of horse-drawn carriages. Hooper, a supplier of bodies to Rolls-Royce and Daimler, had been founded in 1805. The materials they used were mostly wood and fabric, and latterly sheet steel for mudguards and some panels. Even in the '20s, their designs for cars still owed much to the age of the horse – tall and square, with vertical windows, no hint of streamlining. Car dealers would supply finished vehicles or offer customers the option of specifying which coachwork they preferred.

Lyons saw an opportunity to apply the Swallow style to cars. He began with a modest Austin 7 chassis. The low roof, raked windscreen and rounded rear end he designed gave the modest little vehicle a fashionable look. He had them finished in two-tone paintwork, and where the contribution of most coachbuilders reached no further forward than the windscreen, Lyons concealed the radiator behind a curved, plated grille.

Although initially inspired by Walmsley's sidecar, these car bodies were all his own. Incredibly, despite this natural flair for line and style, Lyons could not draw at all, nor was he even much good with his hands. Instead, he relied on trained coachbuilders who could interpret his commands and – just as importantly – had the patience to respond to his fanatical attention to detail. With no craft skill or training, Lyons relied entirely on his keen eye and an ability to communicate it to the craftsmen he drew around him as they shaped the metal to order. Arguably, the lack of training actually freed him from any preoccupation with the internal structures. It was all about the look. Other people worked out how to build it. Steely and determined, his focus gained him the respect of those around him, but he hated interference, especially from his increasingly superfluous partner.

The Swallow car bodies were a hit. Soon, Lyons was getting complaints. 'The chassis from the Austin works at Longbridge [in Birmingham] had started to roll into Blackpool Talbot Road Station in embarrassing numbers. So much so that the station master complained bitterly that his goods yard was becoming completely congested.' In 1926, Lyons convinced Walmsley that they should move the business to Coventry, Britain's Detroit, a bustling, industrial metropolis of workshops and factories with a widely skilled workforce – a legacy of the city's nineteenth-century clock and bicycle trades from which many of Britain's car makers had emerged.

In 1931, Lyons designed his first complete car, a svelte coupé called the SS1, using a chassis and engine supplied by the Standard Motor Company. A few weeks before the launch, he was taken ill with appendicitis. On his return, he was horrified to find that Walmsley, bothered by the practicality of the low roofline, had raised it a couple of inches. Lyons was furious. 'The effect was ruinous to the appearance. The door sill line was two inches above the scuttle and the bonnet giving the top a conning tower look ... I hated it and felt very depressed.' For him, looks were everything, even if it meant sacrificing a little headroom.

It was too late to change it back, but that did nothing to dampen the rapturous reception his first SS received. The *Daily Express* praised its '£1,000 look' although it cost a mere £310. Soon after, Lyons, driven and ambitious, parted company with the soft-pedalling Walmsley, who went off to build caravans. From then on, there was no more interference. A saloon and an open two-seater followed, each with a style that belied its very reasonable price. In bold defiance of the prevailing British tendency to understatement, Lyons adopted raked windscreens, low-slung chassis and gracefully swooping mudguards. When he launched a more upmarket model in 1935, he called it the SS Jaguar. Some in the motoring establishment dismissed them as 'Wardour Street Bentleys', a dig at the less than respectable Soho base of Britain's nascent film industry. Critics who thought Lyons had got above himself also noted that under his long, sleek bonnets lurked prosaic pushro four- and six-cylinder engines from solid but unexciting Standard saloons.

Lyons knew that if he was to gain real credibility he needed to design and build his own engines from scratch. With this in mind, he had already recruited the talent, but the Nazi invasion of Poland put all that on hold. By 1940, virtually all car production was halted until further notice as the entire industry was mobilised for war production. Any diversion from the war effort, such as developing new models for peacetime, was also forbidden. With the government as his only customer, Lyons could not afford to fall foul of them. So he went undercover.

Fire-watchers were volunteers on the home front, charged to keep a lookout for blazes caused by incendiary bombs. Lyons put himself down for Sunday nights and arranged for three others to join him on the same shift: Bill Heynes, Claude Baily and Wally Hassan.

He had hired Heynes from Humber to be his chief engineer in 1934, before SS Cars even had a drawing office, and several years before much serious engineering was under way. But Heynes had found Lyons's ambition seductive; his new boss told him his aim was to create 'one of the world's finest luxury cars'.

Claude Baily was a designer he had lured from Morris in 1940 with the promise of developing a new engine from scratch. Hassan was the wild card. Taken on as a shop boy at the age of fifteen by Bentley, he had soon graduated to mechanic on the Le Mans racers of playboy-financier-driver Woolf Barnato. Through the 1930s he continued to work exclusively on racing cars at Britain's one and only purpose-built race track, Brooklands. With his experience of exotic, hand-built racing engines, Hassan was an unlikely choice for a company aspiring to mass-produce, but he had earned Lyons's respect by getting more power out of the Standard-derived engine in the pre-war SS 100, and for what Lyons had in mind, his pedigree fitted the bill. He wanted some of that Bentley stardust sprinkled on his first in-house engine.

Lyons's secret dream team was complete. As they huddled together in the blackout, listening out for bombers in the night sky, he set down his requirements. No one knew what to expect after the war. Rationing was likely to continue and the chances were that people wouldn't have much money to spend on luxury goods. Nevertheless, he remained devoted to the idea of the high-performance model he had promised Heynes he would build one day.

Heynes found that, with Lyons, his own talents could finally flourish. At his previous employers, Rootes, the wariness of innovation that prevailed was typical of the industry in the 1930s. He recalled the reaction when he showed his independent front suspension for the Hillman Minx to the chief engineer. '"Well, Heynes, who else is using this type of design?" "No one else to my knowledge, sir," I replied. "It's new." "Oh, well in that case I think we had better leave it." That attitude would never have occurred to Lyons, who was all for innovation: being new was an immediate attraction to him.' In the risk-averse British motor industry of the late 1930s, such thinking was heretical.

To Baily's and Hassan's dismay, Lyons insisted that their engine have twin overhead camshafts, which were common on foreign racing engines but rarely seen on mainstream British machines. Even Hassan, who from his Brooklands days had first-hand experience of such machinery, was wary:

> I pointed out that this would be expensive and probably fairly noisy too ... However this didn't satisfy him at all and if he wasn't completely satisfied with anything he would never agree to it. His new engine would have to be good looking, with all the glamour of the famous engines produced for racing in previous years, so that when you opened the bonnet of a post-war Jaguar you would be looking at power and be impressed. He got his way of course – Mr Lyons always did – but I must admit that the rest of us thought it was rather a waste of time and money at that time.

Lyons, always with an eye for style, even cared about how his car looked under the bonnet.

Knowing that the boss always got his way, Hassan realised there was little point in arguing. The others fell into line. As searchlights swept the skies for enemy bombers, the team got their heads down over scraps of paper, by torchlight planning the engine that they would one day build. They and their nocturnal plans survived the war, but what was about to hit them when peace finally came threatened to put Lyons out of business altogether.

2

EXPORT OR DIE

The first peacetime gathering of the Society of Motor Manufacturers and Traders (SMMT) took place on 15 November 1945. It was supposed to be a celebration. The war was over; Britain was on the winning side; and its motor-industry bosses, who had done so well applying themselves to the war effort, deserved a jolly good pat on the back, so thought the society's president, Reginald Rootes.

But Reggie Rootes was not having a good night. The Labour government's president of the Board of Trade, Sir Stafford Cripps – vegetarian, teetotaller and Reggie's guest of honour, was showing little interest in the lavish spread he had laid on. Winston Churchill said of Cripps: 'He has all the virtues I hate and none of the vices I admire.' An ascetic figure, he had embraced wartime austerity with a messianic zeal that he saw no reason to abandon now that victory had been declared.

Cripps was a wealthy barrister, who had also managed a munitions factory in the First World War, whose privilege seemed entirely at odds with his far-left views. He had been expelled from the Labour Party in the '30s for advocating an alliance with the Communist Party. Churchill had cannily made him his ambassador to Moscow, where he distinguished himself by building the alliance with the Soviets after Hitler's invasion of Russia. Later in the war he served as minister for aircraft production, rejoining Labour in time for their landslide victory in 1945.

Now, as the new government's trade commissar, he was on a fresh mission: to explain to the captains of Britain's motor industry assembled in front of him that November night how to do their jobs. In his speech he even told them what they should be making: 'We must provide a cheap, tough, good-looking car of decent size – not the sort of car we have hitherto produced for the smooth roads and short journeys of this country. And we must produce them in sufficient quantities to get the benefits of mass production.'

Undeterred by the harrumphing from his audience, he pressed on: 'This is what we had to do with aircraft engines . . . We concentrated on two or three types only and mass-produced them – not a dozen different sizes in penny numbers. My own belief is that we cannot succeed in getting the volume of export we must have if we disperse our efforts over numberless types and makes.'

To the audience, what Cripps was advocating sounded much the same as what Stalin's industrialists had planned for the Soviet auto industry: collectivisation; a single, utilitarian, state-sponsored design, assembled from standardised components, with all the inherent economies of scale. To Reggie's intense embarrassment, the barely suppressed grumblings now broke out into open hostility, the air thick with howls of derision and actual cries of 'Tripe!'

Cripps waited a few seconds for the audience to calm down, then continued: 'I have often wondered whether you thought that Great Britain was here to support the motor industry, or the motor industry was here to support Great Britain.' Cripps couldn't care less what his audience thought of him; he knew he had them by the balls.

Government rationing of food, clothing and raw materials had been a fact of life for the duration of the war. The outbreak of peace was expected to have made things better and hopes were high. But the new Labour government had to face up to the fact that the war had left the country broke.

Fighting the Axis Powers had swallowed up approximately one quarter of the national wealth. Over £1.2 billion of imports were needed just to maintain wartime levels of consumption. Britain was haemorrhaging money just to survive. The promise of an ambitious social-welfare programme, on which the Attlee government had fought and won the election with a landslide 146-seat parliamentary majority, looked like a pipe dream.

And worse was to come. In the immediate aftermath of VJ Day, the Truman administration in Washington terminated their lend-lease agreement, which had kept Britain supplied with food and raw materials for much of the war. The government's chief economic negotiator, John Maynard Keynes, did not hold back. He called it a 'financial Dunkirk'.

Britain needed hard cash – specifically dollars – to pay for the food, fuel and raw materials it would have to continue to import from the USA, without which there was the very real prospect the country could starve. One of Cripps's first moves was to press-gang the car industry into earning those dollars. And he had a very powerful incentive at his disposal. During the war the government had controlled the supply of steel; now it decreed that to receive any at all, each manufacturer would be compelled to export a percentage of its output. And that figure would soon rise from 30 per cent to a whopping 50 per cent.

Not only did this smack of nationalisation by the back door, when Britain's wilfully independent motor magnates were straining to break free from wartime government control, apart from shipments of cars to the captive markets of the empire, they had next to no experience of exports. There had simply been no incentive. Since 1915 the country's home market had been sheltered by the McKenna duties, a punitive 33.3 per cent levy on imports dating back to the First World War, which effectively choked off almost all foreign competition. It was originally intended to fend off the threat from Detroit, but it would protect Britain's motor industry from European producers as well. Consequently, Britain's car bosses had no experience of export or of serious competition, nor had they any idea whether their cars would sell abroad at all – let alone in America.

Since 1910, road tax, also known as horsepower tax, had been calculated according to engine size, specifically the diameter and number of cylinders. So the industry produced engines that tried to minimise tax charges, with tall, narrow-diameter cylinder bores in which the piston had to make a longer stroke. Long-stroke engines suited Britain's narrow, twisty roads and hills but ran out of puff at higher speeds. They were wholly unsuited to foreign territories, particularly America's endless highways.

There was some logic to Cripps's diktat. Economies of scale through standardisation would theoretically improve industrial efficiency and deliver higher profits. That was Henry Ford's method. But Britain's independent-minded car makers had always fiercely resisted consolidation. Mass-production practices had been adopted but not on anything like the same scale – nor with the same rigour – as Detroit. The network of small workshops and skilled tradesmen that had shaped Coventry's industrial character in the nineteenth century still lingered in the Midlands car industry half a century on.

There were exceptions. Ford of Britain in Dagenham, outpost of the Detroit giant, and Vauxhall in Luton, swallowed up by General Motors in 1925, strove to follow best American practice. Austin and Morris had gone some way to streamline production processes to suit the scale of their businesses, but Hillman, Humber, Singer, Sunbeam, Rover, Triumph and Jowett had all evolved from the bicycle trade. Armstrong Siddeley, Standard, Wolseley, Daimler and Rolls-Royce either sprang from or diversified into wider engineering operations. None of them had the means to invest in modern, mass-production plants. Nor did they see the point. The basic engineering design principles to which most companies' models adhered had changed little since the motor car's invention half a century before. The layout pioneered in the 1890s by the Paris automobile makers Panhard et Levassor became the industry standard: an engine with vertical cylinders in a line, mounted between a pair of steered front wheels driving a pair of rear wheels via a propeller shaft.

Independent suspension, front-wheel drive, monocoque or unibody construction – which combined the body with the chassis – were developments embraced by European firms like Citroën, Fiat, Lancia and Mercedes-Benz in the 1930s, all of which Britain shunned.

And despite being the world's second-biggest car producer by the end of the '30s, Britain's products – with the notable exception of Rolls-Royce – had almost no presence outside the country and its shrinking empire. The industry was stuck in the slow lane and in danger of running out of road.

That night at the SMMT banquet, Reggie Rootes, sitting next to Stafford Cripps as he delivered his highly unwelcome message, had even more reason to be worried than the rest of the room. He had just received a report from his brother Billy in New York. And it made terrifying reading.

The Rootes brothers were talented pioneer car salesmen from the picturesque Kent village of Goudhurst, who in the year leading up to the First World War managed to sell a stratospheric six hundred vehicles. In the '30s they expanded into car making, acquired a clutch of failing marques, including Hillman, Humber and Sunbeam, and forged them into a competitive suite of brands. Hillman was its bread-and-butter model; Sunbeams were for the more sporting; and Humbers conveyed company directors, government ministers and, famously, Field Marshal

Montgomery. His 'victory car', a Humber Super Snipe tourer, had survived being dropped forty feet into the English Channel while being unloaded at a floating Mulberry Harbour on D-Day and took Monty all the way to Berlin. The brothers' passion for motor cars ran deep. 'No other man-made device since the shields and lances of the ancient knights fulfils a man's ego like an automobile,' Billy Rootes claimed. They prided themselves on being adaptable and forward-thinking. If any firm could meet the challenge of the new post-war world order, it should have been the Rootes Group.

But over in America Billy had seen the future, and it had given him a fright. Not only were Detroit's car designs way ahead, their industry had managed to keep some production going. He wrote: 'We have been completely submerged in warfare while America has never been 100% at war.'

While British car design had been on hold, the Americans had roared ahead. Pressed-steel bodies had become standard practice in Detroit. Previously separate parts like radiators, headlights and mudguards had been absorbed into one all-consuming, jelly-mould shape. The profile of a typical American car was no longer 'two box' – one for seating, one for the engine – but had sprung a third: a trunk, or boot. In fact, the term 'box' was obsolete, since Detroit's stylists were now using clay models to mould and sculpt smooth, contoured shapes. American cars had also cruised ahead mechanically. Softer suspension and fatter tyres gave them a svelte, comfortable ride as they barrelled along, effortlessly powered by big, six-cylinder or V8 engines.

Even worse, Billy calculated that the cost of building a car in Detroit was only 10–20 per cent higher than in 1939, whereas in Britain it had gone up an eye-watering 60–80 per cent. He warned his brother that 'the cost of any volume product in Britain today is so ridiculously high that we cannot hope to compete.' His conclusion was bleak. 'It is only in specialised products that we are on an equal footing.' And although he had no idea at the time, it was brilliantly prophetic.

But what exactly were these 'specialised products' that could compete with Detroit and earn much-needed dollars? The Rootes brothers were at a loss. Fifteen miles away from that smoke-filled banqueting hall in central London, at a petrol station in Surbiton, one young man would have the answer, but he didn't know it yet. He was just working out how to build his first car.

3

SUBURBAN TEARAWAY

Around seven o'clock one Friday morning in July 1946, commuters heading to Surbiton Station were taken aback to see a young man with a shock of black, Brylcreemed hair, belted into a gabardine overcoat, at the wheel of a tiny silver vehicle. Its exposed wheels had no mudguards, the unpainted aluminium body looked like an upturned dinghy with a hole cut in it, and its windscreen was no more than a narrow crescent of Perspex, like an oversized nail-clipping. In an effort to ward off unwanted police attention, the driver had strapped on a pair of garage trade plates with red characters on a white background and added a makeshift silencer to muffle the machine-gun crackle of its exhaust.

He headed along Ewell Road towards the Kingston bypass, one of Britain's first arterial roads, built in the late '20s. Wide and smooth, with no speed limit, it made an ideal test track. And there he opened up the throttle. He wouldn't be able to tell exactly how fast he was going because he had no instruments in front of him other than a rev counter. But it was enough to put a big grin on his broad face. John Cooper had built his first racing car, in just five weeks. He was only twenty-three and he was about to turn motor sport back to front – literally.

Racing ran deep in Cooper's blood. Before the First World

War his father Charles had been apprenticed to engine builders Napier in Acton, which brought him into contact with its director, the pioneer racing driver Selwyn Edge, and the exotic world of Brooklands, then the Mecca for Britain's first motorists and aviators. After enlisting in 1914, Charles's time in the Motor Transport Mechanical Cavalry Division gave him access to an even wider variety of vehicles. Gassed at Valenciennes only weeks before the armistice, he discharged himself and in the '20s found work reconditioning ex-army motorcycles.

On weekends he was back at Brooklands, looking after the cars of wealthy playboy racers Kaye Don and 'Ginger' Hamilton, members of the circuit's fast set. For the young mechanic, it opened a window onto a charmed and exclusive world where eye-watering sums of inherited wealth were squandered on extravagant, temperamental machinery. It was easy to be dazzled by the unobtainable lifestyle, but Charles was nobody's fool. Short-fused and famously tight with money, he saved enough to buy a lease on a derelict builder's yard where he built a successful garage and took on whatever work came his way. As John's childhood friend and collaborator Eric Brandon remembers, 'whenever there was a crash on the Kingston bypass the bell of the ambulance would come whizzing down the road ringing its bell ... and then there'd be Charlie Cooper cranking up his breakdown truck and rumbling off in hot pursuit to get the business.'

But Charles was also a dream dad. For John's eighth birthday, he built him a car powered by a lawnmower engine. John loved driving it around the garage and at local carnivals; he was the envy of his schoolmates. When he outgrew it, his father built him a second 'special', with an Austin 7 engine to which he'd added another carburettor. The thirteen-year-old John almost managed an entire circuit of Brooklands, taking it up to 90mph, before being flagged down by furious marshals. As he recalled later: 'It really was quite something; a very quick little car ... but I was caught and given a terrific rollicking!'

The outbreak of the Second World War brought this charmed life to an abrupt end. The fast set dispersed and Brooklands' hangars were pressed into full-scale aircraft production; its massive, banked, concrete corners never to be used in anger again. And while Charles secured lucrative contracts to service fire engines on the home front, John, at sixteen – still too young to be called up – joined a top-secret company under the control of the Admiralty, developing midget submarines. He did eventually make it into the RAF but by early 1946 he was demobbed. With the country still in the grip of rationing and beset by shortages, there seemed to be little scope for the action and excitement he craved.

Before the war, British cars and drivers had achieved only sporadic international success. The last Grand Prix winner in a British car had been Henry Segrave in 1924. And for a few precious years at the end of the '20s, W. O. Bentley's thunderous green machines had dominated Le Mans, until his racer-financier, the buccaneering diamond heir Woolf Barnato, lost interest and pulled the plug.

Throughout the '30s, motor racing remained the preserve of wealthy amateurs. A British driver good enough to turn professional had to swallow his patriotism and sign with one of the foreign factory stables from the emerging fascist states: Mercedes, Auto Union or Alfa Romeo. Only one Brit would make the grade. Standing on the podium after winning the 1938 German Grand Prix in a works Mercedes-Benz, surrounded by officials sporting swastika armbands, Richard Seaman gave a rather tentative obligatory Nazi salute and whispered down to *Autocar*'s John Dugdale: 'I wish it could have been in a British car.'

In post-war Surbiton, where his father was now assembling caravans in the big asbestos shed behind his garage, Cooper junior dreamed of racing. But cars that had survived the conflict were changing hands for double their pre-war value. Motor sport looked like it was going to become even more of an exclusive, rich boys' cadre.

To keep up morale during the depths of the war, a group of racing enthusiasts from the Bristol Aeroplane Company at Filton had formed a motor club. Actual competition was out of the question, so to keep the flame alive they invited speakers from the great and good of motor sport who regaled them with stories of great days at Brooklands and made stirring claims about what to expect if ever things got back to normal. But no matter how much they wished it, there would never be a return to the old order.

In keeping with the spirit of the time, the club members imagined a brave, new, more egalitarian world. They decided to draw up a new set of rules that explicitly favoured the aspiring car builder facing the challenge of scarce materials and rationed petrol. They called it '500 Formula' because it stipulated engines no larger than 500cc and cars weighing no less than 500lbs: 'A minimum weight of 500lbs will allow builders of 500cc cars to construct wheels, chassis and other highly stressed parts from materials which have been adapted from parts already in existence. There is, of course, nothing to prevent the construction of cars from light alloys; in fact builders are advised to incorporate as much light alloy as possible.'

Constructors were encouraged to beg, borrow and adapt, but also to make the most of the plentiful quantities of lightweight materials that the wartime aircraft industry had generated. The 500cc engine limit meant the use of motorcycle engines. And in keeping with the austere times, it decreed that petrol tanks should hold no more than 1 gallon and bodywork was to be 'optional but desirable'.

One hundred and twenty miles away, John Cooper studied the Bristol Motor Club manifesto closely. He didn't have much cash, but there were other resources to hand. Over the years, in the yard behind the garage, his father had accumulated various automotive casualties. Combing through these, John's attention was caught by the remains of a written-off, pre-war Fiat Topolino.

Its rear end had been destroyed in a heavy shunt, but the front was undamaged. Dante Giacosa, its legendary Italian designer, had equipped his 'Little Mouse' with a highly innovative independent front suspension, using the combination of a transverse leaf spring with a pair of wishbones. It was very light yet very effective.

The logical next step might have been to go in search of a whole chassis. But that didn't interest Cooper. The Fiat's back wheels were mounted on a solid axle with a conventional pair of cart springs. He scoured the local garages and scrap yards until he found what he wanted just six miles away – in Walton on Thames, in the garage of Fiat agent John Heath. The bemused Heath, who would later build racing cars himself, was happy to let John have what he wanted – another Topolino *front* end.

Back in Ewell Road, Cooper stripped the wrecks, laid them back to back on the garage floor and proceeded to butt-weld them together. Now he had a chassis with all four wheels independently sprung, a feature not yet seen on the most advanced racing cars.

The four-cylinder Fiat engine was just too big to conform to the Bristol Motor Club formula. In any case, he wanted something lighter, specifically a single-cylinder, 500cc JAP speedway motorcycle engine. But that posed a problem.

For half a century, the conventional layout of a car positioned the driver between the engine at the front and the rear wheels, with the propeller shaft taking the power from one to the other, beneath the seats. But motorcycle engines then delivered their power via a chain.

Since it was not practical to have a chain running from a front engine to rear wheels, Cooper's solution was to fly in the face of convention a second time and simply put the engine *behind* the driver. Much later, when Enzo Ferrari saw Cooper's creation, he would laugh: 'The ox does not push the cart!' Cooper, it turned out, knew better, though his choice, he later claimed, with characteristic understatement, 'was just a matter of convenience'.

Five weeks later, as he blasted along the bypass in the finished product, he discovered his little machine handled like a dream.

4

BRIEF ENCOUNTER

The following weekend, with his pal and helper Eric Brandon, Cooper loaded his new machine onto the back of one of his father's war-surplus US Army Chevrolet trucks and headed to Prescott, a private hill-climb track in the Cotswolds. It was raining hard, but a crowd of diehard enthusiasts wrapped up in ex-War Department gas capes clustered round the strange, new, back-to-front machine. The hill climb was a time trial, one car at a time. When Cooper's turn came, he revved the engine and lifted off the clutch pedal. The car surged forward, then – with a loud bang – came to a stop. The engine mounts had sheared.

Cooper and Brandon retreated to a garage near Leominster where, under torchlight, they scoured the place for something they could use to repair and strengthen the broken mounts. After much searching, they found a track rod from an old bus, hacked off a length and welded up the broken parts.

Next morning they were back. The rain had cleared and Cooper attacked the hill again, dashed into the unforgiving Pardon Hairpin too fast, missed a gear as he tried to change down, over-revved the little engine and bent a valve.

Back at Prescott a few weeks later, John spun the car on

Orchard Corner and snapped the engine mounts again. But its speed and agility were already raising eyebrows.

Cooper came up with a new flexible mount, tried it out on more early-morning runs on the bypass and then they headed south. On Saturday, 7 September 1946, Brighton staged its first post-war speed trials. This seafront event, held on the closed-off Madeira Drive since 1905, consisted of a sprint, from a standing start, down the 1-kilometre straight, against the clock. To make it more exciting, competitors were sent off in pairs. On this bright autumn day, after a seven-year gap, stewards had their hands full; a crowd of five hundred had turned up, double the expected number.

There was no separate class for 500cc vehicles, so Cooper had to take his chances against mightier machinery. As he manoeuvred into position, he found himself pitted against another one-off homemade racer, the exquisitely finished – if somewhat unimaginatively named – Lightweight Special.

He could not help admiring it. It had no chassis; all the parts were bolted onto a stiff, monocoque body of alloy-faced plywood – like an aircraft fuselage. Where the Cooper was cobbled together with parts plundered from wrecks, the Lightweight Special was stuffed with exotic, purpose-built features like rubber suspension and Elektron magnesium alloy wheels, all of which made it astonishingly advanced for its day. At the wheel was its designer, a gangly engineer called Alexander Constantine Issigonis.

Like their creators, the two cars could not have been more different. Issigonis's was the progeny of a cerebral theoretician, each part painstakingly hand-crafted over several years by a tireless, perfectionist control freak, until every last detail met with his satisfaction. Cooper's was the work of a can-do pragmatist, an adapter, improviser, slammed together in a mere five weeks. But there were some key characteristics the two machines did share. Both were extremely light; both had independently sprung wheels; and each in its own way embodied the contrary attitude of their creators.

When the flag fell, the two sped down the straight, neck and neck. Issigonis's 750cc engine was half as big again as Cooper's tiny single-cylinder JAP. But Cooper's was the lighter and more nimble of the two. His time was the fastest of the day for their class. Issigonis came a close second.

It would be another fifteen years before the two mavericks joined forces. When they did, the result would be a perfect synthesis of their two dramatically contrasting personalities, and motoring history would be made.

In October 1947, the final event in the 500 Club's season was supposed to be a circuit race. But in post-war Britain the three race tracks that had existed in the 1930s – Donington, Crystal Palace and Brooklands – were out of operation. A farmer near Towcester whose land had been turned into a bomber base during the war said they could have the run of it for an afternoon. At the time of the Battle of Britain, Hurricanes and Spitfires took off from grass airfields, but as the bombing campaign developed, and with the arrival of US Air Force squadrons, concrete runways replaced them. The standard RAF airfield design was an extended triangle of runway encircled by a perimeter road, servicing the base's buildings and hangars. It made a handy ready-made race track. This one was called RAF Silverstone.

Cooper and eight other teams showed up, unloaded their cars and tried a few practice laps. A man on a bicycle appeared, the airfield caretaker, who insisted they were trespassing on government property. The racers stood their ground. The infuriated caretaker cycled off and returned with a police Wolseley in tow. The constable behind the wheel was grudgingly obliged to do his bidding. Had they arrived a bit later, he told them, they would have been in the clear; the caretaker knocked off for the weekend at noon. As it was, Silverstone would have to wait another year before it could become the new home of British motor sport.

But just as he was pulling away, the policeman made a

suggestion. They could trying calling at Easton Neston, the country house with Towcester race course in its grounds. It was a bit of a long shot, but at this point they had nothing to lose.

The door was answered not by a butler, but by the owner, Lord Hesketh himself, accompanied by a cluster of yapping miniature poodles. He invited them all in, plied them with sherry and said they could have the grounds whenever they wanted. The day was saved.

~

Cooper's tiny car had made its mark. What had started out as a hobby, a diversion from the grim austerity of post-war Britain, seemed to be developing its own momentum. He and his school friend Eric Brandon built a second car. Other drivers were asking if he could build one for them, but Cooper still focused on trying to be a racer – and have fun. For their first event overseas, on the Isle of Man, Cooper decided to raise his game and shoehorned a 1-litre engine into his car. This step up brought him into contact with an altogether different crowd from the brave new 500 racers. Among them were Duncan Hamilton, Bob Gerard, Freddie Dixon and Tony Rolt, all of them promising drivers of the 1930s, their best years stolen by the war, who were hell-bent on making up for lost time.

When the boat docked they drove their race cars along the seafront and parked them outside the Majestic Hotel, where pre-race partying began in earnest.

In no time they had fused the hotel lights, uprooted young trees and planted them round the bar, and Freddie Dixon – well into his fifties – destroyed a piano. The police were called, ordered them all to bed and they meekly promised to retire. However, as soon as the law had left, someone poured petrol and benzol into the swimming pool and set it ablaze. The Majestic had a modest smallholding in its grounds. A pass key was procured and several geese, hens and pigs were introduced into the rooms of unsuspecting guests.

Despite all the attention the hell-raising old guard attracted, all eyes were soon focusing on newcomer John Cooper's car and the replica he had now built for his pal Eric Brandon. Race after race went their way; the lethal combination of an exceptional power-to-weight ratio coupled with the handling advantages bestowed by the Fiat suspension and the position of the engine gave the Cooper its giant-killing competitive edge.

What his design had going for it was something Cooper was blissfully unaware of at the time: it is what mathematicians call a 'low polar moment of inertia'.

Inertia is the tendency mass has to continue in its existing state – be it static or moving in a straight line – unless it is changed by a force. The polar moment of inertia is a measure of the effort needed to make mass turn or change direction. The more mass there is near the front of the car the more effort it takes to change direction. And with an engine right at the back of a car (such as a Porsche 911 or a VW Beetle), more effort is needed to prevent the back end swinging out, trying to continue in the direction it was going before the turn. By positioning the driver and engine close to the centre of the car, Cooper had achieved the compelling advantage of a low polar moment of inertia. Put simply, he could go into a corner faster, break later and accelerate away earlier, lessening the chance of sliding off the track or getting into a spin. Although neither he nor anyone else realised at the time, it would change the way all racing cars were built – for ever.

Characteristically, the modest, affable John Cooper would be at pains to play down the secrets of his success: 'It wasn't that we were doing anything startlingly new, as the fact was that for the first time we combined a variety of known features into one car and made them work very well together.' His knowledge of maths and physics were not taught; they were developed by trial and error.

Cooper was exhibiting both an instinct for innovation and the inner confidence to go his own way, to break the rules. These were the fundamental qualities that would power his generation of British engineers and drivers forward. There was a lot of ground yet to cover and many setbacks ahead, but the seeds were being sown for revolution. Although he was a very different character and on a very different trajectory, Cooper's progress had something in common with that of William Lyons: the confidence to judge by look and feel and to hell with convention.

The clamour from other drivers wanting a Cooper for themselves was not going away. John was willing to oblige but the supply of wrecked Fiat Topolino front ends was drying up. The only thing to do was start from scratch.

John appealed to his father for help. Charles was naturally wary. Back in his Brooklands days he had watched the fortunes of rich, young things disappear in clouds of exhaust. As he saw it, no one had ever made actual money building racing cars, and tying up a lot of capital in an unknown venture was not his style at all. But all his years in motor sport also told him that his son had created something special with real competitive advantage. He grudgingly agreed to John's suggestion of a pilot run of twelve cars. To protect himself from any potential claims, he insisted on setting up a separate business.

The Cooper Car Company was incorporated on 19 December 1947, with John and Charles as joint managing directors. Its product was so different from anything that had come out of a British factory that the established manufacturers of the time would probably not even have recognised it as a car. But word was getting out. Soon buyers would be turning up from as far away as America.

But in the short term, Cooper was not going to solve the

pressing problem posed by the Rootes brothers: what exactly would be those 'specialist products' that would power Britain's assault on export markets? That would be down to a one-legged City banker, a California jeep salesman and a design dating back to the late 1920s.

5

TWO SHEETS OF TIN AND A
BUNDLE OF FIREWOOD

The young ex-US Navy pilot had arrived from California by train. He was early for his appointment, so he hung about on the sidewalk in downtown New Orleans that January morning in 1947, watching the traffic go by. Kjell Qvale (pronounced 'Shell Kervahley') was twenty-eight and living the American dream. Born in Norway, he had arrived in America at the age of ten. 'The only words I knew were "yes", "no" and "stick 'em up".' His family settled in Oregon and in the depths of the Depression he delivered the Portland *Oregon Journal* and sold vegetable graters and phonograph needles door to door, making enough to buy himself a bicycle.

An athletic blond with piercing, steel-blue eyes, he became a track and ski star at school and won a sports scholarship to the University of Washington, but when the Second World War intervened, Qvale enlisted in the US Navy, trained as a pilot and flew every kind of machine going. But it was cars that became his real passion. Back in civilian life, he needed to make some money. With the $8,000 he had managed to save plus some help from a friend's father, he leased premises in Alameda, California and opened a Willys Jeep dealership. But he soon decided he needed a sideline. One of his mechanics had heard of a foreign motorcycle that was going cheap. So Qvale bought a ticket on the Sunset Limited train from San Francisco to Louisiana, with the intention of tracking down the agent.

'All of a sudden, this cute little car pulled up. I had never seen anything like it. The driver got out and I asked him what it was. He said it was an MG sports car. I asked him where it was from. "Made in England," came the reply.'

Qvale had never heard of MG. The only foreign marques he knew of were Rolls-Royce and Mercedes-Benz. In fact, even the term 'sports car' was alien to him. Qvale asked if he could take a ride. It was only a ten-minute spin, but it was enough; he was hooked.

There was nothing new about the MG TC; in fact, quite the opposite. Its design was an evolution of the 1932 Midget, one of the first affordable sports cars to be built anywhere in the world. It could not have conformed less to Billy Rootes's vision of the specialist model Britain needed to break into the US market. It was wilfully archaic, a basic primitive machine. But what Qvale saw in it was a more sociable version of the motorcycle: 'It had no bumpers, no roof, its steering wheel was on the right, but it gave me the biggest thrill of my life.' Its vintage-style 19-inch wire wheels, cutaway doors and open top offered a bracing, wind-in-the-hair ride. He was immediately besotted. And, happily, the driver turned out to be the son of the man he had come to see.

In downtown New Orleans, Jocelyn Hambro cut a most unlikely figure. Born in 1919, he belonged to the third generation of a City of London merchant-banking dynasty who divided their time between Mayfair, Sussex and an estate bordering Loch Ness. When he was thirteen his mother was killed when her motorboat exploded on the loch; her body was never found. Despite this tragedy, he developed an early appreciation of the good life. At Eton he became the school's de facto bookmaker and after going up to Trinity College, Cambridge, he was more often to be found at Newmarket or on a grouse moor. When war was declared he enlisted in the Coldstream Guards. He proved to be an unexpectedly capable soldier and rose to the rank of major. As a tank commander he landed at Juno Beach shortly after D-Day and won a Military Cross for his part in the capture of Hill 309 in Normandy. But then a stray Allied anti-aircraft shell blew off his left leg. For Jocelyn, the war was over, so he joined the family bank.

Pulling in dollars to shore up the post-war British economy was the priority for the City. But the Hambros had no presence on Wall Street; their interests were all in Europe and the Far East. So they decided to bypass New York and go west.

In the summer of 1945, Jocelyn set sail for New Orleans, the largest port in the Deep South, armed with a $10,000 float to establish a trading post from which to import British goods. On no more than a hunch and his own personal enthusiasm, he began with Scottish kippers, but these were judged too small for American plates, rotted in the warehouse and had to be dumped in the harbour. Undaunted, he moved on to jars of honey, which overheated in storage, fermented and exploded. Then there were crystal-glass ornaments, which got smashed en route. Finally, he tried MG sports cars.

There was no reason to expect that these undersized, anachronistic vehicles would be anything other than yet another disaster. American cars in the mid-'40s were all about bulbous curves and chrome; the MG's minimal bodywork had straight sides and sharp edges that had more in common with a veteran Model T Ford. And even in Louisiana, in the Deep South, Hambro soon discovered that established dealers all had franchises with Detroit's big corporations which forbade them to sell imported autos alongside domestic brands.

PETER GRIMSDALE

To begin with, the one-legged former guardsman's modus operandi was more Bishopsgate than Baton Rouge. According to Hambro legend, one illustrious ancestor refused credit to a man with the 'wrong colour socks'. He went bust shortly after. Since many of Jocelyn's potential recruits hereabouts didn't wear socks at all, he had to adopt a more open mind. In Dallas, he signed up a jukebox salesman; elsewhere a beer distributor and a man who sold refrigerators door to door.

The cut was generous: he offered 33 per cent for the distributor against the 20 per cent domestic dealers received. It was still an uphill battle. The MG was just too strange to many American eyes. One potential dealer Hambro approached dismissed the little MG as 'two sheets of tin and a bundle of firewood'.

Not so to Kjell Qvale; for him, it was love at first sight. Then and there, on the strength of that one run round the block and sealed with no more than a handshake, the young ex-navy pilot became the MG agent for the whole of northern California. When he headed home he took six cars with him – and sold them all in a weekend. So he ordered fifty more.

It looked like an extremely rash move. The friend's father who had invested in Qvale's start-up jeep business was furious and the Bank of America refused to give him the same short-term finance to cover his first order of stock. They had never heard of MG, or so-called 'sports cars'. But Hambro rode to the rescue. Since he was also a banker, he was willing to await payment until after the cars had been sold.

Qvale's hunch was right. 'It was the most significant moment in my life,' Qvale wrote later. 'The beginning of everything I would do.'

38

6

An Almost Merciful Relief

The MG's impact on America was out of all proportion to its size and the numbers that reached the country. In 1948 alone, this archaic little machine earned Britain about 4 million badly needed US dollars. By the time it was replaced the following year with the lightly upgraded TD, ten thousand had been sold, three times the number of any previous MG. There was nothing else like it on the American market. It was tiny, stiffly sprung, offered next to no weather protection, added to which it was noisy and had the steering wheel on the wrong side.

None of this mattered to those who fell for it, however. *Car and Driver*'s Warren Weith explained it this way: 'It was a way of life. A wildly different car that you jazzed around in on weekdays and raced on weekends ... A moving spot of colour on a still-drab post war landscape.' Like the Cooper 500 in Britain, the antiquated TC would be a new generation of Americans' entrée into racing. Within two years the tiny Massachusetts-based MG Car Club would morph into the Sports Car Club of America, the national governing body for a whole new type of motor sport.

Back in the English Midlands, where British car makers were struggling to bring their designs up to date, America's love affair with the archaic MG had yet to make its impact. Among Britain's motor barons, struggling to retool their factories for the post-war market, conventional wisdom prevailed: sports cars were a cottage industry, incapable of making serious money. All through the 1930s MG had struggled to justify its existence. Indeed, how it came to survive the Second World War at all was something of an accident, as is how its creator never lived to see its unlikely success.

~

On the rain-drenched night of 4 February 1945 at London's King's Cross Station, Cecil Kimber boarded an LNER train to Peterborough. He only just made it, climbing into the last carriage on Platform 15 just as it departed. Approximately 100 yards out of the station the line climbs towards the long Gasworks Tunnel. The day before, the rails in the tunnel had been replaced as part of routine maintenance. New rails have lower adhesion when wet and can cause the engine's wheels to slip on a gradient. In the damp, smoky blackness of the tunnel, the driver was unaware that not only had his train come to a stop, but that it then started to roll back down the incline. The points just outside the station had already been changed for the Aberdeen Express on Platform 10 to follow. A lone signalman saw what was happening and made a desperate attempt to stop the two trains making contact. But it was just too late. The first bogie of the end carriage had already passed over the points when he threw the lever to switch them, so the wheels at each end of the coach were now travelling on different tracks. It smashed into the locomotive of the Aberdeen train with such force that it threw the carriage upward and into an overhead gantry which sliced through one of the compartments. Cecil Kimber, the founder of MG, travelling by train because he had used up his petrol ration, was one of the two passengers who died that night. It was the end of a life full of inspiration – and frustration.

Kimber had a lot in common with William Lyons. Both men

were boyhood motorcycle enthusiasts who graduated to cars by adding stylish bodies to everyday models. Both were individualists, but unlike the shrewd and independence-obsessed Lyons, Kimber never got to be his own boss. His obituary in *Autocar* recorded that it was 'impossible to dissociate the man and the car'. He created MG, but was always at the mercy of his company's ultimate owner, William Morris and his henchmen.

The name MG, derived from Morris Garages, might well have remained just that – the sign on a workshop in Oxford – but for Kimber's appointment as sales manager in 1921. Born in London in 1888, the son of a failed printers' ink maker, Kim, as he was known to everyone who worked with him, had no formal training after leaving Stockport Grammar School at sixteen. He exhibited a natural mechanical aptitude and a fascination with motorbikes until a severe accident left him with a shortened right leg, which put paid to military service. After a series of posts at various vehicle manufacturers – including Crossley, where William Lyons served part of an apprenticeship – he landed in Oxford during what was a fraught time for the fledgling motor industry. The First World War had left in its wake a slump in the motor trade that would wipe out a number of manufacturers. But Kimber's choice was an astute one, as Morris was on its way to becoming one of Britain's biggest car makers.

Like William Lyons, Kimber had an eye for style; he also had an aptitude for making cars go faster. Decades before the term arrived from the USA, Kimber started to 'customise' Morris's dull but reliable products, transforming them into handsome sporty machines which could sell for up to a third more than the standard car. Although the famous octagonal MG badge was actually the work of his accountant, Ted Lee, Kimber deployed it wherever he could on the car – octagonal instruments, side lights and radiator caps. Wags claimed to be surprised that Kimber hadn't made the engine's pistons the same shape.

His triumph was the 1928 M-Type Midget, a tiny two-seater based on the first Morris Minor. Keenly priced at £175 – £50 more than the Minor – it was the first true budget sports car and a runaway success. For a time, William Morris indulged Kimber because his cars made money. With the success of the Midget, he signed off on MG's move out of Oxford to a new site in Abingdon.

But Kimber was also a keen competitor. MG started to make a name for itself in what was then known as voiturette racing and breaking speed records. In 1931, socialite and future best-selling novelist Barbara Cartland organised an all-women race at Brooklands and her ladies all drove MGs. Even though Morris had become Britain's biggest car maker, he began to fret that Kimber's MGs were getting all the limelight.

However, in 1934, two setbacks slammed the brakes on Kimber's racing ambitions – and ended his autonomy. Brooklands racer Kaye Don, whose cars were serviced by John Cooper's father Charles, was jailed over the death of a passenger while testing his MG before a race. The publicity upset Morris, who had just given his tough new production director Leonard Lord the task of reorganising all his car-making operations – including MG. When Lord made his first visit to Abingdon, Kimber proudly showed him the competition shop where his racing machines were being prepared. 'Well that bloody lot can go for a start,' was Lord's only comment. From then on, Kimber's racing activities were curtailed and MG product development tightly controlled from the Morris headquarters in Cowley.

But all through the 1930s, the Midget remained a steady seller, the only British sports car produced in any numbers until the Second World War put a stop to all car production. Ever resource-ful, Kimber secured for MG a contract making aircraft parts for the war effort, but this perceived insubordination only brought matters to a head. Miles Thomas, Lord's successor as Morris's right-hand man, was dispatched to Abingdon. He didn't mince words with Kimber: 'I told him he better look out for another outlet for his energies.'

It was a textbook example of the prevailing pre-war wisdom of Britain's motor bosses that prized deference over inspiration. Kimber spent the war with a piston manufacturer and he was on business for them when he met his end at King's Cross. His daughter Jean Cook said of his death: 'MG had been his be-all and end-all. It was almost a merciful release – he never quite got over being fired.'

Within a year of the King's Cross disaster, to the dismay of his detractors, Kimber's MG Midget was blazing a trail that would change Britain's motor industry for good.

7

BRICK BY BLOODY BRICK

Leading post-war Britain's export charge was the boss of Austin, Leonard Lord, the man who as Morris's production supremo in the 1930s had tried to shut down Kimber's MG operation. The two were such opposites it is hard to imagine they could ever have worked in the same industry.

'We're not in business to make motor cars – we're in business to make money,' Lord was fond of reminding his subordinates. True to his word, by the late '40s he had turned Austin into the nation's biggest and most profitable motor manufacturer.

Born in 1896, Leonard Percy Lord personified the best and worst of his generation of motor moguls. A bluff, ginger-haired son of a Coventry publican, single-minded, socially awkward, arrogant and blunt, he was also a gifted production engineer. It takes one kind of skill to design a successful car, quite another to organise its production efficiently – and profitably. Failing to accept this inconvenient truth was something that would dog the industry for much of the twentieth century.

In 1923, Lord was supervising production at the engine supplier Hotchkiss in Coventry when it was swallowed up by William Morris. Morris, then Britain's leading vehicle builder, noted how Lord had streamlined the Hotchkiss production processes, so four years later when he bought the bankrupt Wolseley Motors, he sent Lord in to sort out its engine plant. Lord designed multi-spindle drillers which sped up the process of machining engine blocks with great success. So Morris promoted him to managing director of Morris Motors in 1933 and then gave him carte blanche to reorganise the entire Cowley assembly operation plus all its satellite plants.

Lord was a constant presence on the shop floor, the fedora he wore indoors and out pushed back on his head, the brim curled up out of the way of whatever machine he was peering at, his hawk-like gaze drilling into every detail. He turned Morris's plants round in less than two years and put into production a new small car, the Eight – which became Britain's bestselling car between the wars.

Miles Thomas, a fellow Morris manager and later boss of BOAC, remembered Lord with mixed feelings:

> He awoke people to the hard facts of life. Most of them had never worked anywhere except Cowley and were stiff in their attitudes. He swiftly made them flexible. Everyone admired his methods if not his manners. He walked roughly over the toes of anyone who got in his way. He wore a lighted cigarette constantly in the corner of his mouth, blowing off the ash without taking it from his lips.

Lord's reign over Morris did not last. Having transformed the company – and its profits – he expected to be rewarded with shares in the business. But Morris was a control freak, obsessed with total ownership of his domain. He wouldn't give up any of it, so Lord walked out.

He wasn't idle for long, and in 1938 he was headhunted by Morris's deadly rival, Herbert Austin. Miles Thomas, who managed to remain friends with Lord, never forgot Lord's words to him at the time.

'He said: "Tommy, I'm going to take that business at Cowley apart, brick by bloody brick."' It was no empty promise. Lord applied himself to Austin with ferocious zeal. Under his management, the company had a good war. It produced ninety thousand trucks and nearly three thousand aircraft, including Hurricanes and Lancasters, as well as tanks, mines and ammunition. But he never lost sight of the next battle ahead. These lucrative War Department contracts enabled the board to sign off on Lord's plan for a massive post-war investment before VE Day. His new post-war range arrived in 1947, a year ahead of Morris's Minor.

First came the A40s Devon and Dorset, patriotically named after English counties. The all-enveloping pressed-steel bodywork, a dramatic break with the past, owed nothing to British coach-building traditions. Gone was any wood framing, separate running boards or lights bolted onto mudguards.

They were compact little cars with attention-grabbing shapes, all swoops and curves as if moulded in clay – which was how the original renderings were now formed. They were designed with British families and British roads in mind, but government policy decreed otherwise. So, straight after launch, before the home market could get a look-in, Lord had the first eleven thousand Devons and Dorsets shipped straight off to America in packing cases marked 'Austins for Dollars'.

On Madison Avenue, the copywriters and designers went to town. Their artwork did its best to disguise just how tiny the Austin was relative to American machines and tried to make a virtue of their origins. The Devon was billed as having 'the finest craftsmanship of England's largest builder of motor cars' and even being 'the last word in motor car perfection'.

In fact, how the new Austins' look came about was not very English at all, but was down to a most unlikely alliance Len Lord had formed with a part-time cartoonist from Argentina, via Turin.

Born in Buenos Aires of an Italian-Argentinian father and a

French mother, Ricardo Burzi started out in the drawing office at Lancia in Turin, but was forced to leave when it emerged he had a hazardous sideline: drawing caricatures that ridiculed *Il Duce* – Mussolini. For his own safety, Vincenzo Lancia had Burzi moved to a coach-building subsidiary in Paris, but then fate took one of its strange twists.

On a sea passage to New York in 1929, Lancia chanced to meet Herbert Austin. Whether the Italian wanted to offload the politically inconvenient draughtsman or simply do Austin a favour remains a mystery. What is known is that a few months later, Burzi, sporting a green felt hat with a large feather in it – and not a word of English, presented himself at the gates of 'The Austin' at Longbridge.

But, having hired Burzi, Herbert Austin promptly got cold feet about his new man. Like many of his generation who founded Britain's motor industry, Austin was a conservative when it came to style and rejected the radical, flowing lines Burzi sketched for his models.

Only when Lord arrived at Austin did Burzi get the chance to shine, when his new boss told him to come up with a new corporate face for Austin models, which included a then-radical front-opening 'alligator bonnet'. Though it was his work, the affable stylist was not put out when it became known as the 'Lord look'. They made an unlikely pair, the blunt Midlander and the cosmopolitan refugee from Fascist Italy. In June 1940, a few days after Italy declared war on Britain, Burzi arrived at work to find two Special Branch officers waiting for him. Having never got round to applying for British citizenship, he was carted off and interned as an enemy alien on the Isle of Man. For Lord, now heavily engaged with war work, the incarceration of his body stylist cannot have been a priority. Nevertheless, he pulled strings with his new associates in Whitehall, got Burzi released and put him back to work to quietly get on with drafting designs in preparation for peace. So it was that Austin came to have stolen a march on their competitors with modern styling for the American market.

As it turned out, despite Burzi's bold, modern styling, the Devon was wholly unsuited to the American market. Compact on the outside, it was cramped inside. On the highway, the Devon's 1200cc engine and low gearing, designed to pull well at low speeds to cope with British hills, made heavy work of keeping to the steady 60mph that most Americans were used to cruising at. Worse, even at $1,575, the four-cylinder Austin was more expensive than a six-cylinder Chevrolet and even the far larger V8-engined Ford De Luxe.

And yet the little 'British job' was a surprise hit. All eleven thousand units shipped in 1947 were found buyers. And, in the March of 1948 alone, of the twelve thousand British cars shipped to the USA, over ten thousand were Austins. How did they do it?

The reason for this triumph was not so much a timely craze for small cars, but the wave of strikes in 1945 and 1946 that brought the American steel and auto industries to a virtual standstill. By the end of 1947, the desperate American public were prepared to buy anything with four wheels and a roof.

All this brought essential dollars to Britain and desperately needed steel to Austin, but when Lord did his sums it emerged that once shipping was taken into account, the Devon was earning less than it cost to make. This dazzling export triumph was earning Austin its ration of steel but was losing the company money. It seemed like a cruel joke. But Lord couldn't withdraw from the market. Britain needed those dollars and Austin needed the steel that went with them. He needed to pull something else out of the bag. He decided to go and take a look at the American market himself.

Ever since Henry Ford had started producing his game-changing Model T by the thousand – and then the million – forty years before, Europe's manufacturers had been making pilgrimages to Ford's River Rouge plant, the Mecca of mass production, to look and learn. But Lord the production genius needed nothing from Detroit; his path to enlightenment took him to America's showrooms.

It's hard to envisage this austere engineer from Coventry among the neon-lit plenty of post-war America, or to imagine how he could have found any common ground with their taste. This was not quite yet the era of fins, but Detroit was already adorning their products with power-assisted features and pastel colours to tempt a new generation of freshly demobilised buyers. Lord absorbed it all and came back to Longbridge with a plan.

What the American market really craved, he reasoned, was a stylish convertible – modern, futuristic even, stuffed with gadgets, just like a proper American car, only more compact. On the passage home, he did some preliminary sketches to show Burzi the new direction of travel.

It was a dream commission. For a designer who had learned his craft in the *carrozzerie* of Turin, life at the drawing boards of Longbridge must have been soul-destroying. But now Lord was urging him to throw caution to the wind. The result was the Austin Atlantic, and it was like no Austin before it.

In place of the conventional radiator grille was a pair of horizontal slots just above the front bumper. Not one but five chromium strips adorned the bonnet. The line from the top of the front wing swooped downward along the side of the body, over the enclosed rear wheel, to meet the rear bumper. Not one but two 'flying A' Austin mascots stood atop each headlamp fairing and a third headlight peered out from between the slotted air intakes. There was a sloping but ample boot, not seen before on an Austin of any county. And the convertible model had a hydraulic hood, which took twenty-five seconds to fold all by itself. Plus the windows were also powered – another first on a British car – and even the rear screen on the hardtop could be wound down. A steering-column-mounted gear lever and bench seat also made it possible to seat three abreast in the front – albeit three who had come through several years of rationing. There was a choice of radios and, in a final flourish, the dashboard dials were gold-faced.

Beneath this exuberant homage to American styling, however, was an assemblage of the somewhat more familiar. The chassis came from the little Devon and the engine from its big sister, the Hampshire, still a four-cylinder but enlarged to over 2.5 litres. With more highway-friendly gearing, it could be coaxed up to 95mph. In time for the first post-war motor show at Earl's Court in 1948, the Austin Atlantic was ready for launch. 'A car that will bring an added zest to the business or pleasure of motoring,' gushed the blurb.

But at an eye-watering $2,460 on the US market, it was almost double the price of a Devon. Detroit, now back at full output, was offering automatic transmission as well as V8 power for far less money. And, to Lord's dismay, the Americans just didn't get the styling. It looked cartoonish, a miniaturised Yank that seemed strangely shy about its origins.

Of the 7,981 Atlantics manufactured, just 350 found buyers in the USA and only after $1,000 had been shaved off the price. An unkind critic likened it to the failed attempt to market Britain's Diana Dors as an alternative to Marilyn Monroe. After three years, Lord pulled the plug.

But what gave the Atlantic its final push to the scrap yard wasn't what came out of Detroit, but from down the road in Coventry.

8

NEEDS MUST WHEN
THE DEVIL DRIVES

A month before VE Day, William Lyons changed the name of his company from SS Cars to Jaguar. Those once innocuous two letters were now far better known for their association with the Nazis – or, as Lyons put it with his customary titanic understatement, 'a sector of the community not highly regarded.'

He also wanted to give the firm a new image in preparation for his pet project, the 100mph saloon. It was to be powered by an entirely new engine, his firm's first to be designed and built in-house – the one he had begun planning during those fire-watching stints with his team. But it wasn't just a matter of moving with the times. Lyons had much to prove.

Before the war his cars had caused a stir with their swooping wings and rakish lines, but critics had noted that beneath the extravagantly long bonnets were humdrum engines bought in from Standard, a neighbouring Coventry firm that made unexceptional family cars. 'More show than go' was a favourite barb hurled at Lyons's creations. And although his team had worked strenuously to give cars the performance they deserved, Lyons was determined that his next cars would have an engineering pedigree that the Standard-powered cars never had.

But for Jaguar, the massive fixed costs for developing and building a new model from scratch were just the same as for the giants like Austin and Morris, who at least had volume to amortise the huge initial outlay. Lyons, by contrast, was still a minor player and relative new boy among the manufacturers. In his best year, 1939, he had made just over five thousand cars. The company was considered too small to merit a listing in the *Financial Times*. And Lyons liked to run a tight ship. His secretary, Alice Fenton – who had joined him as a teenager – doubled as sales manager, while Lyons opened all the mail himself.

A telling measure of how tight things were, Jaguar's first post-war catalogue measured only 4 × 3 inches. This embarrassed Lyons, who took great pride in his marketing, as the gritted-teeth tone of his explanation shows: 'Severe restrictions on the use of paper have rendered it impossible for us to produce a full-sized catalogue in sufficient quantities to meet public demand for details of the new Jaguar. Therefore this miniature catalogue has been produced in order to give the greatest amount of information to the largest possible number of people, and in this tiny volume will be found all the particulars normally presented in a catalogue ten times the size.'

Size mattered in another, even more crucial way. To make things worse, the minister of supply, George Strauss, announced that the government would stop supplying steel to any car firm that failed to export more than 75 *per cent* of its output. The message was uncompromising: 'Materials must go to the firms that can export and do. And that means those who do not cannot have them. Needs must when the devil drives. And if that results in some firms having to close down, well, it is always regrettable when an organisation which has created a tradition, loyalties and reputation has to disappear.'

Jaguar's future hung in the balance. Lyons had to convince the government he was a player. He drafted a prospectus laying out the company's plans as boldly and ambitiously as he dared, calling his planned 100mph saloon the 'International', detailing the quantity of steel required to get it into production. He took no chances, delivering it in person to Sir George Turner at the Ministry of Supply.

The first post-war Jaguars were indistinguishable from those made in 1939. All the tools and jigs for assembly, mothballed for the duration of the war, had to be refurbished before they could be pressed back into service. But as to what the export market would want, who knew? Lyons had never been to America but he had seen what they were capable of making. He just had to hope that his designs, considered a bit 'nouveau riche' by the British establishment, might find a few buyers in the US even though they were nearly ten years old.

But there was another storm headed Jaguar's way.

Triumph and Riley – both similar to Jaguar in size and output – had gone bankrupt and been bought up by bigger firms. And the omens were far from good. Lyons received a visit from W. O. Bentley – a hero in the industry, but a fallen one. Bentley had built a series of great sporting grand tourers, taken them to Le Mans and won – five times. He had put Great Britain on the map as a maker of fast, superlative cars. Yet despite the glory, Bentley Motors had never made money and, in 1931, after his business was sold from under him to Rolls-Royce, W. O. found a home with Lagonda, where he designed a new engine. But that firm too was in trouble. Lyons knew that he was looking for a lifeline – his engine in a Jaguar body perhaps. But, unbeknown to Bentley, Lyons's own engine was well advanced. Lyons listened politely to the great man, but in the harsh, new, post-war environment, with investment capital so thin on the ground, it was every man for himself.

To escape the quicksand of debt that had swallowed so many of its former competitors, and to remain independent, Jaguar had not only to export but grow. But it couldn't, without tackling the slowest and most labour-intensive side of the business, the one in which Lyons had started out.

To go with the new engine, the 'International' or '100mph saloon' would naturally need a brand-new body. Unlike all the other car firms that had started with engineering, Jaguar, or SS as it was before, had begun by building bodies, but using the traditional coach building crafts. Carpenters chiselled and joined a wooden frame, usually ash, then wrapped it in metal panels. Items like mudguards had to be hand-beaten into shape. What enabled Lyons to charge such competitive prices for his cars was partly down to not having to buy in expensive coachwork or hire designers. He did all that himself. Then, as now, a big proportion of a car's components were made by outside suppliers, whose natural preference was for dealing with the bigger producers. But a dramatic change in the manufacture of car bodies was happening: the future had arrived, and for a small outfit like Jaguar it posed a potentially devastating challenge.

In the late 1920s, a far less labour-intensive process using pressed steel had been pioneered by the Budd railroad-carriage maker in the United States. The new method dispensed with wood altogether – and the carpenters who crafted it – to produce far lighter, stronger body shells. Panels stamped into shape in mere seconds were then welded to each other in a jig, dramatically simplifying the whole process. Suddenly a job that used to take days was done in a matter of minutes, and the end product was both lighter and stronger.

Detroit had switched to pressed steel before the war, as had some European producers like Citroën, but the prohibitive tooling costs of the vast, specially made stamping machines and the welding jigs they required discouraged uptake in Britain. Added to that, the innately conservative British car makers, protected from foreign competition by the prohibitive 33.3 per cent tariffs, had been under no pressure to evolve. Meanwhile, American stylists, liberated from the constraints of traditional wooden frames, could indulge in ever more extravagant shapes. Beside them, the British cars now looked quaint. Not only that, wages had risen dramatically during the war and the costs of hand-crafting traditional wood frames were rocketing. For Lyons to produce the sort of body to go with his new engine, especially for the now vitally important American market, he would have to go for all-steel construction.

A plant capable of producing pressed-steel bodies in Britain started out as a joint venture between the American Budd Company and William Morris in the 1920s. Its 1,600-ton, 28ft-high Hamilton presses shipped from the US could stamp out the whole side of a car in one go. But for many years the development costs were such that they only appeared on high-volume, mass-produced cars. William Lyons built his first all-steel car in 1938, but his company could not afford the huge tooling costs, so he used a multitude of small pressings, some done in-house, others from local workshops, and all welded up by his men.

But after the war, the move to more American-influenced, all-enveloping designs rendered that piecemeal approach redundant. Pressed Steel was inundated with orders from the big firms to supply entire new bodies. Small companies like Jaguar were less of a priority. Lyons would have to get in the queue. Not only that, the bill for preparing the new body for production was now a quarter of a million pounds – an unimaginable sum. He realised he had no choice: for now he was going to have to survive on face-lifted versions of his pre-war cars – exactly what he had hoped to avoid.

The winter of January–February 1947 – the worst that century – cost two precious months of lost production as ports closed and the rail network froze to a halt. Then a fire destroyed 8,000 square feet of the Jaguar factory. Newspaper reports began to suggest that Jaguar's steel allocation could be withdrawn because of poor export performance and that it was headed for extinction.

'Such statements have no authority and are entirely without foundation,' was Lyons's testy rebuttal as he held his nerve. As the lead time for the big 100mph saloon began to stretch into the distance, the pressure piled on him. The 1948 London motor show, the first in ten years, was just months away. There was certain to be a big crowd hungry for excitement, but Jaguar had nothing really new to show. If he didn't have something that would reignite the excitement his cars had provoked in the '30s, Jaguar risked becoming invisible.

So Lyons went back to the drawing board – metaphorically, because he couldn't actually draw. Despite all his duties, and unlike the boss of any other car maker in the world, he still did *all* of the styling. And since he was no draughtsman, he developed a method that was quite unique to him, which he shared with one other man.

Fred Gardner, who had been with him since the Swallow days, was in charge of the company sawmill. Remembered as a rather thuggish, unapproachable character, fond of foul language – something Lyons abhorred – and fiercely protective of his domain, a mark of his status was that he was also one of the very few people his boss addressed by his first name.

There was no initial experiment with scale models. Lyons worked life-size from the start. Inside the sawmill they started with a wire skeleton to define key co-ordinates – the door pillars, the cant rail (the line of the seam between the doors and the roof) and the belt line (which runs just under the side windows and out along the bonnet and boot). Once the overall outline had been agreed, Gardner would substitute a wooden armature, which, under Lyons's direction, would be planed and shaved to his desired shape. Aluminium panels would then be attached but even at this stage changes would be made until the perfectionist Lyons was satisfied. Sometimes he would emerge, his otherwise immaculate double-breasted suit dusted with chalk from having used a stick to mark the wood and metal indicating where he wanted a curve or cut to come.

He made it sound so simple: 'The lines of our cars are arrived at by the direct shaping of panels until they become pleasing to the eye. I have a fairly clear idea of what I want to see and I get the best results working in the full size and assessing the effects and the car itself in the natural environment. Only then can the proportions and detail of the car be determined exactly and these to me are of paramount importance.'

In other words, he was operating like a sculptor, using others to wield their tools according to his strict orders. Bill Jones, one of the metal workers, explained the process to Lyons's biographer: 'Lyons would say: "Right, put me a roof panel on and I want so much shape in it." They would get a lovely highly polished piece of aluminium and roll it and put a nice gentle shape in it. He would come back and say: "Just a fraction more." That's how all these lovely shapes came about.' Lyons would spend hours examining these mock-ups from all angles, positioning lamps to show up the highlights along the curves.

He also insisted on viewing his evolving work outside, but not just in the factory yard. In 1937, he had bought Wappenbury Hall, an imposing thirteen-bedroom Victorian mansion near Leamington Spa. He would have the mock-ups transported there and reassembled on the gravel drive with the house as a backdrop. Only there, he believed, out in the world, could he properly assess his designs. Even then he would ask for more adjustments until he was satisfied. But that summer of 1948 he had a deadline to meet – the London motor show in October.

The shape of the show car took just two weeks. 'It was done more quickly than anything before or since,' Lyons confessed later. But, for all the haste, there was no loss of attention to detail. Lyons had half a dozen radiator grilles made up with just minor differences in the thickness of the bars and shape and tried each one before arriving at the one that worked best for him. Versions of this new 'face' would adorn Jaguars for the next twenty years.

The week of the motor show, Lyons booked every poster space in Earl's Court Underground Station and the sides of 750 London buses. When the doors to the exhibition hall opened on Wednesday 27 October 1948, ninety thousand people flocked through the turnstiles. After the grim years of war followed by prolonged rationing, the crowd were expecting excitement. And they found it on the Jaguar stand: an open two-seater, finished in metallic bronze. It was called the XK120 Super Sports.

Without question it was the star of the show. Among the sensible Austin counties and the promising but utilitarian Morris Minor, the Jaguar, with its long bonnet, raked chrome windscreen, its rear wheels enclosed by low-slung bodywork, oozed speed and excitement. Lyons had completely underestimated the level of interest. As the crowds pressed around the Jaguar stand, he was handed a piece of paper. It was a single order for two hundred cars, more than he had ever envisaged building.

The XK120 was essentially a show car. It looked like the future but its body was hand-built with its ash frame, just as his cars had been in the early '30s, and was not intended for mass production. And although it boasted a promising, racy-looking twin-cam engine, he and his team did not yet know if it could reach the magic 120mph its name suggested. There was nothing for it; the car would have to be re-engineered for mass production – and in left-hand drive, because the order had come from America.

GONE WITH THE WIND

The *New York Times* called him the Duveen of the motor business, likening him to the legendary art dealer 'for his ability to captivate clients with his salesmanship, superb taste and forceful personality'. Max Hoffman knew the value of art. He collected Impressionist works before they were fashionable; he had an eye for style and an instinct for what would sell.

Hoffman arrived in New York in June 1941. He had first fled his native Austria for Paris, then abandoned Europe altogether for NYC after Hitler's armies had swarmed into France. He left behind a successful career as both a racing driver and car dealer.

Born near Vienna in 1904 to a Catholic mother and a Jewish father, he grew up helping his dad make bicycles, shaping and plating the frames. He took up racing, first motorbikes and then cars, becoming a works driver and the Austrian agent for the French Amilcar company. From there he expanded into other French and Italian marques, always with an eye for the most stylish as well as the fastest.

America should have been fertile ground for him. Through the '20s and '30s, the only European cars that sold there were at the very top end of the market. F. Scott Fitzgerald's Jay Gatsby owned a Rolls-Royce, 'a rich cream color, bright with nickel, swollen here and there in its monstrous length with triumphant hat-boxes and supper-boxes and tool-boxes, and terraced with a labyrinth of wind-shields that mirrored a dozen suns.' But those days were gone; Hoffman's timing could not have been worse.

Just six months after he arrived, the Japanese made their surprise attack on the US Naval Fleet at Pearl Harbor. America was plunged into war and overnight the market for all cars, not just for the rich, dried up. To survive, Hoffman had to dust down some of the skills he had acquired as a child. He observed that because of the war effort many more women were now in work, with money to spend but nothing to spend it on. Metal was scarce so he came up with the idea of making costume jewellery out of metal-plated plastic. He borrowed $300, crafted some items himself, put them in a customised display box and took them round Manhattan's jewellers. A week later he had $5,000 worth of orders. Hoffman was an operator; he seemed to know intuitively what would sell. He did so well that by 1947 he was ready to break back into the motor trade and opened his own showroom on the corner of Park Avenue and 59th Street on the upmarket Upper East Side.

To grab attention, he placed in the window a monument to pre-war European exotica, a French Delahaye with coachwork by Figoni et Falaschi, creators of some of the most baroque automotive shapes. His aim was to pick up from where he had left off and import the same French and Italian exotica that he had sold in Austria. But Italy was still under occupation; Alfa Romeo was focusing on smaller cars. And in France, one by one the great marques – Delage, Delahaye and Bugatti – were withering away, taxed out of their home market and too niche to gear up for export. Worse, the first new designs to come out of Europe were all struggling to ape American jelly-mould styling. Hoffman had to find some other product to excite his American clientele.

He soon found what he wanted. The name Jaguar meant

nothing to him. The marque had only been in existence a year and it didn't come with the racing pedigree the continental favourites had in spades. But just as Kjell Qvale had been beguiled by the MG TC, Hoffman saw in Lyons's first post-war Jaguars the classic European style he craved – and at a fraction of the price of those fading French thoroughbreds. William Lyons might have been in a hurry to replace his pre-war designs as soon as possible, but Hoffman detected in them exactly the glamour that he had begun to think had vanished from Europe.

Hoffman set his sights on Jaguar and got an introduction when Lyons made his first trip to America early in 1948. Lyons flew to New York in a BOAC Stratocruiser, a graphic reminder of just how primitive air travel was at the time. Although there were sleeping bunks in the upper storey, he found it was impossible to sleep as the noise from the engines was incredible.

> We landed at Gander Goose Bay, Canada, after an eleven-hour flight. One's first impression was of bleak desolation and it was quite easy to imagine one had landed on the North Pole. We were huddled across the snow into a large wooden shed in the centre of which was a large coke stove which all the passengers immediately surrounded ... It was over an hour before we re-embarked in the 'Monarch' and landed at La Guardia Airport, New York some three hours later. The trip had taken thirteen hours. Nevertheless, after getting to the 'Waldorf Astoria' about 9am and after a cup of coffee, I went to Hoffman's Park Avenue showroom.

The taciturn Englishman was wary of the fast-talking, flamboyant New Yorker who showed off the premises for where his service department would be – a disused warehouse he planned to convert, a job he claimed would be done in two weeks. Lyons was unconvinced. Even he, a fast mover, doubted that it would be possible. Two weeks later, however, when Lyons was back in New York from his tour of America, Hoffman proudly showed him the completed service facility. 'I was quite astounded to see that it had been completed and was being equipped with the necessary service requirements.'

With Jaguar, Hoffman was back in the car business – big time, judging by his comments later: 'There never was such a business as Jaguar . . . I imported cars from England, and I made money. I distributed the cars I imported from England, and I made money. I retailed the cars that I had imported from England and distributed, and I made money.'

Rather too much money, Lyons later decided when he terminated Hoffman's contract, offering a typically euphemistic explanation: 'He was a very good salesman . . . I was later to find that he had some exceptional qualities, although they were to prove by no means favourable to my interests.' But Hoffman had given Lyons new confidence in the overseas potential of his designs. If he could sell them, surely others could. The glamorous Jaguar look that had been regarded as brash and attention-seeking in Britain had the opposite effect in the US. Where other British designs looked dumpy and introverted, Lyons's style fizzed with excitement, nowhere more so than in Hollywood, and in the hands of its biggest screen legend.

It would be Clark Gable's first foreign car. Before, there had been Duesenbergs, Packards and a Lincoln. And after his leading role in the blockbuster *Gone With the Wind* (1939), America's number-one screen idol could afford just about any machine he liked. He had not had his Mark V Jaguar drophead very long when he saw the first publicity shots of the XK120. 'I had to have it like a kid wants candy,' he wrote in an article entitled 'My Favorite Sports Car' for *Road & Track* magazine. The King of Hollywood marched through the doors of International Motors on Wilshire Boulevard and demanded to be the first person in

California to get his hands on an XK. Soon after he took delivery, he drove out to one of Southern California's dry lakes to see how fast it would go. 'To make a long story short, we went through the measured mile course at (the studio will probably cut this out) 124mph (the studio didn't – Ed).' It was not a total puff; Cable criticised the British 12-volt electrics and the 'non-American screw thread system' and lack of provision for cool air in the cockpit. 'But to get the thrill of real sport motoring a fellow has to make some sacrifices.'

Jaguar had found a market no one knew existed. Where the MG TC had the perky simplicity of a motorcycle, Lyons's show car oozed glamour, and with its 3.4-litre engine, three times the size of the MG, it had the kind of raw power to outpace anything Detroit could throw at it. Lyons would eventually build twelve thousand XK120s, 11,800 more than he intended, and even then he would never satisfy demand.

10

LINES IN THE SAND

Sir Stafford Cripps, austere architect of the car industry's export drive and now chancellor of the exchequer, did not make it to Earl's Court in 1948 to see the metallic-bronze XK Jaguar. If he had he might well have shuddered at such brash frivolity, even though more than any other car on show it would do his bidding and bring home the much-needed dollars.

To regain his composure he could have sought out another exhibit, one that heeded his call for automotive utilitarianism. It was barely a car at all; a flat-sided, canvas-roofed contraption that looked as if it had been constructed from Meccano. Even its name had been bolted together rather crudely.

It was called the Land Rover.

In 1945, like many other firms, Rover had no brand-new model ready for peacetime and had restarted car production with ageing pre-war models. Rover's Wilks brothers, managing director Spencer and chief engineer Maurice, had had an interesting war. Theirs had been one of the car firms recruited into the Shadow Factory Scheme, a far-sighted government programme devised in 1935 to create factory space funded by Whitehall but attached to the motor industry so that in the event of war, aircraft production could be ramped up. Rover ran six shadow plants building engines

64

and airframes and for a period even housed Frank Whittle's nascent jet-engine project. Although that partnership was fractious and Whittle was passed on to Rolls-Royce, it would have a lasting impact on the company.

Rover's story is as old as the motor industry, it being one of several marques with deep roots in the Coventry cycle business. In the 1880s, John Kemp Starley invented the Rover Safety Bicycle. With two equal-size wheels and drive by pedal and chain, over 130 years later it is still the standard bicycle design used the world over. But Rover's first few decades building cars were less glorious. Overproduction of too wide a range of models brought it to the brink of collapse in 1930.

Spencer Wilks, a solicitor by training, had joined Hillman after marrying one of the founder's daughters, but left when the Rootes brothers bought the business. He became Rover's general manager in 1929 and brought with him his brother Maurice, an engineer who had done three years in Detroit. Together they salvaged Rover, rationalised its products and carefully recreated the company as a purveyor of modest but refined cars suitable for doctors and accountants. By 1939, they had more than doubled production to just over eleven thousand units.

As the war came to an end, their military work dried up. The pressure was on to get back to cars. But they had been bombed out of their main plant in Helen Street, Coventry. The Rover design team had evacuated to the ballroom of Chesford Grange hotel near Kenilworth. Late in 1944 the Ministry of Supply issued them with a permit to produce precisely 1,108 cars. No detail was too small for the Whitehall bureaucrats. The permit allowed for five hundred 10-horsepower cars, five hundred 12-horsepower cars, a further one hundred with six-cylinder engines and eight 'development vehicles'.

The Wilks brothers wondered if there would still be an appetite for their modestly upmarket products. They also had vivid memories of the Great War and its aftermath, when a slump in demand for medium-sized cars sent shock waves through the industry and killed off many small firms. And petrol was going to stay rationed. Maurice Wilks's answer, he told *Motor* magazine, was to offer alongside their midsize model 'a really small quality car which would appeal to people who had run more expensive types in the past and wished to retain the same standards, even if economy of running forced them to use much smaller vehicles'. The result would be the M-Type, 'M' for miniature.

Like John Cooper, Maurice Wilks found inspiration in Dante Giacosa's Fiat Topolino. They bought one (a whole one) to learn its secrets and within a year his team had their own prototypes on test. The M-Type was an exquisitely miniaturised Rover, a two-seater saloon with a 700cc engine. But before it got very far, it hit two problems, both of them to do with Stafford Cripps. The car might work for a petrol-starved domestic market, but the government had virtually banned sales at home as part of its enforced export drive, and the little car was far too small for North America. And without exports, Rover would never get its steel allocation. Added to that, Cripps had decreed that car firms should concentrate on one model only.

The little M was doomed. Vying with William Lyons in the understatement stakes, Wilks admitted to *Motor* that 'we reluctantly decided that the place which we had foreseen for the M would not materialise.' Early in 1947 it was axed, the promising prototypes broken up and scrapped. Rover would have to carve out an export market by adapting its ageing pre-war model. They had never even built a left-hand-drive car and, more worrying, the 75, a much-needed replacement, was at least two years away.

The winter of 1947, the worst of the century, brought business to a standstill and brought down all the trees on the drive of Maurice Wilks's home, Blackdown Manor. To clear them away, he acquired a war-surplus jeep from a neighbour. When the weather improved he used it to trailer his boat up to his weekend farm house on Anglesey's Red Wharf Bay. He was impressed by its versatility. Four-wheel drive on anything smaller than a lorry was still a novelty then, but the ex-US Army jeep was on its last legs. Joining him in Anglesey one weekend, his brother Spencer asked him what he would do when it expired. 'Get another one I suppose; there isn't anything else,' was Maurice's answer.

It was a light-bulb moment. Could a vehicle like this tow Rover out of trouble? In the sand of Red Wharf Bay, Maurice quickly sketched out with his walking stick the first draft of the Land Rover. On his return to the Midlands he put together a five-man team in the Kenilworth ballroom to bring it to life.

It was a risky strategy for Rover. Essentially it was an agricultural vehicle – a market they knew nothing about. But to the Wilks brothers it was no more than a stopgap, something to tide them over until their new post-war cars came on stream. To get it done quickly it had to use as many existing Rover parts as possible; sourcing components from outside the company meant getting in ever lengthening queues behind other car firms. The body design had to do without expensive presses – the prototype didn't even have doors. Only the most basic curves were shaped over simple wooden formers. And since steel was rationed (every component down to the nuts and bolts had to be covered by a Ministry of Supply permit number), it made sense to make it out of freely available aluminium.

Though the two men had drastically different priorities and probably never met, Maurice Wilks's approach to design bore interesting similarities to that of John Cooper. Wilks's nephew, 'Spen' King, another star of the Rover story who we will meet later, described his uncle as an 'instinctive engineer', unafraid of experimentation, who used the world around him for inspiration. Like Cooper, he also preferred to try things out in the metal first and only if they worked would he then make technical drawings.

Although inspired by the US military jeep, he saw his machine as more of a vehicular Swiss army knife, capable of pulling a plough, or a manure spreader, powering a threshing machine, acting as a mobile workshop – to boldly go where no car had gone before.

Just as the first batch of Land Rover prototypes was being readied, Stafford Cripps made an official visit to the factory. The Wilks team was nervous – the Land Rover flew in the face of the business tsar's mantra of one model per firm. George Farmer, Rover's finance chief, detailed to show him round the factory, decided they should come clean. He made the argument that here was something new that had a future not only for export but also for agriculture, another urgent government priority.

Positioning Land Rover as the farmer's friend turned out to be an inspired move. It had all the attributes Cripps valued – wholesome utilitarian simplicity. So much so that when he became chancellor, he specifically exempted Land Rovers from the 33 per cent purchase tax, a better result than Rover could have hoped for.

Cripps, it turned out, wasn't the only enthusiast. Two months after the Land Rover's unveiling at the 1948 London motor show, the Wilks brothers were in trouble again. They had planned to build one hundred a week; to meet surging demand they would have to ramp that up to five hundred. That December, Rover chairman E. Ransom Harrison reported to the AGM that 'this vehicle will be something very much more than an additional source of production. It may even equal – and even exceed – our car output in quantity.' By the end of 1949, when the all-new postwar Rover P4 75 was ready for launch, Land Rovers were on sale in seventy countries. The stopgap model would outlive the 75 by over half a century.

In the late 1940s, however, for the British buying public a new car of any kind was a pipe dream; waiting lists stretched to five years and more. For the motor trade, the action had moved to the second-hand market.

THIS CHAP WILL GO PLACES

Fitzrovia in central London was once the home of the second-hand car trade. In 1902, Charles Friswell, racing cyclist and entrepreneur, had seen a great future for the motor car and opened Friswell's Automobile Palace on the corner of Euston Road. This ambitious, five-storey emporium was capable of housing over 100 cars plus repair shops and an auction room. Friswell's plan had been to sell new cars but the business soon focused on the burgeoning trade in second-hand vehicles. In the early days of the car, the pace of technological development was such that those able to would frequently trade in for the ever-improving latest models.

Other dealers opened up along the Euston Road but, as traffic increased, parking their wares in the busy street became a problem. Several premises had back entrances in the parallel Warren Street, which had been built a century before to provide access for the Euston Road properties. This quieter side street was where the action moved to, attracting one-man pavement dealers of no fixed abode, who plied their trade on the curb and in nearby pubs. The gangster 'Mad' Frankie Fraser recalled the heydays of Warren Street in his book *Mad Frank's London*:

There could be up to fifty cars and then again some people

would just stand on the pavement and pass on the info that there was a car to sell. Warren Street was mostly for mug punters ... People would come down from as far away as Scotland to buy a car. All polished and shiny with the clock turned back and the insides hanging out. And if you bought a car and it fell to bits who was you going to complain to?

After the Second World War, Warren Street became a Mecca for black marketeers. It achieved national notoriety in October 1949 when the body of a snappily dressed local spiv, Stan Setty, was found wrapped in carpet felt, still wearing his cream silk shirt and underwear, but without his head. *Picture Post* magazine featured the used-car market in Warren Street, opining that 'it attracts a fair amount of the gutter garbage from the hinterland.' It also attracted a gifted young engineering student from the nearby University College London (UCL) called Colin Chapman.

When Anthony Colin Bruce Chapman was born in 1928, his father Stanley owned the Orange Tree pub in Richmond, where Colin's mother Mary had been the barmaid. Shortly after Colin's birth, Stanley bought the Railway Hotel, a larger premises in Hornsey, north London. From an early age Colin dazzled his doting parents. At eight he won a place at the prep attached to the nearby Stationers' Company's School. It was bulldozed in 1983 a few years after becoming a comprehensive, but before the war it was an exclusive establishment. Only twelve boys a year were accepted. In his admission interview Colin was said to have clinched it with his response to the question: 'How many farthings are there in a pound?' He came back with the answer in a flash – 960 – but then took the interview board through the process by which he had worked it out. Clearly this was no ordinary eight-year-old.

For Stanley and Mary, now branching out into catering and acutely conscious of their social standing, this was a win-win, as their son's entry into a prestigious grammar school reflected well on them. As a high-flyer, he would be expected to stay until at least sixteen, whereas most boys left school at fourteen to start earning. His 1938 end-of-year report shows he came top and received an almost equal number of stars (twelve) as detentions (eleven). 'Shows great efficiency in his work – but his impulsiveness leads to far too many detentions,' wrote his form master, prophetically. It was a judgement that would stand for much of Chapman's glittering career.

From an early age he also exhibited the beginnings of a lifelong impatience with correctness. Legend has it that in a woodwork lesson, and having a problem planing a block square, Chapman simply adjusted the tri-square to fit his block.

But there was no question of his abilities. Stan revelled in his son's early achievements, proudly showing off a gun the boy had made that fired matches when he was only eleven. Much to the envy of his friends, his father gave him a gold-lacquered Claud Butler bicycle on which he displayed an alarmingly fearless appetite for speed. When the school was evacuated to Wisbech in the Fens, he was in his element being up close to the skies full of fighters and bombers flying from the nearby bases. It sealed his lifelong interest in both flying and aerodynamics.

He attracted admirers from an early age. One of the first to recognise his potential was his future wife Hazel, whom he met at a dance in Hornsey Town Hall in 1944, catered by Stan. 'I was terribly shy,' she told Chapman's biographer, Gérard 'Jabby' Crombac. 'What attracted me to him was that he seemed so capable in the way he just did everyday things. Even at that age he could always get things done and I remember thinking to myself after our first meeting, "Here is someone a bit different. This chap will go places."'

In 1945, at just seventeen, Colin won a place at UCL to read civil engineering. Stan dreamed of his son designing bridges and tunnels for the brave, new, post-war world. Colin joined the University Air Corps and learned to fly, but lectures bored him. He needed a distraction. He found it two streets away – in Warren Street.

Used cars were all that were available in 1946, all of them pre-war and therefore a minimum of seven years old. This was a time long before MOT tests, and in Warren Street there were a number of scams for shifting stock – even if they only made it a few miles. Stuffing a ladies' stocking down the dipstick shaft could silence knocking engine bearings; rusted-out chassis members could be swapped with a piece of two-by-four timber disguised by a thick smear of grease. Porridge, sawdust or even diluted cement could work temporary wonders on a whingeing differential.

Chapman wanted in, but he needed some working capital to get there first. As part of his civil-engineering studies he had to inspect one of London's many bomb-damaged and derelict buildings, where he spotted a huge forgotten stash of shelving – all made of precious and rationed steel. With a friend, he borrowed a lorry, loaded the booty and took it round London's steel-starved engineering works, flogging it off until there was enough to buy a few cars.

Chapman, by far the youngest of the dealers, with his David Niven pencil moustache and snappy dress, fitted right in. Soon he had amassed a stock of bangers. Since Stan was already troubled by his son straying from his studies and the future he dreamed for him, Colin kept them round the back of Hazel's parents' house.

But when he was still not yet out of his teens, this lucrative double life screeched to an abrupt end. In August 1947, the government, struggling with worsening economic conditions, withdrew the already paltry petrol ration for private-car owners. Overnight, the bottom fell out of the used-car market. Chapman had to sell off his stock at knock-down prices until only a 1930 Austin 7 remained, too knackered to find a buyer. But for the relentlessly resourceful Chapman, a problem could also be a source of inspiration. He needed a new focus for his restless energy and sorting out dodgy cars had taught him more about engineering than his lectures.

The baby Austin was the most significant British car of the interwar years. After nearly going bust in the slump that followed the First World War, Herbert Austin created his tiny 7 of 1922, which saved his company and put motoring within reach of the masses. It would also become the template for the first cars ever made by both BMW and Nissan. It wasn't a revolutionary design, just an ingeniously simplified, scaled-down version of contemporary automotive practice. Its 750cc engine was one of the smallest four-cylinder power units produced, and it was designed to be no wider than a motorcycle and side-car combination, whose owners he was trying to lure. It also became the ideal basis for competitive motoring on a shoestring.

Chapman decided to give his 7 a makeover. He tore off the rotten old wood and fabric body and built a replacement with contemporary materials: aluminium, which was easily available from scrap yards busy breaking warplanes; and plywood, a key ingredient of the RAF's celebrated 'wooden wonder', the de Havilland Mosquito. Aeroplane technology would shape Chapman's ideas much more than the traditional engineering that had failed to hold his attention at university. The 7 took him further away from his studies. He had already failed part one of his maths paper. When he failed it again, he was out of UCL with no degree.

His father was devastated, but Colin, never one to let a setback get in his way, enlisted in the RAF. He would have been obliged to do National Service after finishing university, but having obtained a pilot's licence already, he was accepted as an officer-cadet, which came with much better pay than an ordinary conscript. Within weeks he was flying – and getting paid for it.

With Hazel's help, the 7 was turned into a viable machine

to make the weekly commute between Muswell Hill and RAF Ternhill in Shropshire. The basic petrol ration was restored in June 1948 but only at a notional rate of ninety miles a month. And petrol for commercial purposes was dyed red to help police detect if it was being used improperly. A black market in fuel flourished. Inevitably, Colin had a supply and installed a second tank under the Austin's dash. If he was stopped, the authorities could test the fuel in the standard tank without suspicion.

It was during this time that Chapman had his first brush with motor trials, when he chanced on an event organised by the 750 Motor Club. Formed just before the war, this band of enthusiasts organised competitions for specials built from the plentiful remains of old Austin 7s. It is hard to imagine a more uncharismatic sport. The objective in a 750 Club timed trial hill climb was not so much speed as survival, to struggle to the top of a muddy hillside without stalling or rolling back or getting snagged on a passing tree. A passenger was required as ballast. Since bodywork was kept to a minimum, there was precious little weather protection and a strong likelihood of being drenched in mud. None of this deterred the healthy list of entrants.

A ban in 1925 on racing on any public road in mainland Britain had driven competition onto private land, where opportunities for sustained fast driving were very few. The beauty of trials was that they could be staged anywhere. No track was needed, just some gradient.

Chapman was smitten. He joined, got hold of the rule book and immediately began doing what came naturally to him – reading between the lines; anything to make his car more competitive. He inverted the rear axle so it could be mounted below the springs to give a few more inches of ground clearance on rutted tracks. He attached the mudguards with wood screws and rawlplugs so that they would give easily if snagged on gate posts or tree stumps. Hazel was also put to work on it, with detailed instructions left by Colin while he was flying. She was managing her mother's wool shop and despaired of ever getting her hands clean enough.

With Hazel beside him for ballast, Colin competed successfully in several trials, but like everything in his life it didn't last long. In 1950, he decided to take his chances in an amateur race. The Royal Automobile Club had leased the Silverstone airfield and were gradually turning it into a new permanent circuit. In June 1950, Colin entered his first real track race at Silverstone. It was only five laps long but Chapman in his dumpy, high-riding Austin 7 trials special, now christened 'Lotus', put up a furious fight, blasted past a Bugatti with three times the power and took the flag. Chapman and Lotus were on their way.

His timing could not have been better. More ex-RAF bases were being pressed into service as race tracks. Wide, open spaces, smooth surfaces with few obstructions to crash into – they made ideal venues. The novelty of watching circuit racing caught the public imagination and inspired more enthusiasts to have a go.

Chapman went back to work on his Lotus. While most of the 750 Club racers accepted the limitations of the 1922-designed Austin engine, Chapman brought the full force of his natural engineering nous to bear. He modified the cylinder head to accept double the number of inlets and added a big Stromberg carburettor from a V8 Ford. It gave his car a top speed of 90mph and it was so successful, repeatedly finishing a race half a lap ahead of the rest of the pack, that his competitors grew disheartened. At the end of the year, despite his protests, the club banned his modifications. It would be the first of many run-ins with rule makers. But, like John Cooper, he was starting to be courted by envious competitors asking for parts or whole cars to be built for them.

Up to then, Chapman had not thought of a future for himself making cars. Since resigning his commission with the RAF, he placated Stan by getting a sensible job as a salesman for British

Aluminium. Racing, his father concluded, was just a hobby – an outlet for both his technical and competitive passion. In any case, unlike John Cooper, Colin didn't have a dad with a fully equipped garage. All he had was a semi-derelict former stable block behind Stan's pub, the Railway Hotel in Tottenham Lane, Hornsey.

Despite those limitations, in January 1952, bankrolled by a £25 loan from his now-fiancée Hazel, the Lotus Engineering Company came into being, making or modifying springs, shock absorbers and cylinder heads for Austin 7s and Ford-based 1172 racers. Prices had to be low because the enthusiast-customers were all on tight budgets. Hazel did the packing and the paperwork.

It was a lowly start with modest ambitions. At the time he had no idea where it would lead. The upper echelons of motor sport were far beyond his sort, all the more since he and the rest of the country had just witnessed the high-profile humiliation of the great post-war hope, British Racing Motors, otherwise known as BRM.

12

HUMILIATION

It should have been a day of glory for British motor sport, 26 August 1950. For five years the public had been fed a steady ration of hints about Britain's great new racing car, one that would at last put the nation at the forefront of Grand Prix racing. Now, for the first time, at the *Daily Express*-sponsored International Trophy race at Silverstone, a capacity crowd of sixteen thousand would get a trackside view of the new machine being driven in anger for the very first time.

For Raymond Mays, racing-car driver and constructor, it promised to be the culmination of everything he had been striving for since his first boyhood discovery of speed on the Lincolnshire fens before the First World War. British Racing Motors (BRM) was a consortium of component suppliers to the nation's automotive industry, but it was Mays alone who had been the visionary, the cheerleader and the main source of energy that got BRM to the starting grid that bright English summer day.

From the outset, BRM had one objective: to put Britain where it had never been: at the very top of motor racing, and blast the foreign competition off the road. So advanced, so sophisticated, nothing would match it – well, that was the plan. The technical ambition was awesome. Its 1.5-litre, sixteen-cylinder engine was designed to reach a higher rpm than any previous racing engine – up to 14,500 revs. At 12,000rpm it was expected to achieve 400bhp. Mated to a Rolls-Royce supercharger, a descendant of the one that had given the Spitfire's Merlin engines their extra Battle of Britain-winning *oomph*, it produced so much torque that wheel spin was possible in all five gears.

It was terrifyingly complicated. The engine was in effect two 750cc V8s bolted together. Each of the sixteen tiny aluminium pistons was less than fifty millimetres in diameter. Each bank of cylinders had twin overhead camshafts. The missile-shaped bodywork styled by Walter Belgrove, on loan from Standard, was reminiscent of the pre-war Grand Prix Mercedes which had dominated racing in the 1930s – and so annoyed the patriotic Raymond Mays.

BRM nearly didn't make it to the race. Just two days before the event, the engines in both of their cars blew up. The mechanics who had been working round the clock to ready the machines had been given the weekend off. Someone was dispatched to knock them all up, home telephones still being a rarity in rural Lincolnshire. Engine assembler Dave Turner, caravanning in Skegness, was summoned by the campsite tannoy. Overnight, he and the team built one viable engine out of the two damaged ones. Race sponsors the *Daily Express*, hearing about this last-minute panic, arranged for the reassembled car to be flown by Bristol Freighter to RAF Bicester, close to Silverstone, where it was transhipped to one of BRM's Austin Lodestar transporters for the final few miles, flanked by police outriders.

Despite all the patriotic fervour, for this great occasion the services of a seasoned French racer, Raymond Sommer, had been retained by BRM. A telling indication of just how far behind Britain had slipped was the view, reluctantly accepted by Mays, that only a Continental driver would have the skill and experience necessary for handling such a powerful machine.

On the starting grid, in front of the crowded grandstands, Sommer lowered himself into the sleek, pale metallic-green machine. Of the nineteen starters, nine were Italian machines – Alfa Romeo, Maserati and Ferrari. Engines were started, swathing the racers in blue-grey exhaust. Tazio Nuvolari, the veteran Mantuan driving ace, dropped the flag, the revs of the combined field soared to an explosive cacophony and the machines surged forward – all except the BRM, which remained stranded on the start line. Frantically, Sommer re-engaged first gear, then tried second. It was hopeless. The drive shafts had sheared the moment he lifted the clutch; the enormous torque of the V16 too much for them. Mechanics rushed to assist, but Sommer spread his hands, levered himself from the cockpit and stepped away. A group of spectators near the start line jeered and threw halfpennies at the car.

Scenting a great British disaster, Fleet Street piled in; the *Sunday Pictorial* leading the charge with the banner headline: 'FLOP. FOUR YEARS, EIGHTEEN MEN AND £160,000 ... WENT TO BUILD THE RACING CAR THAT WOULD NOT START'.

In the weeks that followed, a protracted war of words raged between Mays and his suppliers over who was to blame. The defective part was isolated and questions were asked about its manufacture and inspection. Surely this was just an unavoidable consequence of trying out new and unproven technology? That was the team boss's explanation to his increasingly restive backers, but behind closed doors, doubts were voiced about Mays's leadership of the whole venture.

Among the hard-bitten, war-weary industrialists on his board, Mays was something of an exception. The only child of a doting and prosperous Lincolnshire wool merchant, from an early stage in his charmed life he styled himself as an extrovert. At his prep school, as he recalled in his autobiography, *Split Seconds*, he 'always liked to be well turned out, and it pleased me when "scruffy" boys were told off for being untidy. Colours attracted me enormously and blue was always my favourite – a preference that the headmaster seemed not to share when one day I appeared in blue socks and with a blue handkerchief in my breast pocket.'

In his youth he developed two passions: motor racing and music hall. His father Tom's enthusiasm for motoring meant that young Raymond got to ride with his mechanics when they tested his cars across the deserted fenland byways. 'These speed bursts', he recalled, 'were to me the supreme thrill ... bringing the realisation that to race was the great ambition of my life.'

In 1918, after schooling at Oundle, he was commissioned as a subaltern in the Grenadier Guards, choosing a suite at the Grosvenor Hotel over Chelsea Barracks. But he never got to see battle. The guards were en route to Cambrai when the armsitice was signed.

He resigned his commission and went up to Cambridge to read engineering, but found little time for lectures and claimed his tutors only knew his name for his achievements behind the wheel rather than a desk. His father Tom hoped he would take over the family business, but Raymond's ambitions were either for the race track or the stage (among his motor-racing trophies nestled a silver cup from a dance competition at the Casino Ballroom in Skegness). Precocious, passionate and brimming with confidence, he made little attempt to cover up the fact that he was gay, and the otherwise deeply conservative automotive world turned a blind eye, beguiled by his boundless charm and drive.

Mays, always a patriot, was determined to win in a British car, even if it meant building his own. But in the 1930s the successes he enjoyed with his first venture, English Racing Automobiles (ERA), were only in the junior voiturette classes of the sport. In Grand Prix, Mercedes-Benz and Auto Union were bankrolled by Hitler, and Alfa Romeo by Mussolini. Nothing came near. But as soon as victory in Europe was in sight, Mays resolved to right that wrong and raise Britain's game. If he could recruit the combined forces of the nation's motor industry to back him, he could seize the moment and finally take Britain to the top.

What he had not quite bargained for was how remarkably unscathed the Italians emerged from defeat, as if the war had barely distracted them. Not only were Alfa Romeo and Maserati back, they were joined by a third. For two decades, Enzo Ferrari had presided over the Alfa Romeo team; now he had struck out alone building cars under his own name.

On 2 March 1945, some weeks before VE Day, Mays sent a letter to each of the captains of Britain's motor industry, alerting them that he had appointed himself spokesman of a movement that as yet existed primarily in his own fertile imagination. 'I have given a good deal of thought to the future of motor sport in this country, particularly motor racing,' he wrote

> This has been inspired largely by the import of the innumerable letters I am constantly receiving from servicemen all over the world . . . It is only fitting that this superiority should be perpetuated as a gesture to the technicians and servicemen who have made our victory possible – no less than the masses who have patently endured so much.

This patriotic call to action did the trick. Within days he had commitments from the bosses of electrical suppliers Joseph Lucas and the component giant Rubery Owen. Others soon fell into line. The unveiling of Britain's first true Grand Prix challenger took place on 15 December 1949. Despite the Mays predilection for glitz, the occasion was redolent of the straightened times. The location was a freezing briefing room on RAF Folkingham. Mays and a few of his backers sat in their overcoats in front of a large and rather crumpled Union Jack that had been pinned on the wall for the occasion. In front of them, shrouded by a silk parachute that had somehow escaped being converted into lingerie, was the machine that Mays believed would finally give Britain its entrée into top-level racing.

From the moment the BRM was revealed, the clock was ticking. An impatient public wanted results. For five years they had been promised a car that would win on the track. Mays and his team fought so hard to get their machine up to speed, but it would be another eight years before a British car won a Grand Prix – and it wouldn't be a BRM. What went wrong? How could a team led by such a seasoned and passionate advocate, backed by the driving forces in Britain's automotive industry, fail so spectacularly?

Hindsight offers a variety of answers for BRM's shortcomings, but the most telling evidence can be found in an obscure intelligence report published by His Majesty's Stationery Office (HMSO) Technical Information and Document Unit just before the end of 1948. Its author was a 25-year-old prodigy named Cameron Earl.

The notion that British was best had taken a serious beating during the Second World War. While patriots could proudly point to the prowess of the Spitfire over the Messerschmitt ME 109 and Frank Whittle's achievements with the jet engine, those with a deeper knowledge of the technology behind Hitler's war machine knew there was much to be envied – and learned.

The purpose of the British Intelligence Objectives Subcommittee (BIOS) when it was formed in 1945 was to extract as much technical detail as could be gleaned from surviving German engineers while the Allied occupation gave them the authority to do so. Over the next two years the BIOS sent twelve thousand experts to gather information about German industry and technology and produced over three thousand reports, all published by the HMSO.

Cameron Earl's BIOS mission, No. 3,219 (yes, someone numbered them), was one of the last. History does not recall how he wangled it, but it probably attests to a very determined, single-minded character who could flash his brilliance to great effect. Clever, persuasive and pushy, Earl was one possessed with the right stuff to help deliver Britain's motor-racing renaissance.

He grew up in Scarborough where a fellow pupil at the Falsgrave Junior School recalled: 'he was very clever . . . He never came out to play. He was always doing homework to get on in life.' His first move when given a new bicycle was not to go for a ride but to take apart the three-speed Sturmey-Archer gear set it came with – and put it all back together. Assigned to the tank unit in the Royal Armoured Corps, he soon complained about the shortcomings of the machines. 'Well if you think you can do so much better, get on with it,' he was told. Four months later, Earl was working in the experimental wing of the Tank Design Department. By the end of the war he had risen to the rank of captain and had been drafted into Intelligence. Like Mays, Earl had been put out by the overwhelming supremacy of the Nazi motor-racing machine. Now he was well placed to unearth its secrets. He managed to wangle himself an assignment to Germany to track down the surviving best and brightest of the Mercedes team. According to S. C. H. Davis, motoring journalist and winner of the legendary 1927 Le Mans, Earl told him he was compiling it 'for the few people actively engaged in the construction of GP racing cars'.

The report, 'Investigation into the Development of German Grand Prix Racing Cars Between 1934 and 1939', ran to some two hundred pages. The cornucopia of technical detail leaves the reader in no doubt about the awesome technical prowess of the triumphant Mercedes and Porsche-designed Auto Union racing teams that blitzed all comers through most of the 1930s. More tellingly, Earl also describes in depth the attention to detail of the organisation, management and financing behind the teams that helped them win race after race wherever in the world they were sent.

Had he digested the report, even the determined Raymond Mays with the captains of Britain's motor industry behind him might have been tempted to throw in the towel. Earl noted that, in 1939, the Mercedes-Benz team kept a minimum of *twelve* race-worthy cars at the ready, with sixteen spare engines:

> Eight large diesel lorries were permanently attached to the experimental workshop for transporting the cars and equipment to the circuits. One of these was equipped with a mobile workshop complete with lathe, borer, welding plant and a shock absorber test jig. A second lorry was supercharged for use in transporting urgently required spares when necessary.

In 1951, the newly launched *Autosport* magazine had the inspired idea of asking Earl to comment on BRM's performance so far. His praise for the technical ambition of the machine was tempered by a warning of the extensive development such a complex design would need. He also expressed alarm at the number of suppliers Mays had recruited, warning how it could inhibit the rapid and constant development such a design would need to attain and maintain competitiveness. Earl would never find out just how perceptive and prophetic his words were, because the following June he was killed, at the wheel of one of Raymond Mays's old ERAs.

But on that humiliating summer day in 1950, the spectators coming away from Silverstone after BRM's disastrous debut could have been forgiven for deciding that Britain was better off out of high-end motor sport. But it wasn't all bad. Later in the day, in the 500cc race, Raymond Sommer had a much happier time at the wheel of one of John Cooper's amusing little cars, only to be beaten to second place by another Cooper driver, an unknown new boy by the name of Stirling Moss.

13

WIN ON SUNDAY –
SELL ON MONDAY

Stirling Moss's motor-racing pedigree was impeccable. Both his parents had raced cars – his father Alfred had competed at Brooklands and Indianapolis in the 1920s; and Aileen, his mother, had been Ladies National Trial champion. A prosperous and resourceful London dentist, Alfred ran a chain of seventeen surgeries and designed some dentistry tools. During the Second World War, fed up with having to herd the family to an outside bomb shelter during the night-time Blitz, he invented and patented what became the Morrison Shelter, a cage-like contraption that could be fitted over a bed. It was named after the then Home Secretary Herbert Morrison, who ordered 350,000 to be distributed to poor families.

The Moss family lived in a substantial Thames-side property near Maidenhead where Aileen raised ponies, which Stirling and his little sister Pat fielded in gymkhanas. When Stirling was ten, his father bought an old Austin 7 as an economical runabout for shifting hay bales. Stirling quickly mastered it and was soon charging around their land frightening the ponies. But his childhood wasn't entirely charmed. Scarlet fever and nephritis, a kidney

disease, caused him to miss two years of education – and helped
to make him a failure as a scholar.

Alfred's hope that Stirling would follow him into the family
business soon evaporated when he saw his son's school reports.
Although he was good at sports, Stirling hated his public school,
Haileybury, where according to him anti-Semitism was rife. Even
though his grandfather had abandoned the Jewish faith to marry
a Christian and changed the family name from Moses, he was
still a target.

The kidney disease excluded Stirling from National Service (it
also made him a lifetime teetotaller), so, after leaving school at
sixteen, Stirling's parents suggested the hotel trade and he started
by training as a waiter – he even adopted the name Toni in a bid
to fit in. But he hated the drudgery and had no aptitude for it. His
only passion, apart from girls, was driving, but his parents were
having none of it. Aileen had made it a condition of accepting
Alfred's hand in marriage that he give up racing and her business-
minded husband knew from first-hand experience that there was
no money in competitive driving. You either had to have a garage
or a private income. But shortly after the war, Alfred bought himself a pre-war BMW 328 sports car. Although it was a ten-year-old
design, the 328 was still a competitive machine. In 1947, Stirling
persuaded his dad to let him have a go at a few minor speed trials
and showed immediate promise.

The route back from one such event took the Mosses
past Cooper's Surbiton garage. On the forecourt was one of
John Cooper's first 500cc cars, which were making a name
for themselves. Alfred Moss knew Charles Cooper from their
Brooklands days and was persuaded to stop and have a look.
Stirling was smitten and his father too couldn't help being
impressed by the miniature racing machine. Shortly after this
encounter, Stirling's parents relented. Alfred said he could have
a year to prove himself and the family would support his efforts.

To his sister Pat's dismay, their horse box, hauled by an ancient Rolls-Royce shooting-brake, was converted into a car transporter. Donat Muller, a German POW who had been allowed to work on the Mosses' land and stayed on after the war, acted as mechanic. But Stirling was also made to contribute: 'I had to sell my tent, my bicycle, my radio and other things, and I had to pay my own expenses.' One other stipulation was he would have to wear a crash helmet – unheard of then – supplied by Herbert Johnson of Bond Street, who also made Pat's riding hats.

Stirling's first actual circuit race was on an airfield at Brough near Hull. It was typical of the many circuits that were springing up all over the country on former wartime air bases. The 1-kilometre track was laid out on the runway and perimeter road. It was organised by the Blackburn Aircraft Motor Club. Stirling and his father transported the car by night train, but had to drain the fuel tank for the journey, so they carried the fuel in cans in their suitcases. With petrol still rationed, the cars ran on methanol mixed with acetone and castor oil.

On the day, the rain was so heavy that the organisers considered cancelling the event, but five thousand spectators turned out to watch the three heats. As it happened, they were in for a treat. In his heat and the final, Moss, at eighteen the youngest driver by far, was uncatchable. Then, finding that the events had finished earlier than anticipated, the organisers decided to stage an extra eight-lap race for the top six drivers. But in the scramble to stage it the field was flagged off before Moss was ready. Undaunted, the youngster set off after the others and one by one picked them off until the race was his. 'BROUGH RACE WON BY BACKMARKER' was the *Daily Mail*'s headline, which described the event as 'a new thrill'.

'Road-racers hurtled their machines round the treacherous surface of the rain-sodden track ... and the handling of his car brought eighteen-year-old S. Moss of London out ahead.' Stirling's prize was £15 and a beer tankard. By the end of 1948,

Moss had claimed eleven wins out of fifteen starts. There was no turning back now.

Stirling's timing was impeccable. Silverstone and Goodwood were open for business, riding the crest of a wave of new interest in motor sport. His parents started to accept the inevitable: this was going to be Stirling's future. But where would it lead? He convinced them that he should try his first race abroad.

The Circuito del Garda was a very Italian event. First held in 1927, the 8-mile circuit was made up of spectacular country roads and cobbled streets that swooped in and out of hillside villages and round blind bends. Moss, his parents and a mechanic travelled in the family's Rolls-Royce, towing his sister's horsebox with the Cooper aboard. What the Italians made of this sight one can only imagine.

As well as a wealth of driving talent, and despite being on the losing side in the war, Italy already dominated the top end of motor racing. With the Germans out of action and only spo-radic competition from the French, their teams mostly raced each other. At Garda, the list of entrants read like a *Who's Who* of Italian racing aristocracy: Villoresi, Bonetto, Tadini, Bracco, Bianchetti and Sterzi in Ferraris; Biondetti, Carini and Romano in Maseratis; Taruffi and Macchieraldo in Cisitalias; and Serafini in an OSCA. Moss in his Cooper was the only foreigner. When he dropped the horsebox ramp and unloaded his tiny machine, derived from a pair of crashed Fiat Topolinos, the Italians were highly amused. He recalled: 'They laughed at my Cooper which it must be confessed, did not measure up in any dignity and impressiveness to those lovely thoroughbreds of Italy and France. They had never seen a racing car like it before and to them it was a joke.'

What made the Italians so good at motor sport is not easy to pin down. Cameron Earl explained Mercedes-Benz's pre-war supremacy as a combination of massive investment, meticulous organisation and attention to detail. Here, motor racing induced a national fervour among the *tifosi* that bordered on the religious.

Undaunted, Moss prepared for the race, but the gulf between what Britain could offer against the Italians was plain. Moss resolved to drive as steadily as he could, as close to the limits of the little Cooper's potential would allow, and stay on the road. The race was in three heats. First he surprised everyone by qualifying third and then proceeded to hold his position against far more powerful V12 Ferraris. As bigger cars failed to shake him off and several retired, Moss got through to the final round and came home third. 'What an ovation I got,' he said. 'The jeers became cheers.' A competitive Englishman in a British car – albeit a tiny one – was a novelty.

Novelty was soon to prove a problem for Moss as he attempted to raise his game closer to home. Sceptics saw a young upstart in a tremendous hurry to earn his spurs, which likely meant an accident was waiting to happen. This was a time when speeds were rising – and so would the number of fatalities.

Sports-car events then were as popular as open-wheeled racing, particularly in Europe. Top-line Grand Prix drivers all found time to compete in them. Manufacturers liked them too because the cars in the race were much the same as what was sold to the public. 'Win on Sunday, sell on Monday' went the maxim. But Britain had nothing to compare with France's Le Mans, Italy's Mille Miglia or Sicily's Targa Florio. And, as with Grand Prix, British cars had not featured since the Bentley Le Mans victories of the 1920s.

In 1950, the Royal Automobile Club, the governing body for motor racing in the United Kingdom, revived the historic Tourist Trophy race using a circuit in Northern Ireland. An anomaly of the 1925 ban on competitions on British public roads was that it did not extend to Northern Ireland. So County Antrim got its own road circuit near the village of Dundrod.

It comprised eight miles of very fast and very narrow country roads, bordered by steep grass banks and sturdy stone gateposts, with a liberal sprinkling of telegraph poles along the way. Among the other excitements were sudden dips, an outrageously tight hairpin, blind brows and a hair-raising downhill section known as the Deer's Leap with a tight right-hander at the bottom. And if that wasn't enough of a challenge, the particularly abrasive asphalt surface chewed up tyres during the six-hour event.

Desperate to compete, Stirling Moss approached all the companies planning to field teams in the race. But there was a problem, as he told his biographer, Philip Porter: 'None of them would trust me. They thought I was going too fast for my experience and if I was going to have an accident and kill myself, they didn't want me to do it in their car.' But Moss did have experience at getting his way, and was not about to give up. What's more, there was a particular machine he wanted to try. Racing drivers are not necessarily car enthusiasts and Stirling Moss simply saw cars as a means to an end. But one machine that had excited him on sight was William Lyons's creation, the XK120. 'It was so beautiful-looking; everybody wanted to have one but you couldn't buy them. They all had to go to America for dollars.'

Moss knew of one person who owned one: the journalist and racing driver Tommy Wisdom. He also knew that Wisdom had been booked to drive for another team in the TT and that many years ago, Moss's father had lent Wisdom a car. Perhaps he might return the favour.

Wisdom recalled: 'I was taking high-octane refreshment in the Steering Wheel Club, London's Mecca of motor racing folk, when a fresh faced curly-haired youngster ... came along side, drew up a barstool and dropped a broad hint ... An hour later I found I had accepted, subject to his father's okay, the persuasive Stirling's proposition that he should drive my XK in the TT.'

William Lyons, still a newcomer to motor racing, with a

machine that had been designed primarily as a show car, was wary of the new kid on the grid and was not happy as Moss struggled on the first day of practice with the barely familiar car on the unknown circuit. The ingénue was up against far more experienced drivers and more race-bred cars from Aston Martin, Allard and Frazer Nash. Had he bitten off more than he could chew? The next day Moss set the fastest lap – in the dry. But then, as the race started, so did the rain, which got steadily worse as the day wore on. Wind blew the beer tent over and a huge marquee into which the press had retreated collapsed. But the few hardy spectators who remained at their posts witnessed a virtuoso performance of driving in the wet. By lap two Moss was in the lead and pulling away from another Jaguar piloted by Leslie Johnson, a driver noted for his wet-weather skills. But the pack was never far behind Moss, so with an hour to go his father Alfred held out the 'Faster' sign, whereupon his son obliged by putting down the fastest lap of the race. Stirling, untroubled by the appalling conditions, wasn't even driving on his limit and cruised to victory.

As Moss explained later:

Because it was wet I think it helped me. When it's really wet you don't have adhesion and neither do the bigger engine cars such as Allards so they couldn't use their horsepower. Our brakes were really limited at the time because of the technology [disc brakes had yet to arrive] but when it's wet you can't use the brakes hard anyway. So there were quite a lot of things going for having a car of that type.

Typically, Moss, a master of understatement, goes to great lengths to make a virtue of the car's limitations – the XK had not been designed for competition. But reading between the lines it is very clear that what else was at play was a formidable natural talent tempered by a self-control that belied his age.

One of those who could read between the lines was William
Lyons. That night, at the after-race reception in the Grand Central
Hotel in Belfast, he offered Moss a contract to lead the Jaguar
racing team the next year. It was a big risk for the wily but cautious Lyons, who nevertheless recognised in Moss a rare maturity
for his age. A reminder of the young driver's youthful charm, however, shines through in a letter written to Lofty England, Jaguar's
seasoned team manager, shortly after the TT: 'I am enclosing a
cheque which I would like you to split up into three £5 for each
of the boys and with the remaining £10 would you buy yourself
something to remember the occasion by . . . Please thank Mr Lyons
and Mr Heynes for allowing me to drive the XK and tell them I
am looking forward to the next time! Cheerio, Stirling.'

Lofty's response is a similar piece of quintessential Britishness.
Having served as mechanic to many of the best drivers of the
1930s, he knew how to recognise talent. In his reply, he expresses
his appreciation for Stirling thinking of the mechanics, but he
attached a cheque for £10, explaining: 'I have received all the
reward I require in the knowledge that you were satisfied with
the car and the very satisfactory result which was obtained
through your efforts . . . I was most impressed with your general
attitude to motor racing, which was something reminiscent of the
days gone by when I worked for Seaman.' This was praise indeed,
for Richard Seaman had been the only Englishman to be a Grand
Prix contender in the 1930s.

A few hours after that celebration at the Belfast hotel, another
milestone was passed. It was Moss's birthday. He was twenty-one.

14

ENDURANCE

Moss's performance convinced Lyons that he should get serious about going racing. The Dundrod TT win demonstrated that, in the right hands, the XK120, conceived as a show car, had real competitive potential. But racing carried huge reputational risks. Failure could have a knock-on effect on the company's growing international sales. What's more, only outright wins produced worthwhile publicity.

Lyons would also be going up against the likes of Enzo Ferrari, a man with three decades of racing behind him; first as a competitor, then a team manager, and now, like Lyons, patron of his own marque. But where Ferrari only sold cars to finance his racing obsession, Jaguar's core business was building and selling cars for the road.

But Jaguar was now on a roll. From just over a thousand cars made in 1946, it delivered six times that number in 1950, three-quarters of them for export. Lyons's 100mph saloon, the pressed-steel-bodied, XK-powered Jaguar Mark VII, had just debuted at the London motor show. But the stakes were high. The XK was the first ever Jaguar-designed engine. It couldn't afford to fail.

A sharp lesson in the reputational hazards of competition had already been graphically taught by the high-profile failure of BRM, not just at its debut but in several subsequent events. Despite the backing of Britain's motor magnates, Raymond Mays' promise to finally place Britain at the top table of motor sport had proved spectacularly undeliverable, fuelling doubts that the British had the know-how to get there. If Britain couldn't make a viable Grand Prix car, what hope was there for its sports cars?

The world's most prestigious race at the time was Les Vingt-Quatre Heures du Mans, better known simply as Le Mans. Run over closed public roads since 1923 (with a ten-year interruption between 1939–49), the enormous 8.4-mile circuit included a 1.9-mile-long straight and several sharp right-angle corners. Each car had a pair of drivers and by the early 1950s, with cars *averaging* close to 100mph for the entire twenty-four hours, it was a truly brutal test of mechanical and human stamina.

For the British, the significance of Le Mans was massive. It was the only international event in which they had achieved any consistent success – five Bentley wins between 1923 and 1930. It was also the only motor race outside the United States to which Americans paid any attention. And that interested Lyons.

But at Le Mans in 1951, Jaguar would be taking on bigger, much more powerful cars. The 24-hour race was not only about surviving to the finish; top speed could be decisive. More power could be extracted from the XK engine, but would that be enough to put Jaguar at the front of the field? There was another way. Bill Heynes, Jaguar's engineering chief, persuaded William Lyons to sanction the construction of what was in effect an entirely new car around the XK engine; a sports car, but one designed specifically with Le Mans in mind. It would mean a completely new light-weight frame and a more streamlined body. The latter requirement was a challenge for Lyons. He alone had overseen the shapes of all his cars. He saw himself as the artistic custodian of Jaguar style. But aerodynamics was a science, not an art. The 3.4-litre XK would be going up against 4.1-litre V12 Ferraris. Two miles of every lap were taken flat out down the Mulsanne Straight. Top speed mattered. Any advantage to be found through making the car more slippery could make up for the power deficit.

~

Malcolm Sayer had never worked in the motor industry. Although he emerged from Loughborough College in 1938 with a diploma in automobile engineering, he saw his future at the Bristol Aeroplane Company, where he thought pay and prospects would be better. Given that only a year later Britain was at war, it was a shrewd choice. He was born in Cromer, where his father taught maths and art. Both disciplines would be fundamental to Sayer's vocation. At college he was seen as an eccentric: he owned a Bentley which he christened 'Boadicea', but couldn't afford the petrol and drew cartoons for the student magazine.

At Bristol Aeroplane Company he warmed to the rarefied discipline of aerodynamics. Aircraft shapes are deceptively simple. The end product may have aesthetic appeal, but their graceful curves are arrived at through hundreds, even thousands, of calculations for key factors such as weight, lift, thrust and drag. Sayer, a natural mathematician, was in his element. Within months he had improved the wing performance of Bristol's Blenheim bomber and pioneered groundbreaking 'reverse flow' methodology to improve the air-cooling of its engines.

When the Luftwaffe bombed the Filton factory, several of Sayer's colleagues were killed and a photograph was taken of him with his head bandaged holding the large lump of shrapnel responsible. He stayed on at Bristol after the war was over and he married during the exceptionally cold winter of 1947 that brought Britain to a halt. His wedding photo shows him wearing a flying jacket and a duffel coat for the occasion.

Always a mercurial character, he accepted the job of setting up an engineering department for the University of Baghdad and took himself off to Iraq, only to find when he got there that the department was only a proposal. But his time there was not wasted. He later claimed that he honed his knowledge observing the behaviour of wind on the dunes in the Iraqi desert.

Still uncertain about his future, he abandoned his wife and child for several months and disappeared to France, living rough and busking. When he reappeared at his parents' home, he told them he was going to be an artist.

But Sayer had not lost interest in cars, and through the diaspora of ex-Bristol engineers he heard that Jaguar was looking for someone who knew about aerodynamics. It was only a short-term contract, £5 a week, and he would have to clock in and out just like the men on the production line. But it was work that interested him.

Sayer had to tread a difficult path. Creating a shape for the then unnamed competition version of the XK120, he was effectively replacing a design that had been an international sensation at the 1948 Earls Court motor show. And while Lyons's motivation for getting into racing was to enhance Jaguar's engineering pedigree, ultimately it was all about sales. The racing car needed to be recognisable as a Jaguar and look like the models people could see in the showroom and on the road.

Creating an aerodynamic shape for a car could be more challenging than designing an aeroplane, as Sayer explained in a lecture he gave called 'The Shape of Cars': 'The design cannot follow as precise pattern as that for, say, an aircraft in nice laminar flow air because the car operates in turbulent air almost entirely, and near the ground – at least it should – which give an entirely different set of conditions.'

The XK has very distinctive styling features: a swooping line from the top of the front wing down under the door handle, and a curved, tapering bonnet. Sayer's challenge was to make an aerodynamically viable shape that still hinted at those stylish curves. He put the headlamps behind Perspex covers that followed the curve of the bodywork, compressed and widened the radiator grille and flattened the sides of the body. One concession was to include a gentle dip in the line between the front and rear wings to act as a 'waist', echoing the original car's swooping line.

The overall effect was rather as if a model of the XK120 had been carved out of soap and then used for a vigorous wash until the more pronounced outlines had been smoothed away. Sayer's aerodynamic requirements retained a whiff of Jaguar. It was a compromise, but a happy one. It could only be whispered, and well out of earshot of William Lyons, but it even made the original look a little dated. The name also became streamlined, as the awkward XK120-C (for competition) became the C-Type – the first of a dynasty of Jaguar 'letter' cars that survives nearly seventy years on with today's F-Type.

How the shape got from drawing board to metal was also a big change for Jaguar. There was no sawmill mock-up or 'up a bit, down a bit'. To translate the aerodynamic deductions Sayer made into three dimensions, he would break them down into a series of horizontal and vertical slices. The vertical cross sections were called the body line and the horizontal were known as the water line, as if it were the outline a shape makes when partly submerged in water. This way he could reduce a surface that might curve in two or three directions to a series of mathematical co-ordinates; dots, in effect, for the craftsmen in the sawmill to join.

Sayer was anticipating what CAD (computer-aided design) would do in thirty years' time. But in an age before computers, what he handed the craftsmen was a booklet full of calculations from which they could bring his shape to life.

As well as his gift for mathematics, Sayer exhibited an almost mystical understanding of aerodynamics. When a Jaguar driver demanded that the little Perspex windscreen in front of him be shortened by two inches so he could see over it rather than through it, Sayer told him it would cut their top speed by 4mph, which is exactly what happened. He was also sceptical about the value of wind-tunnel testing for cars, where, as he pointed out, 'the wheels are not rotating, the engine is not running'. For him, nothing but real-world testing could show what happened to the air around a car as it overtook another or made sudden changes of direction. He poured all this thinking into the C-Type's slippery bodywork, which, combined with engine tweaks and a lighter frame, made it capable of 140mph.

But Lyons was still taking an astonishing risk. Not only would this be the untried C-Type's first competitive outing, Jaguar was up against nine Ferraris. Briggs Cunningham, an American who had discovered sports-car racing first with an MG TC, was fielding a team of his own creations powered by 5.5-litre V8s. Juan Manuel Fangio, the Argentinean legend, was behind the wheel of a 4.5-litre French Talbot-Lago and the rest of the field were a motley collection of lesser machines, including a previously unheard of German entry called Porsche.

As if to express his confidence in the cars, Lyons had his team of C-Types registered and licensed for the road and driven the 500 miles from Coventry to Le Mans by his team mechanics.

The other person staking everything on Jaguar was Stirling Moss, impatient to make his mark as a top-line driver. One of the signature features of the race was the 'Le Mans Start': the cars were lined up at an angle to the track in order of engine size and the drivers were positioned on the opposite side. When the flag dropped, they had to sprint across the track, jump in and get moving. Moss was twenty-second on the grid, but had practised his starts repeatedly. He beat most of the other drivers across the track and passed fourteen cars before the first corner. Team tactics were for Moss to act as hare to the Ferrari hounds, and by lap five he had taken a commanding lead and set a new lap record of 105.232, impressive for a young driver new to Le Mans in an untried car. To his satisfaction, he discovered that the Jag would easily cruise down the Mulsanne Straight at a steady 140mph, with power still in reserve. He hoped that by not caning the car it would keep going through the twenty-four hours. But it was not to last. In the dead of night, in the rain, Moss's engine expired.

It was a long, dark, drenching 3-mile walk back to the pits. Before daylight, a second C-Type retired. The mood in the Jaguar pits became tense as everything now rested on the survival of the third and last car. But Moss had done what was required: he had worn out the Ferraris and French Talbots that had given chase, leaving the way open for his Jaguar teammates Peter Walker and Peter Whitehead to take the chequered flag.

The press was unanimous in saying that it was Moss who had made Jaguar's win possible by luring the competition to go hell for leather and breaking the Continental challengers. But the real focus was on the car itself. That Jaguar could come out of nowhere and beat the bigger, more powerful Ferraris with a new and untried car was a huge coup. After the BRM humiliation, it offered fans back home something worth hoping for – that maybe Britain could be a contender after all.

For Moss, it would also mean that his road to glory was going to get more crowded. The fact that Britain at last had an international race-winning machine for the first time since the Bentley era in the '20s was not lost on his elders – drivers whose best racing years had been stolen from them by the war. Bitter and battle-hardened, they were spoiling for a fight.

15

Eton, Sandhurst – and Colditz

A racing driver's motivation is quite simple: it comes down to an overwhelming determination to win. Balancing that is the application of skill, reconciling raw, competitive aggression with sensitivity to the behaviour of a car and the road and weather conditions. The ingénue Moss excelled in all these areas. He was a new breed of driver, ahead of his time. Teetotal, super-fit, early to bed, managing his sporting life like the business it would soon become, this grown-up approach would irritate contemporaries who cherished the more cavalier, amateur traditions associated with the sport. But speeds were rising; cars were becoming lighter and nimbler. Moss knew that if he looked after himself he had years of competitive racing ahead of him. It was the modern way – and it didn't impress the old guard.

The Second World War had brought the curtain down on Brooklands' fast set – the moneyed, aristocratic gentlemen (and gentlewomen) drivers who squandered their trust funds on the pursuit of speed. As teenagers, Duncan Hamilton and Tony Rolt were among the last of that era, angling for a drive on the hallowed concrete banking. A natural mechanic, Hamilton as a youth exasperated his well-heeled parents by borrowing and dismantling any car he could get his hands on. His father enrolled him in the Chelsea College of Aeronautical and Automobile Engineering, where he hoped Duncan's talents would lead him towards a decent job. But cars remained a weakness. His parents had already banned him from having his own after a series of lunchtime races round Chelsea with fellow students attracted police attention.

Brooklands became his playground. To get past the gate, he used to climb into his college overalls, fill a bucket of water and barge through the queue, ordering them to make way. Affable and persuasive, larger than life in every sense, he was making good progress with Brooklands regulars like Billy Cotton the band leader when the war intervened.

The navy rewarded his appetite for adventure. During the abortive Allied Norwegian campaign in 1940, he was fished out of the sea when HMS *Glorious* was sunk, only to find himself back in the water a few hours later when HMS *Curlew*, the cruiser that salvaged him, was bombed by the Luftwaffe. Rescued again, a shell then put him in hospital for five months. In the Fleet Air Arm, he narrowly escaped being shot down flying Lysanders over occupied Holland to collect SOE agents. Less physically threatening was the occasion when he was nearly court-martialled after his dog ate a set of documents, postponing naval action by several days.

~

Tony Rolt's war was no less colourful. Barely a year after winning the British Empire Trophy, Rolt, a Sandhurst graduate and lieutenant in the Rifle Brigade, was in Calais with the British Expeditionary Force. For three days his brigade held up the 10th Panzer Division from advancing on Dunkirk, for which he received a Military Cross (MC) – and detention in Germany for the rest of the warm, where his exploits continued unabated.

Rolt attempted no less than seven escapes from five camps, one of which took him just metres from the Swiss border, all of which would earn him a bar to his MC. He was transferred to Colditz in 1943. There he masterminded a rooftop airborne escape plan involving the creation of a glider, christened the 'Colditz Cock'. Constructed behind a false wall in the castle attic, it was to be powered by the gravitational force of a falling bath of concrete. The venture was thwarted by the arrival in April 1945 of Allied liberators.

~

More serious and steely, Rolt was in many ways the opposite of the rumbustious Hamilton, but they shared a furious desire to make up for those lost years. They launched themselves at the post-war motor racing. But the wins were few and far between, in ageing and inferior machinery. Together, perhaps as a result of their war-honed perseverance, they gravitated naturally to long-distance endurance racing in which they made a good pair. Old enough to remember the Bentley glory days that fired their childhood imaginations, they set their sights on Le Mans. The 24-hour race required stamina and determination. Driving flat out down the Mulsanne Straight, hour after hour in the dark, and sometimes in the rain, called for a cool head and a stiff dose of bloody-minded resolve. Rolt and Hamilton more than fitted the bill. In 1950 and 1951 they distinguished themselves by finishing well up the field, making the best of inferior machinery. But time was ticking on. Both men were now in their thirties, being hounded by the likes of Moss and the next generation of drivers coming on stream. At this stage it did not matter to them what nationality the car was; they had both resorted to Continental machinery in their quest for victories. But now, finally, there was a British car with the speed and reliability to win Le Mans. Fortunately, their dogged determination and staying power had attracted the attention of Jaguar team manager Lofty England. He asked them to join the team.

In 1953, there was even more pressure on Jaguar. After their historic win in 1951, the next year was a wipeout. Malcolm Sayer's modifications to make the C-Type's bodywork more slippery starved the engines of ventilation and caused them to overheat. It was a lesson in how capricious the new science of car aerodynamics could be. And to press home the humiliation, a surprise entry that year by a resurgent Mercedes team won first time out.

There were sixty-nine entrants from nineteen different marques. As well as more British teams trying their hand at the big race, Jaguar now faced opposition from three Italian teams: Ferrari, with 4.5-litre V12s; supercharged Lancias; and Alfa Romeo's revolutionary Disco Volante, so named because of its flattened, splayed body shape. American Briggs Cunningham was also back with a team of big V8s.

Jaguar had the same size 3.4-litre XK engine but now the C-Types, back to their original shape, were shod with revolutionary new disc brakes, a British invention. If they couldn't match the Ferraris' speed down the straight, at least they could brake harder and up to 100 yards later.

At last, Rolt and Hamilton were in with a chance, albeit in the same team as the youthful Moss. But then – disaster. In practice their car had worn the number 18, the same as another entrant. For the officials of the Automobile Club de l'Ouest, who organised the race, this was too much; their rules had been flouted. Rolt and Hamilton were disqualified.

Inured to disappointment, they did the sensible thing and drove into Le Mans town and found a bar in which to drown their sorrows. All was going according to plan until Jaguar's team manager Lofty England appeared in front of their table. The officials had been mollified (25,000 francs had changed hands) and they were back in the race.

What happened next is a matter for debate. Rolt, a disciplined if driven character, later claimed somewhat unconvincingly that he had had nothing to drink. Team boss Lofty England concurred, putting it thus: 'Of course I would never have let them race under the influence. I had enough trouble with them when they were sober!'

According to Hamilton's own memoir, appropriately titled *Touch Wood*, in the few hours left before the start, hot baths and several cups of coffee were taken, but when the caffeine began to make his arms twitch, he supplemented cognac.

Within an hour of the start, Moss claimed the lead but his Jaguar started to misfire. A four-minute pit stop while the plugs were changed followed by a second stop to replace a blocked air filter put him down to twenty-first. Would the other Jaguars suffer the same faults as Moss? Mechanical problems were contagious among teams; what one car suffered often afflicted the others. Rolt and Hamilton pressed on into the night, duelling with the dominant Ferraris for the lead. In the early hours of the morning, BBC commentator Raymond Baxter looked in on the Jaguar pit: 'It was silent, the tension palpable.' He decided to leave them to it, but then Hamilton's wife Angela saw him and greeted him with a warm smile. 'Oh, hello, Raymond, would you like a cup of tea?'

Moss fought his way back up through the field, a heroic dash that would surely break the car, but as in 1951 he was doing the same sterling job of wearing out the opposition who gave chase. Hamilton, in the lead, nearly ended their race with what is euphemistically termed an 'unsafe release'. Rushing to get back out before the second-place Ferrari came past, he cut across a back-marker braking for fuel. They missed, inches apart, and he was also lucky not to be disqualified. By dawn, fewer than half the cars were still running. Mist descended and threatened to cause chaos on the track. One Ferrari crashed and the driver was killed. When Hamilton pulled into the pits for a handover he told

Rolt he had just experienced the worst three hours' driving of his life. With eight hours to go, Peter Whitehead and Ian Stewart's C-Type was fourth, Moss and his co-driver Peter Walker were back up to third, harrying the second-placed Ferrari. And when that expired it was left to an American, Cunningham, to split the leaders. The Rolt–Hamilton Jaguar was well in the lead when, at 130mph, a bird smashed into its windscreen and broke Hamilton's nose. But even that was not going to stop them. This was a drive of a lifetime.

They took the chequered flag after 2,555.04 miles, the first time a car had averaged over 100mph throughout the twenty-four hours. Moss and Walker clawed their way up to second after an epic drive. The third works Jaguar finished fourth, and another privately entered Jaguar came in ninth. For William Lyons, it served notice that Jaguar was no flash in the pan. Not only had he won against the massed ranks of Ferrari, but all his team had finished. He immediately sent a telegram to the newly crowned Queen Elizabeth informing her of the great news. In his book, *In the Track of Speed*, Moss recalled the French spectators, rewarded with such a tense spectacle, chanting 'Elizabeth, Everest, Jaguar', 'linking the three great events of the year.'

For Rolt and Hamilton, the scale of the victory went a long way to make up for those lost racing years they would never get back. There would be other races and other victories, but none quite like this.

WHEN AUSTIN MET HEALEY

Victory on the track made Jaguar's name worldwide, particularly in the United States, but the Coventry company was never able to make enough XKs to meet demand. MG had the same problem.

Conventional motor-industry wisdom held that sports cars were at best loss-leaders and at worst money pits. The men still at the helm of the big companies – Austin, Morris and the Rootes Group – had been around long enough to remember what happened to Bentley, and Sunbeam, the only British marque to have won a Grand Prix. No sooner had their cars crossed the finish line than bankruptcy and liquidation were looming in the rearview mirror.

But two men who almost certainly never knew of each other's existence – Sir Stafford Cripps, the socialist chancellor of the exchequer, and Kjell Qvale, the Alameda car dealer – had changed all that. In the post-war dash for dollars to shore up the British economy, the wilfully British semi-vintage MG, unloved by Leonard Lord and ignored by William Morris, had found its way to America and – like a later British curiosity, Monty Python – confounded everyone at home with its stateside success.

And far from being a passing craze, America's love of the British sports car was showing no sign of flagging. Even as the pressure to export was relaxed and steel rationing lifted, Jaguar and MG were discovering that their only problem was making enough cars to meet demand.

Leonard Lord's Austin Atlantic was a personal failure for which only he could take full responsibility. He had thought he could second-guess American taste, micromanaged the design with Ricardo Burzi and came up with what would become widely regarded as one of Britain's ugliest cars. It was a painful irony that the MGs which he had so tersely dismissed before the war when he was at Morris were a runaway hit.

It is easy with hindsight to pillory Lord for his thinking behind the Atlantic. With the government holding car makers to ransom by rationing steel to export performance, desperate measures were urgently needed. The unsuitably slow and cramped Austin Devon had initially sold well in America. But this happened to be during a brief period when US domestic cars were in short supply due to an epidemic of industrial action in 1945–46. The Austins earned Britain those much-needed dollars, but since they didn't produce a profit they were just an elaborate form of currency exchange.

As it turned out, modestly sized British saloon cars would never find enough of a following in the United States to make it a worth-while market. Billy Rootes's warning to his brother in 1945 had been spot on. Detroit would always win because their economies of scale were bigger and their overheads per car were lower.

Leonard Lord understood this better than most. As a production engineer, his route to success was by making more cars with fewer hands, smoothing the production process into seamless mass production. But in the worldwide export market this was not enough. The Atlantic, his answer to Billy Rootes's prescription of a 'specialised product' for the US market, had failed. Austin had no product the Americans wanted and Lord had been left with a surplus of A90 engines. Salvation came at the London motor show in 1952, from a man possessed of just the same passions and aspirations Lord had so despised in MG's Cecil Kimber. His name was Donald Healey.

Born in 1898, two years after Lord, Healey grew up in the tiny Cornish village of Perranporth, where the dwindling fishing business was augmented by frequent shipwrecks. As a boy he witnessed bounty washed ashore including enough candles to keep the village lit at night 'for the next four or five years' and huge barrels of wine. 'If they didn't leak they had to be sent to the Board of Trade, but marlinspikes soon saw to this, bucketsful finding their way into the village. The local drunks had the time of their lives, lying open-mouthed beneath their personal leaks until insensible.'

Donald inherited his father's appetite for speed – albeit on a penny-farthing bicycle – and he embraced the local talent for scrounging. He was still a boy when, from the abandoned remains of an early motorcycle engine and some bicycle parts, he assembled his first vehicle for riding up and down the sands. He also converted his father's first car, a Panhard et Levassor, to generate electricity for the family's general store and some of the nearby cottages. But the magazine *Flight*, which arrived every week by horse-drawn delivery from Truro Station, convinced Donald that aviation would be his calling.

By the age of sixteen he had an apprenticeship with the Sopwiths, who had taken over a defunct ice rink in Kingston upon Thames, moving on to the Mecca of Brooklands to build the legendary Sopwith Camel. Once the Royal Flying Corps was formed, Healey couldn't wait to join up and lied about his age to enlist. But two gruelling years' service in France, culminating in being shot down by friendly fire on one of the first ever night-bombing missions, dulled his passion for flight and he made his way back home to Cornwall.

There, he opened a garage in his home village, next door to

the family shop. Among the features he introduced was one of Cornwall's first petrol pumps. There were only three cars in his village, one of them his father's, so he developed a sideline hiring out chauffeured cars and charabancs. The irrepressible Healey also built electric organs and radios, which he sold under the locally inspired name, Perraphone.

But it was cars that came first. By his own admission, he was never a fast driver, but his passion for long-distance competitions took him to the first European rallies, culminating in a spirited attempt at the 1931 Monte Carlo Rally in an Invicta. Before he was even half way, he sideswiped a telegraph pole, knocked the rear axle several inches out of place and jammed one of the brakes. So he sawed through a rod to free it and drove on for a further three days over the Alps and down into Monte Carlo on three brakes and won the event.

Rallying as a sport was still in its infancy. It was less about top speed than endurance – of both car and driver. Knowledge of the machinery and a capacity to improvise was what frequently stood between survival and retirement. This experience gave Healey what he believed was his advantage when it came to building cars later on: 'The basic difference between some of the highly qualified automobile engineers, who have achieved their learning without any real practical experience of working on cars in a garage or at the roadside, and those less qualified – like myself – who are in essence practical engineers.'

Keen to apply his expertise to design, Healey headed to the Midlands where he prepared competition cars for Riley, moving on to Triumph, where he became technical director. Both Riley and Triumph were driven by people who put passion before profit, Healey noted. By the outbreak of war, both companies had folded, only to be swallowed up by bigger, harder-headed manufacturers.

After VE Day, Healey, now in his late forties, decided to start his own company and make cars bearing his name. He and his father put up the £20,000 capital needed and, in 1945, in the corner of a factory in Warwick making cement mixers, the Donald Healey Motor Company was born. Since permits for rationed steel were hard to come by, he did what he had learned to do on the bounteous beaches of Perranporth and begged or borrowed whatever parts he could lay his hands on to build his first machines.

He produced a tiny number of machines, but they showed great promise. His practical, no-nonsense approach to design combined with his competition experience meant that Healeys performed well in all forms of competition. The Riley-engined Healey Silverstone, named after the former airbase turned race track, included several innovative design flourishes such as a retractable windscreen and a spare wheel that doubled as a rear bumper. A no-frills, open two-seater, it wasn't cheap at £990 – double the price of an MG – but it at least scraped under the 66 per cent purchase tax applied to cars over £1,000. Donald drove it to second place in the 1949 Alpine Rally, its first competition outing.

But like other enthusiast sports-car makers, Healey soon found his passion was getting him into serious debt. One of the first Silverstone customers was a wealthy American racer, Briggs Cunningham, who shipped it home on board the *Queen Mary* and shoehorned into it a Cadillac V8 engine. Healey thought he saw an opportunity: to build cars solely for the US market fitted with American engines. That way he could earn dollars, avoid some of the Ministry of Supply's rationing and sell a more powerful car. In December 1949, he set sail for New York. During the crossing, he spotted a man on deck with a stereoscopic camera for taking 3D photographs. Naturally curious about any new technology, Healey started interrogating the photographer, who introduced himself as George Mason, president of the Nash-Kelvinator Corporation, to which Healey answered: 'Well I'm president of the smallest motor manufacturing concern in the world.'

When Healey explained the purpose of his mission, Mason, whose company produced cars and refrigerators, warned him that he might be disappointed, as Cadillac was having enough trouble meeting its own demand for engines. Mason added that if Healey were unsuccessful, he should get back in touch with him. Mason was right, and when Healey contacted him from Detroit, he sent a private plane to fly him to his estate. For the Cornish sports-car maker, operating out of a cement-mixer factory, this was another world.

Mason disapproved of his US competitors' reliance on excess chrome and excess power. Nash had a workaday, utilitarian image which he tried to maintain into the glitzy 1950s. Selling points included unusual features like seats that folded to make a double bed, which made it a hit with courting couples, and supposedly fuel-efficient, streamlined bodywork, which critics likened to an upturned bathtub. Mason was also keen to steal a march on Detroit and add a European-style sports car to his line-up, but the only engine they had on offer was an iron-block six-cylinder, Nash's quixotically named 'Dual Jetfire'. Healey admitted that 'it was one of the heaviest engines I'd ever been associated with', but since he now owed the bank £50,000 he decided to seize what looked like an opportunity.

Healey confessed all to his new American friend, who told him not to worry. Nash would pay off his overdraft and put up the money for the prototype development. It is a tribute to Mason and his number two George Romney (father of the 2012 US presidential contender Mitt) that they were willing to take such a risk with this upstart Brit who didn't even have a factory to himself, and also to Healey's charm and energy that the Nash-Healey ever happened. As it turned out, Nash got far more than it dreamed of when one of its Healeys came fourth in the 1950 Le Mans, piloted by Duncan Hamilton and Tony Rolt.

Nash had ridden to the rescue, but Healey knew that the car

was expensive and really no more than a 'halo' model to attract showroom attention to Nash's otherwise dull line-up. And there would be no market for it outside the US. To survive, Healey decided he needed something 'faster, lighter and cheaper'.

It was on one of his frequent visits to America on Nash-Healey business that he realised there was a gap in the burgeoning sports-car market. Between the 120mph XK Jaguars and the 80mph MGs that had effectively jump-started America's passion for sports cars, there was scope for something that would do 100mph, built using as many existing bought-in components as possible.

Austin had the A90 2.5-litre four-cylinder engine. Unlike the Riley engine, it was a simple, sturdy, no-frills design that went into a variety of machines including pick-up trucks and tractors – as well as the ill-fated Atlantic. Off the shelf, it was much cheaper to buy than the Riley motor and there were plenty available.

Gerry Coker was still in his twenties when he joined Healey. He had a background in body engineering and was taken on to supervise the fitting of the Nash-Healey coachwork to the chassis. He had done some sketches of cars, 'just fun stuff, as a hobby', when Healey told him about his plans for the new car. 'He said give it a try, see what sort of a shape you can come up with.'

Coker was always defensive about his skills. 'I wasn't a stylist, I was a body engineer,' he was fond of reminding people. But like William Lyons, he had a natural flair for style. To do the Hundred body he did as he was trained and made a full-size, side-elevation technical drawing and pinned it to a wall. 'A stylist does a picture, to make it look better than it will be, with huge wheels; well we didn't have time for all that and this was the only way I could do it so what you saw is what you got. I designed the whole car, the dash, the seats.'

The result was one of the most effective sports-car designs ever created. Coker also devised a windscreen with an adjustable rake which when lowered could add another 6mph to the top speed.

When Donald Healey saw the design he didn't like the front grille, but the 1952 London motor show was less than a week away; it was too late to make changes. So he had the car parked with its front end close to a pillar with a couple of pot plants either side. As it turned out, Healey had completely underestimated Coker's design. The Healey Hundred was a show-stopper. A barricade had to be put up to keep back the crowds that surged around it. Elbowing his way through came Leonard Lord.

By now Lord was the boss of the newly formed British Motor Corporation, a merger of Austin and Morris. Having finally made peace with his former boss and nemesis, the ageing William Morris, and merged the two companies, Lord ruled over Britain's biggest car company, with 40 per cent of the market. He spent some time peering at the sleek machine, powered by the engine from his ill-fated Atlantic. His response was typically blunt. He told Healey: 'You'll never make it. You'll have too many orders.' In Lord-speak this was high praise.

The motor baron sat in the passenger seat and Healey, the upstart car builder, got in beside him. It was a short conversation. Lord told him: 'We can build two hundred of these cars at Longbridge, whereas the best you can do is twenty a week at Warwick.' Then and there a deal was done. That night Coker designed and made a new badge. By the following morning the Hundred had a new name – Austin-Healey.

The American response was beyond expectations. In the first year, 80 per cent of output went to the US, with 60 per cent of that just to the West Coast. Ten thousand Austin-Healey 100s were produced in two years, more than double Jaguar's XK output and eclipsing all other sports-car production.

Lord's decision to build the Healey at Longbridge was a signal that the age of the mass-produced sports car had arrived. Standard-Triumph followed with the TR2, which sold nearly as many as the Healey, and the Rootes Group with the Sunbeam Alpine.

Sports-car building had always been derided as a niche activity, powered by passion rather than profit. You could make a small fortune – if you started with a big one. The naysayers, William Morris, Leonard Lord and Miles Thomas, were not wrong; there would never be enough demand in the home market to justify production in serious numbers. But this was a new era where the fortunes of Britain's car makers would be decided not at home but on the worldwide market.

Lord and his fellow motor barons were also belatedly absorbing what Cecil Kimber had discovered twenty years before when he produced his first MG Midget. Sports cars derived from mainstream models were actually simpler and cheaper to make than standard cars. They used fewer parts yet could be sold at a premium because, as William Lyons had discovered with his sidecars, style sold. And, as he famously said: 'It doesn't cost any more to make something pretty.'

In the years since the end of the war, Britain's car industry had reinvented itself. Pressed, unwillingly at first, into a frantic export drive, it hit the seemingly unachievable targets set by the government and arguably saved the British economy from near collapse. By 1950, it had miraculously overtaken the far bigger American auto industry as the world's number-one exporter of cars. In 1937, Britain accounted for just 15 per cent of world car exports; five years after the war, over 75 per cent of British car production was going overseas. Despite having wholly unsuitable cars for the all-important American market, British car makers opened up a previously untapped appetite for two-seater roadsters that even Detroit had overlooked. British sports-car output expanded twentyfold and even then didn't meet demand. The trail blazed by MG and Jaguar, followed up by Austin-Healey and Triumph, showed that relatively straightforward, uncomplicated engineering and some eye-catching bodywork could put a shine on the balance sheet.

The message was clear, style made money – in the export market at least. But what about the home market? Even into the '50s it was still struggling to emerge from the strictures of rationing.

THE BLONDE'S BOMBSHELL

Austin-Healey and Jaguar clothed their machines in organic, flowing curves that bore no resemblance to British machines that had come before them. They were show-stoppers; they inspired immediate and universal appreciation. Their design was favourably compared with the finest bespoke Italian *carrozzeria* worn by Ferraris and Maseratis.

Yet the XK120 and the Hundred, emphatically two of the most exciting and seductive car designs of the 1950s, were each the vision of individuals with no aesthetic training. Lyons's eye for line and style was innate – like perfect pitch. Perhaps it was thanks to being born not in an industrial heartland but in Blackpool, Britain's leisure capital, and into a musical family, that fuelled his exuberance. Coker was much less prolific. He only designed two cars in his life, the Hundred and its little brother, the Austin-Healey Sprite, both tributes to his natural flair for style.

Yet if these bold creations were the first fruits of a new British automotive design language, it would take time to impact the nation's mainstream car styling. The Second World War had a pervasive influence over British design and taste that would last well into the 1950s. The whole nation was mobilised in the battle for national survival. Rationing and shortages affected all classes and pressed people into a kind of enforced solidarity in which any excess was seen as unpatriotic. The wartime government had introduced the prescriptive Utility Scheme for the standardisation of clothing and furniture, functional designs that eschewed all frippery. The privations of the home front meant that any excess or indulgence was frowned upon, and this sentiment persisted into peacetime when some rationing became even tighter. The irrepressible Stafford Cripps championed this design ethic as a guiding principle for the new egalitarian order the Labour government of the late 1940s was striving for, and saw it stretching into every corner of daily life. 'Good design can provide us in our homes and our working places with pleasant articles which combine good construction and fitness for their purpose with convenience in use and attractiveness in shape and colour.' This wholesome prescription filtered down to the motor industry as it belatedly turned its attention to the domestic market. Chrome was kept to a minimum and the most common choices of colours – black, grey and fawn – were almost masochistically dull. Big engines and high speeds had negative connotations of excessive consumption and waste of scarce resources. Even at the top end of the market, Bentley, under the wing of Rolls-Royce, played down any hint of glamour or frivolity. In its publicity the cars were depicted in front of industrial backdrops, chimneys and cranes, with two men of substance alongside in serious conversation. 'Take a Bentley into partnership' was the strap line.

One person who wasn't buying any of this socialist austerity was the new wife of the boss of Britain's oldest car company, Daimler. The self-made, twice-widowed Lady Norah Docker decided to lead a one-woman campaign to 'bring happiness and glamour into drab lives', bankrolled by her compliant, besotted third husband, Sir Bernard Docker.

Born in 1906, above a Derby butcher's shop, Norah ran away to London with dreams of the stage, by her own admission 'an

artificial blonde among thousands of artificial blondes searching for stardom'. She became a dancer at the Café du Paris off
Leicester Square, customers paying £1 a time to take a turn with
her round the dance floor. She married the boss of wine mer-
chants Hennekey's, who died in 1945, then wed the 69-year-old
chairman of Fortnum & Mason, who tragically died two years
later in 1948. Consoled by Bernard Docker the Daimler boss, she
married him in 1949.

Immediately Norah caused a stir by holding champagne-fuelled
'anti-austerity' parties on her new husband's yacht *Shemara*, not
only for her rich friends but also on one occasion seventy members
of a Yorkshire miners' club, for whom she danced on the quarter
deck. 'The dear boys, I just loved them. It proved to me conclu-
sively that the social barrier exists only in the mind.'

Her sound bites were a gift to the popular press and she spoke
her mind, even when it came to her husband's business, telling an
interviewer: 'I was ashamed when I married Bernard to discover
that both at home and abroad the Daimler car was in danger of
becoming a relic.'

Lady Norah was dead right. Founded in 1896, using designs
licensed by the German company of the same name, Daimler qualified as Britain's oldest motor manufacturer. King Edward VII, the
first British royal motorist, was a Daimler owner and for half a
century it continued to be the first choice for the royal household.
But profits always eluded the company and by 1910 it had been
absorbed into the Birmingham Small Arms (BSA) conglomerate
in a deal engineered by Bernard's industrialist father Dudley, who
appointed his son managing director on his deathbed.

Like their royal patrons, Daimler had shown little inclination
to move with the times. Their range-topping Straight Eights were
ponderous, 3-ton limousines, usually painted black, whose contours harked back to nineteenth-century carriage designs. Bernard
was stung into action. Dazzled by his new wife's flair for style,

he made her a director of BSA's recently acquired coach-building branch, Hooper, installed a drawing board in their Mayfair home and put her to work alongside their dismayed chief stylist, Osmond Rivers.

The result was a massive touring limousine with 7,000 gold stars hand-painted on its flanks by a heraldic artist. The radiator and hubcaps were also gold-plated, 'because chrome is so hard to come by,' so Norah explained. The interior was upholstered in hand-woven silk and fittings included a Cartier cut-glass cocktail set and a set of gold-trimmed crocodile luggage in the boot. It stole the 1951 London motor show and made worldwide headlines, with photographs of Norah posing with the car. While the British establishment shuddered, the general public applauded. 'Not one rotten tomato was thrown at us,' Norah noted when she used the vehicle for shopping trips. For each subsequent motor show, Bernard sanctioned a further four show cars, culminating in the Golden Zebra, a curvaceous coupe trimmed with six zebra hides and sporting an ivory dashboard.

But the attention Daimler got through Norah's show cars did not translate into sales, though the indifferent performance was masked by a boom in BSA's motorcycle division. A new, smaller model, the Conquest, was introduced at her behest she claimed, but sales were modest. Although the show cars included innovations such as headlights faired into the bodywork and even double-glazing – an automotive first – the basic engineering remained resolutely dated. And not all the publicity that Daimler's celebrity stylist garnered was positive. With her higher profile came reports of extreme behaviour, such as a drunken fist fight in a casino in Monte Carlo over several thousand pounds of disputed winnings, this at a time when a maximum of £25 cash per person could be taken out of the country. The BSA board grew restive, notably when Norah, opening Daimler's new Paris showroom, billed the company for £7,910 worth of couture for the occasion.

When it transpired that the royal household, sensing trouble ahead, had quietly shifted allegiance from Daimler to Rolls-Royce, matters came to a head. In April 1956, the Dockers flew to Monte Carlo for the wedding of Grace Kelly to Prince Rainier, taking two of the show cars with them. The BSA board seized the moment and voted Bernard off. And to drive the point home, Norah's five cars were summarily stripped of their finery and sold off.

Furious, the Dockers went out and bought a new Rolls-Royce and continued to hit the headlines during their long and messy fall from grace. Norah, whose quick temper could be inflamed by alcohol, fell out with her new friends the Rainiers. On discovering that her son was not invited to the christening of Prince Albert, she tore up a Monégasque flag and earned a life ban from the principality. Daimler never recovered. A few years later, Britain's oldest car marque would be swallowed up by the comparative upstart Jaguar.

With the fall of the Dockers, the British establishment breathed a collective sigh of relief; they were an aberration best forgotten. But, in an albeit loud and crass way, Lady Norah had made a point. British design had to wake up. With the honourable exception of William Lyons, the middle-aged men who ran Britain's motor industry were uniformly blind to the post-war public's emerging appetite for glamour. In her own way, Norah was only following what Detroit had discovered: that glitz attracted attention and attention translated into sales.

Had Norah taken time out to study the history of British design theory, she would have recognised what pioneer industrial designer Christopher Dresser was on about in his influential 1873 work *The Principles of Decorative Design*. Addressing those 'who seek a knowledge of ornament as applied to our industrial manufacturers', he claimed that beauty had a commercial value and therefore was an important element of design:

John Cooper, with his father Charles, standing with one of his first rear-engined 500cc cars in the late 1940s. Created from a pair of crashed Fiat Topolinos, it would go on to revolutionise car design.

Desperate for much needed dollars to salvage the British economy after the Second World War, British car makers threw everything they could at the US market. The most successful export was the least likely. The MG TC, a pre-war design, not even available with left-hand drive, was an unlikely hit in America and it started a craze for British sports cars.

Alamy

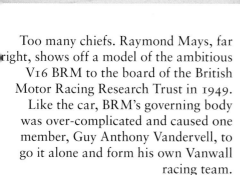

Export or die. A40 Devons bound for America leave Austin's Longbridge plant in 1947. The wartime camouflage is still visible on the factory walls.

Too many chiefs. Raymond Mays, far right, shows off a model of the ambitious V16 BRM to the board of the British Motor Racing Research Trust in 1949. Like the car, BRM's governing body was over-complicated and caused one member, Guy Anthony Vandervell, to go it alone and form his own Vanwall racing team.

Getty

Hollywood star Clark Gable collects his XK120 from Jaguar boss William Lyons in 1948 – the first one to arrive in California. Lyons only planned to make 200, but such was demand from America that 12,000 were produced.

In the Austin Design Office at Longbridge, stylist Dick Burzi, left, and Austin boss Leonard Lord discuss the finer points of their ill-fated Austin Atlantic. Styled especially for the US market, it failed to impress the Americans.

After the failure of the Atlantic, Leonard Lord teamed up with Donald Healey, right, to mass-produce his Austin-powered 'Hundred' sports car.

Loyal customer. Queen Elizabeth is reputed to have owned over thirty Land Rovers during her reign.

On a one-woman mission to 'bring happiness and glamour back into drab lives', Lady Norah Docker stole the 1951 London motor show with the limousine she styled for her husband's company, Daimler. Seven thousand gold stars were applied to its flanks. The establishment were shocked and within a few years the Royal Family ended their half-century of Daimler ownership.

Mastering understatement. Rover's stylist, David Bache, was reprimanded by his bosses because his designs were too eye-catching. Reined in, he produced this – the P5, which ran from 1958 to 1973. In the background is an early attempt at what would become the all-conquering Range Rover.

Duncan Hamilton, nursing a broken nose and windscreen from a 140mph bird strike, gives co-driver Tony Rolt (in sunglasses) a lift on their victorious C-Type Jaguar at the 1953 Le Mans.

Best friends Mike Hawthorn and Peter Collins at the height of their powers at Silverstone in July 1958. By the end of the year Hawthorn would be Britain's first Formula 1 world champion, but it was a hollow victory; Collins was killed at the German Grand Prix, two weeks after this photograph was taken.

Moss refuels in his Vanwall. His drive helped the team win the 1958 Formula 1 constructor's championship, the first ever by a British car, but he missed the driver's prize by one point, to Hawthorn in a Ferrari.

Body designer Frank Feeley, right, discusses the proposed shape of the 1953 Aston Martin DB3S with his boss, David Brown. Brown was the scion of a Huddersfield engineering business who bought both Aston Martin and Lagonda in the late 1940s. Feeley, who had joined Lagonda at fourteen, became one of the leading British car body designers of his day.

Stirling Moss, at the wheel of an Aston Martin DB3S at Goodwood, 1956. Throughout the 1950s, it was customary for Formula 1 drivers to compete in sports car races and Moss took part in rallies as well.

First at last. Vanwalls line up on the front of the grid. In 1958 they would win the Formula 1 constructors' title but team owner Guy Anthony Vandervell's success was soured by the death of one of his drivers, Stuart Lewis-Evans, in the season's final race at Casablanca.

One of Alec Issigonis's first sketches in 1956 of what would become the Mini. Britain's greatest car designer always drew free-hand, leaving the technical drawing to his faithful team. Even though this is one of his first studies for what became the Mini, many details of the finished car are already there.

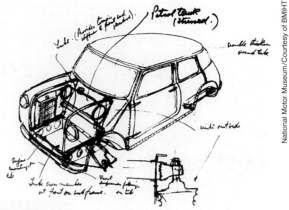

Issigonis with two of the very first production Minis outside the 'Kremlin' – Austin's Longbridge headquarters.

Alec Issigonis and John Cooper first met when they raced their home-made cars at the 1946 Brighton Speed Trials. Fifteen years later, they joined forces to create the Mini Cooper. By that time, Issigonis had transformed small car design and Cooper had revolutionised the shape of Formula 1 machines.

Game changer. Stirling Moss takes John Cooper's rear-engined Formula 1 car to victory in the 1959 Argentine Grand Prix. Enzo Ferrari dismissed the radical design: 'The ox does not push the cart.' A year later he, too, was putting his engines behind the driver.

Mike Hawthorn's Jaguar D-Type leads the Moss-Fangio Mercedes-Benz at the 1955 Le Mans. Shortly after this was taken another Mercedes crashed, killing over eighty spectators and injuring more than 120. Mercedes withdrew from the event, leaving Hawthorn to claim an easy but troubled victory. After the race he was accused of setting off the chain of events that caused the accident.

Steve McQueen gets aboard his 1957 Jaguar XKSS, one of only seventeen made before a fire gutted Jaguar's factory and destroyed the remaining cars.

Masters of the world. Together, Colin Chapman and Jim Clark claimed two Formula 1 Championships and a ground-breaking win at Indianapolis in 1965. Only a decade before, Chapman had founded Lotus in a stable block behind his father's London pub. Despite being total opposites, the gifted, introverted Clark and his irrepressible team boss were an unbeatable combination.

Crowd pleaser. The E-Type breaks cover in 1961.

The author with his father's brand new Rover 2000 in 1965. David Bache's design was a complete break with company tradition.

January 1964, Ringo Starr, stranded at a Paris airport and late for a show, gets a lift in one of the Minis competing in that year's Monte Carlo Rally.

Paddy Hopkirk and Henry Liddon en route to victory in the 1964 Monte Carlo Rally. When a journalist knocked on his hotel room door to say they had won, Hopkirk thought it was a prank.

Sean Connery as James Bond relaxes beside his gadget-laden Aston Martin DB5 during the filming of *Goldfinger*. The smash hit film made Aston Martin world famous, but the tiny builder of hand-made cars was in no position to capitalise on its sudden fame.

Corgi Toys were better placed than Aston Martin to capitalise on the *Goldfinger* phenomenon. They sold over 2.5 million of these exquisitely detailed models, which even came with a working ejector seat.

Minis evading the Turin police in *The Italian Job*. Fiat offered the filmmakers free cars, but screenwriter Troy Kennedy Martin would not be persuaded: 'The Minis came through the film as a powerful symbol of what we can do in Britain; they were the most remarkable elements of the story.'

The 1968 Jaguar XJ6. It was William Lyons's last design for the company he founded in 1922, and the one he considered his finest.

High hopes. For two decades, Rover had toyed with combining the best qualities of their cars with the off-road capability of their Land Rover. The 1970 Range Rover effectively invented a new type of car, the SUV. Four-wheel drive and a hundred miles an hour, all for £2000.

We may even say that art can lend an object a value greater than that of the material of which it consists, even when the object can be formed of precious matter as of rare marble, scarce woods or silver or gold. This being the case it follows that the workman who can endow his production with those qualities or beauties which give value to his works must be more useful to his employer than the man who produces objects devoid of such beauty.

William Lyons knew this intuitively. Detroit's British satellites, Ford and Vauxhall, responded by adopting American styling cues. British car stylists had to raise their game – but how? Another person in the public eye with strong views about car design was the husband of the new queen. The Duke of Edinburgh's first automotive love had been an MG TC, before he traded up to a Lagonda. In 1955 he went to Longbridge to inspect the Austin factory. By then it was one of the most modern automated car plants outside Detroit, the crowning achievement of production wizard Leonard Lord. It boasted an imposing new office block which wags soon dubbed 'the Kremlin'. Despite being the boss of all of BMC and one of Britain's top industrialists, the blunt publican's son was painfully awkward in the presence of nobility and left the tour to his more urbane deputies, George Harriman and Joe Edwards. When he joined them for lunch in the directors' dining room in the Kremlin, Lord got off to a bad start by telling the duke that on her estates the queen should use an Austin Champ (a heavy and unsuccessful jeep-like machine built for the army), rather than the Land Rover she was so fond of. An awkward silence then ensued, which Lord broke by inviting Philip to see the styling studio and look over their latest designs.

Despite the debacle with the Atlantic, Lord and his chief designer Ricardo Burzi had pressed on with more cars named after more counties – the Somerset and Hereford had replaced the Devon, Dorset and Hampshire – all of which bore some family resemblance to the axed coupe.

According to Joe Edwards, the duke was not impressed. 'They're no good. You will never sell them,' he told the stunned executives. Lord had met his match in bluntness. Philip's comment hit home. The following day, Lord commissioned the leading Italian *carrozziere* Pininfarina to give all Austin designs a radical makeover. Ricardo Burzi's 25-year reign as Austin's chief stylist was over, though he survived at Longbridge into the 1970s.

Leonard Lord was not the only British motor magnate to have struggled to find the right look for his cars. At the Standard Motor Company, Sir John Black, the man who had supplied William Lyons with engines and chassis for his first SS cars in the 1930s, had been quick to see that times were changing after the war. He had acquired the failed Triumph company and with it came a promising stylist, Walter Belgrove, whom Donald Healey had championed during his time as chief designer there. Belgrove, unlike many of his peers, was an art-school graduate; he was the first British stylist to use clay models and distinguished himself by applying some streamlining to his designs. While the war was still raging, Black directed him to look towards America for inspiration, but also told him where to find it closer to home, as Belgrove recalled: 'The best looking Yankee car is the Plymouth and the best place to study one is outside the American Embassy in London. I suggest you take yourself off to Grosvenor Square. The place is swarming with embassy vehicles . . . come back only when you have got all you want, and don't get shot.'

Belgrove duly travelled to London, installed himself on a park bench in Grosvenor Square with his sketch pad and somehow evaded arrest as he made a detailed annotated drawing. As well as capturing the shape and detail, he added notes about how the boot lid opened to the full width of the body and pointed out how the door hinges were concealed. This became the template for Standard's first post-war car, the Vanguard.

Nervous about committing wholly to this radical design departure, Black hedged his bets and also commissioned the venerable Mulliner coachbuilding company to produce two, more traditional, designs for Triumph – the Renown and Mayflower. Possibly, Black was reacting to America's surprising embrace of the MG TC, because the 'new' Triumphs were unashamed throwbacks to the 1920s and 1930s; their 'razor-edge' design as it became known was tall and boxy. The Renown body was even built on a traditional wooden frame.

Unfortunately these 'retro' designs had none of the MG's charisma. On arrival in America, the Mayflower suffered almost as dismal a reception as the voyagers on the eponymous ship. And the Vanguard, like the Austin Atlantic, a forced marriage of American style and modest British chassis proportions, was also a flop.

Black then sidelined Belgrove and hired Amercan industrial designer Carl Otto to update the Vanguard. Meanwhile, Belgrove got the job of producing a Triumph sports car to get in on the American craze for them. A rush job, he was given ten weeks and a budget of £16,000 to spend on tooling for the bodywork. The result was the Triumph TR2, a workmanlike design with none of the Healey's flair, but it performed well – and sold. When it emerged that Otto's Vanguard renderings were deemed 'too American', Belgrove was given the unhappy task of toning it down.

Fed up with being messed about by the mercurial Black, Belgrove went freelance in 1955, before giving it all up to run a post office in Dorset. From then on, Standard-Triumph followed Austin's lead and sought help from an Italian, Giovanni Michelotti.

It is easy to pillory Lord and Black for their seemingly misguided pursuit of scaled-down American looks, or for Black's attempt to reincarnate a pre-war look. Both men approaching retirement found themselves in the eye of a style revolution. During the 1920s, the boxy basic shapes of mainstream car styling had been almost uniform throughout the world, until pressed-steel technology made more organic forms possible. But after the war, car styling set off in two diametrically opposed directions: one profoundly sensible, functional, modest, utilitarian; the other rebellious, brash and aggressive, informed by jet aircraft and juke boxes. Detroit, having been the first to embrace the bulbous forms afforded by pressed steel, forsook them in the early 1950s for sharp-edged fins and heavy doses of chrome. Advances in glass production enabled windscreens to be curved like the canopies of jet fighters and as paint quality improved, sombre shades gave way to loud pastel hues and extravagant two-tone finishes.

While British coachbuilders dwindled as manufacturers concentrated more of their styling in-house, the Italian *carrozzieri* managed to stay afloat and control the direction of their country's car styling, incorporating some American influence but preserving a lightness and simplicity of line in everything from Fiats to Ferraris.

Caught between these two impulses, the next generation of British stylists in post-war Britain, whose ageing masters were as old as the car itself, faced a daunting challenge. So it must have seemed to a young draughtsman at Longbridge, sketching out the dashboard of Austin's A35. His name was David Bache.

No Style, Please,
We're British

David Bache was born in Germany, where his father Joe, a former Aston Villa captain, was the coach with VfR Mannheim. His elder brother had worked for Austin and was instrumental in the birth of BMW's first car, an Austin 7, known there as the Dixi. After his parents returned to the English Midlands, young David wanted to go to Birmingham College of Art, but his brother warned his parents off the idea, as Bache recalled: 'My brother said, "Look, if he goes to college he'll be in the army at eighteen, but if he becomes an engineering apprentice that'll be deferred for a couple of years."' So he joined Austin as an apprentice and did the rounds of the departments, ending up in Ricardo Burzi's design office. He served his time at the drawing board and got to work on the Austin A30, styling its dashboard.

At the time, Leonard Lord had flirted with the idea of getting some American expertise into Austin. Raymond Loewy, famed for designing the Lucky Strike cigarette packet and beautifying Coca-Cola vending machines, sent over Bob Koto. The American's renderings didn't please Lord or Burzi, but Koto showed the men of Longbridge how to sculpt body styles using clay rather than wood and metal, as was the tradition in Europe. Bache, the frustrated artist, was transfixed. In 1954, when he got his big break, a job at Rover, at twice what Austin were paying him, he brought the new clay methods with him.

Rover had been saved by the runaway success of the 'stopgap' Land Rover and the Wilks brothers had successfully launched their first all-post-war design, the 1949 P4 75. Like Black and Belgrove at Standard, they too had looked to America for direction – but not to Detroit.

Based in South Bend, Indiana, Studebaker started out making wagons in the 1860s. In 1946, they stole a march on Detroit by introducing the first car to have a proper boot or trunk. Virgil Exner's landmark design effectively changed the basic car shape from two boxes (engine and body) to three (engine, body and boot). Impressed, the Wilks brothers acquired a pair of Studebaker Champions and conducted what is known in the motor industry as a 'tear down' on one of them – dismantling the car to discover how it was built. Since the Champion wheelbase was almost the same as the new Rover P4's, the dismantled Studebaker body was grafted onto a prototype chassis and used as a mobile laboratory that was soon christened the 'Roverbaker' by Wilks's team.

As Maurice Wilks and his body engineer Harry Loker sketched out their first thoughts about how the new car would look, several design details migrated from the Studebaker to the new Rover, including doors which closed against the central pillar and the distinctive protruding, sloping boot. Inside was a bench front seat capable of seating three abreast and a gear lever mounted on the steering column, out of the way of feet and legs. Exner had added to the Studebaker a personal design flourish – a feature, controversial even in America, of an aeroplane-inspired nose cone. Even this was echoed in the new Rover with a radical third headlight or 'pass lamp' right in the centre of the grille.

Although the new car, looking nothing like Rovers past, was

well received, that third, erroneously named 'Cyclops' lamp as it came to be mistakenly known, was unloved by regular clientele. A hasty facelift swapped it for a more conventional grille that harked back to pre-war Rovers. But car styling, having moved glacially in the 1930s, was speeding ahead in the '50s. Organic curves made possible by pressed steel rapidly gave way to straight lines and sharp corners – and fins. The Wilks brothers concluded that they needed someone concentrating full-time on what Rovers should look like – someone from a different generation.

Bache, still under thirty when he joined Rover, regarded himself as a stylist at a time when the term implied frivolity, especially at Rover, where he noticed that everyone seemed to be an engineer of some sort. His job was prosaically described as 'member of the drawing office with responsibility for exterior appearance'. But what he found at this much smaller company was a more convivial atmosphere.

'The difference between working at Austin and Rover was chalk and cheese,' he recalled later. Leonard Lord was a 'roughneck' who liked to intimidate. Bache had witnessed the Austin boss summoning a senior manager over just to stamp out a cigarette he had let drop to the floor of the design office. At Rover he found that 'the standards and quality of work was everything'. He developed a deep respect for his new boss, Maurice Wilks. 'He was quite sensitive and always appreciated nice quality things. He'd never order anyone to do anything. He would always *suggest.*'

But Bache's exuberance soon ruffled feathers in Solihull. He arrived in his Jaguar XK120, which was frowned upon, so he swapped it for one of Rover's more stately products. His eye for style didn't stop at cars. As a hedge against sudden redundancy, he kept up a sideline in tailoring and, though not exactly approved of, it wasn't uncommon in Rover's drawing office to find a manager coming by to be measured for a suit.

His first job was to give the P4 a mild makeover, which gave it a further decade of active life, but soon he was entrusted with the task of coming up with the shape for a completely new smaller model, internally known as the P5. With the Land Rover doing so well, another car line was feasible.

In 1954, Bache persuaded his new bosses to let him attend the Paris Motor Show to gather inspiration. It was a defining experience. One machine that caught Bache's eye was France's one and only luxury performance car, the new Facel Vega *grande routière*, a clever blend of European and American styling. It had a straight-through belt line running from the front to the rear lights, nearly flat flanks and a panoramic curved windscreen. He also admired another transatlantic joint venture, a Chrysler bodied by the Torinese *carrozzeria*, Ghia (whose design for VW, the seminal Karmann Ghia, would appear a year later).

Enthused, Bache took this inspiration back to Solihull and applied it to his first renderings for the new Rover. Like the Chrysler Ghia, it sported a pronounced semi-oval radiator grille with a thick chrome surround and thin roof pillars with a wraparound windscreen. With his newly recruited team of clay modellers, he produced a dramatic, lifelike, quarter-scale model. But there was a problem.

My design for the P5 had been finished in clay and painted and so on and everybody had said they liked it but Maurice Wilks still hadn't seen it after three weeks. No comments of any sort. I came in one Monday and Frank Underwood [his immediate boss] said that Maurice had come in on the Saturday and spent nearly two hours looking round that model, didn't speak to anyone, just looked at it. Later he sent for me. He sat behind his huge desk and said: 'That's a very beautiful model you've produced. I know everyone is most impressed with it. But we can't make it, you know. And I'll tell you why we can't make it. Because it's a head turner, and the Rover Company doesn't make head turners. We like to make vehicles which pass unobtrusively and are not noticed.' Of course I was absolutely floored. We had to retract ourselves and do something far less exuberant.

To Bache, this was the dead weight of tradition coming down from the older generation, stifling his creative flair. He had seen the future and knew what it needed to look like, so he thought. The P5 was now on hold and he was farmed out to the team who were preparing a revamp of the Land Rover, now approaching its tenth year. For the snappily dressed stylist, this was something of a comedown.

The Land Rover was a brutally functional machine, more of an agricultural vehicle than a road car, the most unstylish vehicle imaginable. Bache swallowed his pride and got to work. There was not much room for manoeuvre, as all the basic co-ordinates were fixed. But he made subtle adjustments to the metal, giving the wheel arches a more car-like curve, adding sills under the doors to conceal the chassis and introducing a small curve along the body's waist line which made the sides less flat. They were small cosmetic touches, but their overall effect domesticated the machine without compromising its off-road abilities. The job was done in six weeks; the Wilks brothers were satisfied. Lesson learned, Bache was back in favour. He was elevated to chief styling engineer and given a better studio with a turntable that would enable the construction of full-size mock-ups of future designs.

Meanwhile, Rover product plans had changed again. Having committed to the ever-popular Land Rover long-term, Spencer Wilks concluded that they lacked the space to build enough of the smaller car to be profitable. So the P5 grew to be a larger, lower-volume, more imposing car that would sit above rather than below the P4. Here at last Bache was able to feed some of that Paris show influence into his work – albeit more discreetly this time. The new

P5 bore a passing family resemblance to the P4, but there was more than a hint of the Facel Vega and the Chrysler Ghia that had so inspired him. The turret, the section of the car that comprises the roof and windows, became much more of a glasshouse, with wraparound windscreens front and rear to give the interior an open-air atmosphere. The front end kept the traditional Rover radiator grille but, in another nod to the Paris show exotica, the vertical spokes were recessed within a deeper chrome surround. Bache had learned his lesson from Maurice Wilks, but had also stuck to some of his guns, cleverly blending the new into an overall design that had great presence but didn't shout about it.

Inside, there was plenty of traditional woodwork, but the instrument pod that carried the speedometer and other dials had a distinct aviation influence, and the steering wheel was dished so the central boss sat further away from the driver. The seats themselves were also more sculpted and extremely comfortable. The end result was a design that had a clean simplicity all of its own. As per Maurice Wilks's instruction, it did not draw attention to itself, but it was distinctly modern and had an imposing presence.

John Bolster, writing in *Autosport*, approved: 'The Rover 3 Litre is for the man who cannot bear anything cheap and flashy. He buys a car knowing that he will be living with it for a long time, and he chooses it because it will give him smooth silent travel in an atmosphere that does not affront his good taste.'

Evidently, the 3 Litre's appeal didn't end with men. Two early adopters were none other than the queen and her mother. Bache had proved that he could be restrained and worked within the Wilks design ethic. But a quirk of Rover heritage was that during the 1930s, the line-up included 'sportsman' or 'coupe' versions of their main model with a slightly lower roofline. Wilks asked Bache to do the same for the P5. He delegated the task to one of his team, Tony Poole, telling him to make half a dozen sketches, and to make one really extreme using thicker windscreen pillars and compound curves in the screen. To Bache's surprise, the Wilks brothers opted for it – a rakish, American-style hard-top roofline, so futuristic that the team nicknamed it Dan Dare, after the *Eagle* comic's science-fiction hero.

Bache's journey is a telling indication of the quandary Britain's car makers found themselves in in the late 1950s. Austerity was being blown away by rock and roll. Sensible was giving way to stiletto. Commercial television was beaming images of American affluence into living rooms all over the country. And across the Atlantic, Detroit's big beasts were locked in an arms race to deliver the tallest tail fins and the most chrome. On a visit to their British outpost in Luton, General Motors president Harlow H. Curtice insisted that, for the 1957 Victor, Vauxhall should adopt a design from their Michigan styling studios which aped the latest American crazes. Vauxhall's engineering boss Maurice Platt was not at all comfortable with the extra weight and cost involved, but noted ruefully that 'no one felt sufficiently reckless to suggest that the panoramic windscreen was a costly gimmick of uncertain acceptability outside the United States.' Platt and his team gamely got on with the job, while Vauxhall's copywriters spun Detroit excess into cheerful British common sense. 'The Victor's road vision is such that the tips of all four wings can be seen by the driver.' *Country Life* magazine was unconvinced, pronouncing the new look 'most disturbing', but for an emerging group of Brits who saw Americana as the only antidote to British fustiness, Vauxhall's motorised juke boxes found favour. Meanwhile, the Rootes brothers retained the services of American industrial designer Raymond Loewy for their mid-'50s Hillmans and Humbers, while Standard-Triumph, after the departure of Walter Belgrove to the Post Office, followed British Motor Corporation to Italy and hired Giovanni Michelotti. Outside of Rover and Jaguar, Britain's mainstream car makers were still some way off championing home-grown design.

While British passenger cars in the '50s suffered something of an identity crisis, however, an entirely new design ethic would take shape in a different corner of the industry – one that was nothing to do with style but was all about performance.

19

A RUGGED OLD BUGGER

The previously rarefied world of British motor sport had been democratised by the 500cc Club revolutionaries. They had invaded abandoned aerodromes and with a few hay bales repurposed them as race tracks. Young engineers whose horizons had been expanded by wartime aircraft production had embraced new techniques and materials and used them to reinvent the most basic principles of automobile design. John Cooper and Colin Chapman, like the emerging generation of musicians who would change Britain's soundtrack, were busy breaking rules and overturning time-honoured conventions whereby good things supposedly only come to those who wait, dismissing decades-old customs and practices. But to the wider public, their names didn't register. Jaguar had made its mark at Le Mans, but to most people a racing car still meant Ferrari or Maserati.

Stirling Moss had grabbed the attention of a nation in need of national heroes. Never before had a British racing driver become a household name, courted by manufacturers to promote their machines through the many and various forms of competition Moss willingly campaigned. Britain now had three permanent motor-racing circuits: Silverstone, Brands Hatch and Goodwood. All he needed was the right machine to match his potential.

In the inaugural Formula 1 World Championship, at Silverstone, in the summer of 1950, in front of King George VI and a capacity crowd, Alfa Romeos topped the leader board. Ferrari won the four subsequent British Grands Prix. Meanwhile, BRM continued to carve out a reputation for itself as unreliable and uncompetitive. As Britain's great new hope, Stirling Moss was desperate to race in a British car. But despite Raymond Mays optimistically issuing a press release saying Moss would drive for BRM in 1952, the young star, wisely, never signed the contract. As Moss saw it, BRM had ruined everything. Having got the public very excited, they had let them all down with a car that failed to deliver. They had spent a fortune and got nowhere. 'There was a feeling that a British car would never win a Grand Prix,' he lamented, and resigned himself to campaigning in a Maserati.

Another individual sharing Moss's and the rest of the nation's disappointment with BRM was Guy Anthony Vandervell, an early backer of Raymond Mays's venture. Like Mays, GAV, as he was known, was born wealthy, was public-school educated, single-minded and similarly obsessed with racing. But there any resemblance ended. GAV had no airs or graces; one associate summed him up as 'a rugged old bugger'. It wasn't always that way, however. His despairing father had given up hope of passing on the family electrical business to him and sold it on to Lucas in 1926. Too headstrong to accept the authority of the company's new bosses, and after a row over expenses, GAV severed all connections and went his own way. He might have joined the other rich playboys burning up their inheritances round the banking of Brooklands, but for one last attempt by his father to make an honest man of him. Vandervell senior installed GAV as a director of a tiny widget maker, the O&S Oilless Bearing Co., which inhabited two wooden buildings in the London suburb of Willesden. The timing couldn't have been worse, as the Wall Street Crash had just plunged the world into a deep depression.

Despite this, GAV set about chasing business to keep the little company afloat. In 1930, he got wind of a new engine bearing being developed in Cleveland, Ohio. Big-end bearings are semi-circular metal shells that separate the spinning crankshaft from the engine block and are critical to the smooth running of a vehicle engine. But they were also expensive and time-consuming to replace. Each one needed to be cast and shaped to obtain an accurate fit. The Cleveland Graphite Bronze Company's thin-wall bearing dramatically simplified the process. In this mundane component, GAV immediately saw his future.

He headed to Ohio and presented himself at the office of Ben Hopkins, the company boss and inventor of the thin-wall bearing, in the hope of buying a licence to manufacture it in Britain. But Hopkins was unconvinced. How could a two-bit outfit like O&S have the means to produce his invention? Having come this far, however, Vandervell wasn't going to be fobbed off. Finding himself back in Hopkins's outer office, he took up residence on a sofa and waited. And waited ... On the sixth day, Hopkins, worn down by the Englishman's persistence, relented; the deal was done. And by the end of the 1930s, every bearing in almost every British car engine was supplied by Vandervell. War work boosted his output to half a million units a week and by 1945, the one-time playboy racer was a major player in the British motor industry.

When Raymond Mays's letter arrived just before VE Day, touting for backers, GAV was one of the first to sign up. But as the first heady excitement subsided he soon became a vocal critic of BRM's governing trust, with its many stakeholders. As development of the new car dragged on, he decided that BRM needed some actual competition experience. Enzo Ferrari, whose brand-new V12s were already winning races, used GAV's bearings. In 1949, he persuaded the Italian to sell him a car. He had it repainted British racing green, called it the 'Thin Wall Special' and entered it in the

1949 British Grand Prix with Mays named as driver. Only a few months short of his fiftieth birthday and preoccupied with his own slowly evolving creation, Mays had little appetite for racing the Italian machine. After a few laps he handed it over to another driver, who spun off, injuring some spectators.

The following year, when the BRM failed so spectacularly on its debut, GAV's exasperation boiled over. He decided the only way to beat 'those damned red cars' was to go it alone.

Vandervell's approach was the opposite of BRM's. Whereas Raymond Mays surrounded himself with pals from his 1930s racing days, GAV looked to the new generation of post-war upstarts. The first to catch his eye was John Cooper.

Cooper had graduated from 500cc to 1- and then 2-litre machines. His cars were enjoying success in the Formula 2 class of races using a Bristol engine that was one of the fruits of Allied reparation – a design seized from BMW in Germany. The gruff, autocratic Vandervell and the amiable, self-taught, young *garagista* made an unlikely pair, but their approach was very similar. Both were opportunists, driven by practical rather than theoretical ideas, and they were eager to learn from the competition and ready to beg, borrow or steal wherever they could. GAV shipped the thin-wall Ferrari down to Surbiton and told Cooper to build something on the same lines.

Since there was no competitive British engine available, Vandervell had to come up with his own. He gave the job to motorcycle makers Norton, where he also happened to be a director. The result could not have been more different from BRM's dauntingly complicated V16. It was a four-cylinder, essentially four Norton Manx engines joined together and bolted onto a Rolls-Royce B-series engine crankcase. With the engine slotted into Cooper's improvised chassis, the new machine was ready to race in the 1954 season under a new name – Vanwall. The engine showed promise, but Cooper's Ferrari-derived chassis and simple cigar-shaped bodywork were not good enough to put Vanwall, as GAV had called his new team, on the front of the grid. So he went talent-scouting again. This time to the stable block behind the Railway Hotel in north London.

20

THE MOONLIGHTERS

In 1952, Colin Chapman, with the help of a £25 loan from his fiancée Hazel, had set up Lotus as a limited company. 'Automobile and component manufacturers. Racing car design and development' was how the company letterhead optimistically described the business. There was next to no capital and almost all of those put to work in the stable block were volunteers, many of them moonlighting from day jobs – including Chapman himself. With its band of helpers improvising with whatever they could lay their hands on, Lotus had more in common with one of Britain's newly formed skiffle bands than a car manufacturer. Chapman's school friend Bob Hester, who lent a hand, recalled that the facilities ran to a sink but no toilet or heating. In winter, any warmth came from welding torches and frenetic physical exertion; in 1953–54 some 100 Lotus kits were produced. Completing the job themselves saved customers the 33 per cent purchase tax that was slapped on all finished cars. Chapman's charm, energy and ambition were seductive, and for his band of young enthusiasts, the stable block behind Colin's dad's pub was an exciting refuge from grey, bombed-out post-war London.

Several of these eager helpers were moonlighting from apprenticeships in the aircraft industry, among them Mike Costin.

Colin still had his job at British Aluminium, and I was at de Havillands. I'd do a full day's work there, eight till six, then drive my Austin 7 from Hatfield to Hornsey, get there for 7.30pm, work through till around 2am building up Lotus Mk6 kits, and then drive home for four hours' sleep. Then back to de Havillands with various bits that needed heat-treating and stuff like that, and my pockets full of cigarettes to bribe my work-mates to do it.

Chapman's familiarity with aeronautical engineering dated back to his time in the RAF. This, together with his readiness to question all the received wisdom about car design, made him receptive to Costin's ideas from this far more exotic engineering world. He began to see a car's frame not just as a chassis holding the wheels and the moving parts, but as a three-dimensional 'space frame', like the skeleton of a fuselage. The one they built for their next design, the Lotus Mark VIII, at a mere 35lbs, was extremely light.

When it came to the design of the body for the Mark VIII, Costin suggested that Chapman consult his older brother Frank, who was in charge of de Havilland's Aerodynamic Rectification Department in Chester.

Frank's passion was all aeroplanes; he claimed to have little time for machines that ran about on the ground. He had worked on the world-beating de Havilland Vampire, the company's first jet fighter. When Mike introduced him to Chapman, Frank, true to his name, told Chapman exactly what he thought of his designs – too heavy and un-aerodynamic. But instead of being affronted, Chapman, a magpie when it came to other people's ideas, invited Costin to look at a model of the new Mark VIII's body. The initial shape for the Mark VIII, as envisaged by his team, was no more than a skin stretched over the hard points of the lightweight frame.

Frank took the model away and went to work with his slide

rule. He then applied plasticine to Chapman's model until he had evolved a shape that conformed to his calculations. The result bore no resemblance to the original that lurked under the plasticine, nor any car that had come before. It was a fluid, swooping shape that hugged the road, low at the nose, rising to a pair of rounded fins at the rear. The rear wheels were completely enclosed. Chapman was pleased. The design was attention-grabbing and futuristic, another V-sign to convention. They built a full-size prototype.

But Costin fretted about how stable the car would be at high speeds. Creating a shape to minimise drag was one thing, but ensuring the car stayed very firmly on the ground was precisely the opposite of what he had learned to do for aircraft. Once Chapman's bodybuilders created a full-size aluminium shell and mounted it on the Mark VIII frame, it was ready to race. But Costin insisted it was tested first under his supervision. So on a grey, windy Sunday morning they trailered the car to a deserted airfield. As is done with a fuselage in a wind-tunnel test, Costin attached small tufts of wool to the car's body surface so he could observe the movement of air while the car was in motion. Since they had no access to a wind tunnel, he would just have to watch from trackside as it made a series of runs.

The information was useful, but he wanted to get more of a close-up view of how the air behaved around the front wheel arch. So de Havilland's star aerodynamicist had the Lotus mechanics strap him to the bonnet of the Lotus, so he could peer over the side and watch the wool threads as it was driven at 100mph.

With its space-frame chassis and aircraft-inspired body, the Lotus Mark VIII was truly revolutionary. Chapman's typically counter-intuitive guiding principle was, as he put it, to 'simply add lightness'. It owed nothing to conventional car design and everything to aero-engineering. And even with a humble production MG engine producing 85bhp, it could easily manage 125mph.

On Saturday 17 July 1954, Chapman drove the machine from

the Hornsey stable block up to Silverstone and entered it in the seventeen-lap 1,500cc support race for the British Grand Prix. It was the first competition of the day and the track was battered by wind and rain. On the grid alongside Chapman and the usual collection of keen amateurs was a full-blown professional team. Porsche was just beginning to emerge on the racing scene. They arrived from Stuttgart in force, with a squad of three meticulously prepared 550 Spiders (to become infamous as the car in which James Dean died a year later). Leading the team was Germany's top driver, Hans Herrmann. With their high-tech 4-cam engines, they should have cleaned up. But Chapman prevailed, the part-time car builder at the wheel of his own machine with a second-hand MG engine cruised ahead of the pack of professionally prepared German machinery. The works Porsches were no match for the British upstart. Perhaps it was the weather, or the fact that all the attention was on that afternoon's main event, but the motoring press barely noticed history being made.

Chapman collected his prize, drove back to London and the following Monday was back at his desk in St James's Square, selling aluminium. It would be another year before he quit his job to go full-time at Lotus.

But one person who did get to hear about Chapman's car was Tony Vandervell.

GAV was impatient with the pace of Vanwall progress. Never mind that it was a new car with a new engine, he wanted to win races. He was the same age as Enzo Ferrari, but the Italian had three decades of team management under his belt.

Derek Wootton was a driver for Vanwall – in that he drove the lorry that transported the cars to the races. He suggested to GAV that he talk to Frank Costin, the designer of the Lotus Mark VIII's body. It says so much about the seemingly gruff, autocratic Vandervell that Wootton the lorry driver felt able to speak up and that the boss was receptive.

GAV invited Costin to come and give his car the once-over. Costin didn't mince his words. He said the engine was fine but the rest was a 'load of rubbish'. In his view, the Vanwall didn't just need a better body, it needed a better chassis and better suspension. He told GAV to send for Colin Chapman.

Chapman had not had much to do with motor-industry bigwigs. Having been rebuffed in an attempt to buy a new engine from Ford, he had proceeded to go round to Ford dealers buying enough parts to build one all of his own. He was used to going his own way, swimming against the tide and treading on toes to get what he wanted.

In the presence of Vandervell he was more circumspect than the blunt Costin. He need not have worried. GAV liked people to speak their minds. He had responded to John Cooper's down-to-earth enthusiasm, but what he saw in the young aluminium salesman was something else – a sharp theoretician with an impatience for conventional wisdom. And, like Vandervell, Chapman was a man in a big hurry.

By Christmas 1955, Chapman had redesigned the chassis and suspension and sent Costin a set of drawings with instructions to him to start thinking about the shape. What evolved was more fuselage than racing-car body, a teardrop shape from above with a long, drooping nose that finished in an oval aperture not unlike the mouth of a jet engine.

At last, six years after BRM's troubled debut, it looked like Britain's long-suffering Formula 1 fans might have a competitive green car to cheer on. GAV's next challenge was to lure the driving talent he needed to win.

CATCH THIS DODGER

Stirling Moss was the first post-war British racing driver to be spoken of as a future world champion. But by the mid-'50s, he was no longer alone. Closing in fast were two more young men, dashing blonds with ladykiller looks and reputations to match. They were Mike Hawthorn and Peter Collins. Through the '50s, the three of them would battle each other for the ultimate prize – to be Britain's first Formula 1 world champion. And at the end of the decade, only one would emerge alive.

Although born in the same year, 1929, Hawthorn was different from Moss in almost every other way. A platinum blond, standing 6ft 2, too big to fit in a Cooper 500, he towered over the slight, prematurely balding Moss. And beside the organised, disciplined, teetotal technician, Hawthorn was a throwback, in a flat cap with a broken peak, bow tie, tweed jacket and cavalry twill trousers. Smoking a pipe, he looked more at home propping up the bar in a pub off the A3 than at the wheel of a racing car. On the evening before a race, while Moss was tucked up for an early night, Hawthorn would frequently be up larking about into the small hours.

Hawthorn and his father followed a similar path to the Coopers. In the 1920s, Leslie Hawthorn's passion for motorcycle tuning and racing brought him south from Yorkshire to Feltham, twenty miles away from Brooklands, where he opened the TT Garage.

Leslie was known as a character, a hard drinker and a womaniser, prone to after-hours high jinks. One night in 1936, he lodged his protest against the introduction of speed limits by removing all of Feltham's newly installed 30mph signs. But he made a success of the TT Garage, branching out into cars, and had a good war ferrying aircraft for the Air Transport Auxiliary – good enough to send his young son to Ardingly College in 1942.

One of Mike's best friends there was Bill Cotton, son of Billy the band leader (and amateur racing driver) and a future BBC controller. They met in the school band, Mike playing the bugle, Bill the drums. 'He was always a bit of a tearaway and I had to be careful because if there was going to be any trouble he'd get away with it and I wouldn't,' Cotton recalled. Showing no sign of any interest in studies, Mike never made it into the sixth form and celebrated his early departure from school in 1946 by tearing round the cricket pitch in an Austin 7 stolen from the school's resident sergeant major.

When Mike turned fifteen, Leslie added a year to the age on his licence application and gave him a 125cc James motorcycle. He also signed Mike up for an apprenticeship with lorry manufacturers Dennis Brothers in Guildford, in preparation for one day inheriting the TT Garage. But gainful employment took a back seat to the young man's burgeoning social life. His group of friends called themselves 'The Members' and their raison d'être was 'bikes, booze and birds', each of them determined to outdo the other in all three fields.

Fearing that the motorbike would send Mike to an early death, Leslie swapped it for a car, a Fiat Topolino. He had sold a few Italian cars before the war and supplied Topolino bits to the young John Cooper. But having four wheels instead of two did nothing to tame Mike, who got through tyres and precious rationed fuel at an alarming rate. Mike's daily route to Dennis Bros included a particularly sharp bend on the A3, beside the premises of an engineering firm, whose manager told Leslie that every morning all his lads gathered outside just to watch a certain little blue Fiat take the corner flat out. Despite a volcanic outburst at this news, Leslie, himself a tearaway in his youth, recognised his son's enthusiasm as something to be harnessed rather than squashed. So he bought him a Riley Ulster Imp and together they went racing.

They shared the driving, but not for long. On his first outing, at twenty-two years old – in a seventeen-year-old sports car – Mike showed extraordinary promise. By the end of 1951, out of sixteen races he'd scored an astonishing twelve first places, four seconds, one third and one fourth. Having burst onto the motor-racing scene, he would remain at its centre for the next nine years.

~

The third man was Peter Collins, from a family of road hauliers in Kidderminster. Like Mike, he ended his schooldays prematurely following some motorised misbehaviour; in his case on fairground dodgem cars during school hours. And he too was apprenticed with a view to taking on the family business. Like Moss senior, Collins's father helped him buy a Cooper 500 in which Peter instantly showed promise. He had dazzling looks, effortless charm and an easy way with people. Unlike Moss but more like Hawthorn, he treated the whole thing as an adventure into which he had blundered almost by accident. He loved all forms of driving and claimed to be as happy at the wheel of one of his dad's Leyland trucks as a tiny Cooper. He enjoyed his life outside racing, particularly with women and boats. He also struck up a deep friendship with Hawthorn.

~

Fleet Street was an early supporter of Britain's motor-racing renaissance. In 1948, *Daily Express* motoring correspondent Basil Cardew, noting that 100,000 spectators had descended on the newly opened Silverstone circuit for the first post-war British Grand Prix, had persuaded his bosses to sponsor a race. Other papers followed suit, now that motor racing was no longer a niche sport full of foreign names and places and there were some British heroes to cheer on.

Hawthorn in particular made great copy. And his success considerably widened his horizons. For him, the life of a racing driver was one big adventure. His childhood friend Neil McNab provided motor-racing historian Chris Nixon with this vivid snapshot of Mike's life off the track when they flew to a race with BRM at Monaco in one of Leslie Hawthorn's war-surplus Fairchild Argus planes which Mike had learned to fly:

We landed near Paris and grabbed a cab to Fred Payne's bar in the Rue Pigalle, where we immediately got stuck into some champagne. In those days, half bottles of bubbly were about ten bob each and we got through an astronomical number. Fred's place was next to a brothel and there were always several tarts in the bar having a drink and looking for business. The more we drank the better looking they became and we got very pissed, eventually going next door with two of the girls, who were by now looking very good indeed. A while later Mike suddenly appeared in my room stark naked and said: 'I'm getting bloody bored with mine. Why don't we go and see what else is going on? We might find some better looking girls than ours.' We were both very big blokes and pretty fit, so we went into some of the other rooms to see if we were missing out on any good crumpet. We'd just lift the bloke off his tart, have a look at her and drop him back on again. What a furore that started!

According to McNab, the naked Englishmen were lucky to leave the premises intact. The next morning, exhausted and hungover, they flew on to Nice. When they arrived in Monaco, Raymond Mays was already having trouble with the engine of yet another problematic BRM, so decided to withdraw – a disappointment that must also have come as a relief.

Despite all the attention the three British drivers were getting on and off the track, they were driving at a time when one star burned so brightly he put all competition in the shade. Although in his forties, the Argentinean Juan Manuel Fangio's combination of consistency and spectacular pace on the track and gentile maturity off the track was an example that all three struggled to match. Moss endeavoured to learn from him:

'I followed Fangio very, very closely, watched what he did,' Moss explained later.

The whole art of driving a racing car is keeping it balanced. Acceleration, steering and braking are all inclined to unbalance a car but Fangio could somehow go closer to the edge of disaster than anyone else because of his feel. When you go into a corner with a powerful grand prix car, you steer on the throttle, you use the steering wheel to present the car to the corner. Then you use the throttle to balance the car, to hold it on its limits. He had the gift of balancing a car like that, more so than anyone else.

In April 1952, Cardew delivered the headline Britain had been waiting for: 'ENGLISH GIANT BEATS FANGIO'. 'A fair-headed giant of an Englishman, practically unknown in international motor racing, beat the reigning world motor racing champion Juan Fangio, at the Goodwood international car meeting yesterday.'

Hawthorn's reward would be a contract with Ferrari, the first of his generation to get a drive with a winning team. It was a fantastic vote of confidence in the youngster. Moving to a foreign *équipe* had another advantage: being based abroad meant Hawthorn could avoid being called up for National Service. It was also the beginning of a very unhappy relationship with the press.

After the war, two years of National Service was compulsory for men between the ages of seventeen and twenty-six. Stirling Moss's childhood nephritis meant he was exempt. Hawthorn also suffered from a chronic kidney problem which would almost certainly have ruled him out had he got himself tested. But first as an engineering apprentice and then once out of the country racing, technically he couldn't be summonsed. Peter Collins had got round the problem by going to work for Aston Martin's French distributor in Paris. Yet it was only Hawthorn who took the flak.

In 1953, Hawthorn delivered Ferrari seven wins in Grands Prix and sports-car races. Internationally, he was now Britain's most successful driver. But at home his fame generated more criticism. A question in Parliament about Hawthorn's status set off a press feeding frenzy. 'CATCH THIS DODGER' ran a *Daily Mirror* headline. The rest of Fleet Street, sensing a rich new seam of indignation, piled in.

In 1954, a fiery crash at a race at the Syracuse Grand Prix left him with second-degree burns over his legs and a few weeks later, as he was recovering, his father was killed in a road accident. When he returned to Britain for the funeral, he faced more questions as to why he was not being served with his call-up papers.

Back at the wheel despite his burns, he continued his season with Ferrari. Despite the appearance of glamour, life at the top of motor racing in the '50s was not as exotic as it might have appeared. Start and prize money were Hawthorn's only source of income; the team paid no retainer. He also found that Enzo Ferrari expected to be repaid for the hospital bills for his burns treatment in Italy.

Another example of how far the lifestyle of racers and their girlfriends had yet to go can be glimpsed through Hawthorn's girlfriend Moi Kenward's telling recollection of waiting for news of the race, not from the trackside but in her bedsit in Earl's Court. She didn't want to miss the BBC news on the radio, but had run out of money for the electricity meter. So, to conserve what power she had left, she turned off all the lights and read by candlelight until it was time for the next bulletin.

Hawthorn was not the only British driver who succumbed to the lure of Italian machinery. In 1954, Moss scraped together £5,000, mostly from his family, and bought his own Maserati 250F, but his season was fraught with bad luck. Then he got an offer he could not refuse.

Just ten years after its factories had been flattened by Allied bombs, Mercedes-Benz had come back fighting. Cameron Earl's intelligence report had underlined how the German team's success in the 1930s had been down to engineering and organisational finesse, backed by a formidable corporation. Despite the war, nothing had changed.

Not only was their Formula 1 machine highly competitive, their sports car was truly radical. Rather than being derived from a road car like Jaguar's C-Type, it was essentially a wide-bodied version of their Grand Prix car.

The German team's resurgence had caused bitterness. Only a few years before, when Mercedes won Le Mans, the French had refused to play the German national anthem and had hung up a banner remembering Robert Benoist, a driver who had joined the Resistance and been killed by the Nazis. But Moss's run of bad luck with inferior machinery had worn him down. Unlike Ferrari, Mercedes was offering a retainer of about £20,000. Another inducement was that Fangio had also joined Mercedes. He was still the man to beat, but at least now Moss would have the same tools to work with. Before he signed, Moss insisted on trying the car first at Germany's Hockenheim circuit. It was different and challenging but fantastically powerful. But that wasn't all that impressed him.

'As I clambered out of the car, rummaging in my pockets for a handkerchief or a rag to wipe my face, a mechanic suddenly appeared, bearing hot water, soap and flannel and a towel.'

Moss signed.

Picture Post magazine ran with the headline 'THE GERMANS CAPTURE STIRLING MOSS'. Although it raised some eyebrows, the press did not round on Moss, who seemingly could do no wrong. *Picture Post* followed up with a feature on the Mercedes team headlined 'THE MASTER RACERS'.

~

In April 1955, Hawthorn turned twenty-six; he was now too old for National Service. He had publicly stated that he would never drive for 'any Kraut team', so he was pleased and proud to accept an offer from William Lyons to lead the Jaguar sports-car team. At last there was a chance to prove his patriotism once and for all in a British car capable of delivering him victory. And with Moss – his greatest British rival – in a German car, the year's Le Mans had all the makings of a memorable event.

It would be, but not in the way any of them could have envisaged.

22

COOKING WITH SALT

On 11 June 1955, the Jaguar team arrived at the Sarthe circuit outside the city of Le Mans, intent on bagging their third win. Their D-Type looked spectacular. Malcolm Sayer had given it an aeroplane-like tail fin, ostensibly to enhance straight-line stability down the 2-mile Mulsanne Straight. While aerodynamicists debated its actual value, there was no question that it was a great piece of styling, which pleased the boss, William Lyons.

There was a strong turnout from Britain, with Peter Collins driving for Aston Martin, and a team of Austin-Healeys – smaller, slower cars in search of a class win. But Mercedes looked formidable. At Le Mans, top drivers were usually paired with someone from the second tier of racers. But Mercedes decided to pair Moss with Fangio, the dream team, though a special adjustable seat had to be fashioned to accommodate the chunky Argentinean and the comparatively elfin Brit. To compensate for the Jaguar's superior disc brakes, their 300 SLR had a fiendish secret weapon. The silver car's entire rear deck behind the driver's head was hinged at the rear and could be raised to act as an air brake. To cope with the 30mph corner that lurked at the end of the flat-out Mulsanne Straight, the air brake gave the Mercedes drivers an extra 200 metres to stay on full throttle.

To dissipate residual bad feeling, Mercedes had recruited an international team for the event. Alongside Moss and Fangio, Karl Kling was the only German, who was partnered with Frenchman André Simon, and American John Fitch drove with the second Frenchman on the team, Pierre Levegh, a Le Mans veteran who had once famously attempted the full twenty-four hours alone.

On the day of the race, the conditions were ideal. The air was warm and the track dry as the drivers lined up across from their machines. When the flag dropped, Fangio, who was to go first in the lead Mercedes, jumped into his car and got the gear lever stuck up his trouser leg. He eventually got away – at the back of the pack. Still, it did not take long for him to find his way up to first place – ahead of Hawthorn, but only just.

In his book, *Challenge Me the Race*, Hawthorn wrote of being momentarily mesmerised by the legend of Mercedes superiority. 'But then I came to my senses and thought, "Damn it, why should a German car beat a British car?" As there was no one in sight but me to stop it, I got down to it and caught up with him again.'

The two masters diced with each other. This was personal; Hawthorn had already snatched his historic first Grand Prix victory from the Argentinean. But it was a good-natured scrap, as both men, though insanely ambitious, had a sense of fun – and a desire to please the crowds. When one shaved a second off the lap record, the other would counter, their averages inching up past 120mph for the whole 7-mile circuit, touching 190 down the Mulsanne Straight as they ran side by side, wheel to wheel, thrilling the crowd.

Coming up to thirty laps, Hawthorn was due to hand over to co-driver Ivor Bueb and he looked out for the pre-arranged signal from the Jaguar pits. There were no pit lanes then; drivers simply pulled over to the side at the point along the pit counter wherever their team had taken up residence. Watching from the other side of the track by the start-finish line was British author Douglas

Rutherford. In his widely praised thriller *Grand Prix Murder*, published that year, he had discovered a rich source of material in the world of international motor sport, so he was back to research a follow-up. Even with his fertile imagination, however, he could not have conjured up the spectacle he was about to witness.

At 6.27pm, Hawthorn had just overtaken Lance Macklin's much slower Austin-Healey when he braked heavily and steered right for the pits. Macklin, fearing a shunt, swerved left to avoid him and crossed the centre line of the track and into the path of the first of two Mercedes-Benzes closing in at over 150mph.

In the first Mercedes was Le Mans veteran Pierre Levegh. The fifty-year-old Frenchman's 300 SLR clipped the left rear wheel of the Macklin Healey, sending it straight towards the safety bank opposite the pits. The bank should have slowed it, but the Mercedes was already airborne. It passed right over Rutherford's head, 'still in one piece and identifiable as a car with a driver aboard. It seemed to fly on as leisurely as the horses going over Becher's Brook.' Thirty yards later it slammed to earth, bounced onto the concrete stairwell structure of the grandstand and exploded, sending the engine, wheels, suspension and shards of burning magnesium bodywork scything through the defenceless crowd. Eighty-three fatalities were recorded, including driver Pierre Levegh who was killed outright; a further 100 sustained injuries. In over half a century of motor racing, nothing of this scale had happened before.

Despite the rear end of his Healey being completely destroyed, Macklin escaped unscathed, and Fangio – coming through at about 150mph just seconds later – drove through the unfolding carnage. Hawthorn, distracted by the sight of the Mercedes hurtling through the air to his right, came to a halt several yards down the road from the Jaguar pit. He leapt out, panic-stricken. Team manager Lofty England, knowing that they were not allowed to change drivers outside the pits, nor to reverse the car, coerced the distraught Hawthorn back behind the wheel for another lap before handing over to co-driver Ivor Bueb.

Hawthorn was by his own admission near to hysteria, even before the scale of the tragedy was apparent. He wrote later of how, wandering in a daze behind the pits, Duncan Hamilton and his wife Angela caught up with him, steered him to their caravan and poured a drink down him. 'Duncan talked to me like a father, trying to calm me down.' It shows what a blur those moments were to him, because Hamilton was out on the track racing; it was Tony Rolt's wife Lois and team owner Rob Walker who had talked him down with a large brandy. When Hawthorn claimed it was his fault, Walker told him it was nonsense and made strenuous efforts to convince him that what had occurred was, in motor-sport parlance, a 'racing accident'.

The message must have got through, because Hawthorn got back in his Jaguar. Clerk of the course Charles Faroux made a controversial decision – the race would continue. Stopping it would clog the roads with departing spectators just when they had to be kept clear for the convoys of ambulances ferrying away the casualties.

Moss was leading by three laps when, at 1.30am, Alfred Neubauer, their team manager, flagged him into the pits. In Stuttgart, after a midnight emergency board meeting, the directors of Mercedes-Benz had decided to withdraw from the race. Advised of Neubauer's orders in advance, Jaguar team manager Lofty England judged that their cars would continue. To do otherwise, he felt, would be to suggest they thought Hawthorn was in some way responsible.

With the Mercedes gone, Hawthorn and Bueb cruised to an easy victory at an average speed of just over 107mph. Hawthorn did what he thought was expected, gave his co-driver a victory hug, smiled and swigged the champagne. It was victory for a great British driver in a great British car in the world's greatest sports-car race. Not only that, his friend Peter Collins had come second in another British car, an Aston Martin. They did not yet know how many had been killed.

Hawthorn's brave face for the cameras should be seen in the context of that time, when memories of the war loomed large and it was considered bad form to dwell on losses. Outward displays of grief did not do. Motor racing, after all, was accepted as dangerous. Moss would later defend the sport of that time because he passionately believed the danger gave the drivers more responsibility. He also said driving without danger was like 'cooking without salt.'

But in the days that followed, recriminations began. Fangio, closing in to lap his teammate Levegh, had seen it all. He and Lance Macklin agreed privately that for the good of the sport no one should be blamed for the accident, but then in a statement to the French investigators, Macklin said Hawthorn had braked 'too sharply'. Challenged as to whether Hawthorn had made a mistake, Macklin hedged: 'In an affair of this kind it is difficult to speak of responsibility. Hawthorn no doubt committed an error but the real responsibility was the speed of our cars.'

For a press in search of a scapegoat, Macklin's comments set off a wave of criticism of Hawthorn in the European press, the French in particular, whose veteran driver Levegh had been at the wheel of the Mercedes. On behalf of Jaguar, team manager Lofty England issued a robust rebuttal: 'As a result of close questioning of the Jaguar pit personnel and others who witnessed the occurrence, there is no evidence to establish that Hawthorn acted in any way contrary to accepted racing practice.'

Back in Coventry, William Lyons had agreed with his publicity manager that all the advertising space they had reserved in the British daily papers in case of victory should be cancelled. But he could not help feeling cheated. Le Mans was the reason he had gone into racing. Racing for him was only worth it to promote his road cars; it was not an end in itself as it was for Enzo Ferrari. Despite Jaguar's extraordinary success, bursting into sports-car racing and taking on the top teams from a standing start and proving his company's pedigree, Lyons's interest in competition had waned. As it happened, he had stayed away from Le Mans that year as he had suffered his own very personal tragedy.

Now in his mid-fifties, Lyons had begun to consider his succession. His only son, 25-year-old John Lyons, was being groomed to take over the reins from his father. After National Service and an apprenticeship at Leyland, he had started work at Browns Lane and, despite being the boss's son, had become very well liked. A week before Le Mans, he was thirty miles south of Cherbourg en route to the circuit at the wheel of a Jaguar Mark VII service car when he was killed in a head-on collision with a US Army truck. The task of informing William of the death of his son fell to team boss Lofty England, who said it was the most unpleasant thing he had to do in all of his life. Despite the tragedy, there was never any suggestion of Lyons withdrawing from the race.

~

Moss had a stellar year, coming second to his teammate Fangio in the Formula 1 World Championship, winning the British Grand Prix, Italy's Mille Miglia and Sicily's Targa Florio, the last with Peter Collins as co-driver. Despite the supremacy of the 'Old Man', Fangio, the British drivers were all regular winners at international events, with Moss now very much the leader.

At the end of the year, Mercedes-Benz pulled out of motor racing altogether, not to return as a Formula 1 team until 2010. Fangio signed with Ferrari. Moss was once again without a team.

He still yearned to be at the wheel of a British car, but was it worth the gamble? In November 1955, he organised a 'beauty contest' and tried out both the Vanwall and the redesigned BRM back to back on the same day. Both showed promise. At a dinner he hosted for motoring journalists at the Royal Automobile Club in Pall Mall, he stated:

> I believe the Italian Maserati will have the best chance of winning the World Championship next year, and I have a chance of driving Number One for them. But there are some promising British cars that have been built during the past twelve months and you know that the dearest thing to my heart is to win the World Championship in a British car.

He then posed a question: 'It is now really a choice of Maserati or Vanwall or BRM. What would you do, gentlemen?'

Moss put it to a vote: British or Italian? Of the sixteen writers present, the vote was seven for Britain, nine for Italy. He put all his hopes in Maserati.

23

THOSE BLOODY RED CARS

Having made his name in sports cars with Aston Martin, Peter Collins struggled in Formula 1 with substandard British machinery from BRM and Vanwall. Salvation came in 1956 with a drive for Ferrari, alongside Fangio. At last, Collins had the means to show what he was made of, but racing with a top team had its downside. Fangio, now a three-time world champion, a first in the history of motor racing, had the casting vote when it came to tactics.

At Monaco, Collins showed immediate promise, holding second behind Moss. It was plain to see that on the demanding street circuit, where skill was more important than speed, with the right tools, Collins was a potential champion. Fangio, having a bad weekend, had started fifth and was driving so hard to get back on top he damaged a wheel, and on lap forty was forced to retire. After fourteen more laps, Collins, still running second, was brought in and ordered to hand over his car to the Argentinean.

It was normal practice at that time that if the number-one driver had retired he could take over a teammate's machine. Collins was furious but powerless, but it made him all the more determined to shine. He won the next two Grands Prix in Belgium and France and by the time the Formula 1 circus descended on Monza for the Italian Grand Prix, Collins was in with a very real chance of the championship. If he won the race *and* drove the fastest lap, the prize would be his.

Collins was lying third when Fangio retired. The 'Old Man', as he was affectionately known by his youthful rivals, had been the biggest single barrier between the British brat pack and championship glory. Now all that stood in the way of Collins's victory was Moss, leading in his Maserati.

What Collins did next would be the signature move of his racing career. At the end of his 34th lap, he pulled into the pits for a tyre inspection. But instead of staying seated at the wheel, he stepped out of his car, grabbed a dismayed Fangio and pushed him towards it. Initially, Fangio tried to resist, but Collins was determined. The flabbergasted Argentinean took off, finished second and secured his fourth World Championship.

His actions brought Collins plaudits. Said the Italian evening daily *Momento Sera*: 'The British driver Peter Collins who gave up his car and the world championship to Fangio set an example of nobility, style, class and sporting dignity which was unmatchable.'

Fangio was awed: 'I do not know whether in his place I would have done the same. Collins was the gentleman driver.'

When motor-racing journalist Bernhard Cahier pressed Collins on why he had let his chance of the championship slip from his grasp, he replied: 'It's too early for me to become World Champion – I'm too young,' adding that he wasn't ready for all the obligations that would come with such an award.

The priority for Collins was to live in the moment and enjoy the life of the playboy racer, a long way from driving trucks in Kidderminster. Both he and Hawthorn saw themselves as amateurs, whereas the teetotal Moss regarded himself as a professional and even had his own manager. Collins was having too much fun to care, but Hawthorn despised Moss's business focus and was not averse to referring to him by his grandfather's name – Moses – a subtle anti-Semitic jibe which was tolerated then as it wouldn't be now.

In 1957, after a whirlwind one-week courtship, Peter Collins married Broadway actress Louise King and the couple took a flat in Modena from Ferrari for a peppercorn rent of 500 lire a week. Unlike Hawthorn, who would only speak his native tongue, Collins was a natural linguist who knew French from his time in Paris selling Aston Martins, and he quickly picked up Italian so he could communicate better with the team. He also befriended Ferrari's son Dino, who was almost the same age but bedridden with the nephritis that would soon kill him. Collins spent a lot of time with Dino. If he went to a film, the next day he would tell Dino all the details, frame by frame. When Dino died, Enzo was devastated. Ferrari moved Collins into the flat over the Ristorante Cavallino where Dino had lived. For a month Ferrari was inconsolable and visited his son's grave daily, as Collins's wife recalled: 'Eventually Peter went in to see Ferrari, and in effect told him to snap out of it. It made him angry that he was neglecting the company, spending so much time in this endless mourning. People couldn't believe that anyone would have the guts to say something like that to Ferrari, but actually he accepted it, and was much lighter after that.'

For all his boyish charm, Collins could exert a confidence and maturity that Ferrari admired and that marked him out from the more emotional Hawthorn, who was also now signed to Ferrari. But rather than seeing themselves as rivals, they behaved like a team within a team, a dazzling duo sometimes resented by the rest of the men.

Writing in the *Sunday Times*, Godfrey Smith heralded the start of the 1957 Grand Prix season by focusing on the three competitors with a fighting chance of being Britain's first ever world champion: 'Photographed at speed, Moss looks half asleep. He is in fact a text book stylist, immaculate in his calculation and control of any situation ... Collins is the playboy, with his yacht and a connoisseur of Nuit Saint Georges ... Fluent in French and tries at Spanish so he can talk to Fangio. Hawthorn crouches, teeth bared above the inevitable bow tie, an indomitable scrapper.'

For 1957, judging the Vanwall finally to be championship-winning material, Moss joined a home team. Into the seat he vacated at Maserati stepped Fangio, from where he won his fifth championship. Yet again, Moss was runner-up. He had bet on British machinery and lost, but he stuck with Vandervell's team for 1958.

Despite having won an extraordinary five championships, Fangio was back. But early in the season, at the non-championship Cuban Grand Prix, came a most unexpected twist. Hours after setting the fastest lap, Fangio was kidnapped at gunpoint from Havana's Hotel Lincoln by members of Fidel Castro's revolutionaries. They hoped to get the race cancelled, which would give their cause worldwide publicity.

Undaunted, Cuba's dictator, Batista, ordered the race to go ahead while police hunted for the F1 star. Fangio's captors gave him his own bedroom, a radio so he could listen to the live coverage of the race and even a TV to watch the highlights while they spoke at great length about their struggle. Fangio had no interest in politics but later confessed to sympathy for their cause and remained good friends with his captors after they let him go, calling the whole incident 'another great adventure'.

Then, in July, at the French Grand Prix in Reims, Ferrari driver Luigi Musso was killed. During the race, Fangio, now forty-seven, had a realisation: 'I had intended to come to Europe for one year only, in which I never expected to win any races. And now I had raced F1 for ten years and won five championships. Suddenly I thought to myself that I would be stupid to carry on doing it.'

Struggling with a broken clutch pedal, he managed to come home fourth, stepped from his Maserati and told his mechanic:

'It's finished.' A new era was about to begin; for the first time in motor-racing history, the championship would go to a British driver. But which one?

Hawthorn was now more focused. Surviving all the bad press over National Service and Le Mans, plus the loss of his father, had matured him. Although he got along very well with Collins's new wife and the three of them spent a lot of time together, Hawthorn asked Peter not to bring Louise to the next races, since they tended to stay out later and party more when she was there. Collins ignored the request and proceeded to race even better than before, walking away with the British Grand Prix. But it was to be his last win. At the Nürburgring for the German Grand Prix, he lost control at the Pflanzgarten corner and crashed. Thrown from his car, he smashed into a tree and died instantly. In the days before seat belts and roll bars, being separated from a crashing or burning car could be a blessing. Not this time.

Devastated by the loss, Hawthorn accompanied Louise back to London for the funeral. Neither of them made any attempt to cover up their grief.

'He was my best friend and that's it,' was all he would say to the press pack that greeted them. All the fun was gone out of the sport – from here on it was a job he had to get done.

The duel between Hawthorn and Moss to be the first British F1 world champion was now about to be played out at the last Grand Prix of the season, in Casablanca.

Moss in his Vanwall was eight points behind Hawthorn's Ferrari. To take the championship, Moss had to come first and set the fastest lap. But even then, if Hawthorn came in second, the title would be his. Tony Vandervell, now in his sixtieth year, had put everything he had into the 1958 season. Two more British drivers, Tony Brooks and Stuart Lewis-Evans, were on the Vanwall team; their job would be to keep that second place from going to Hawthorn. Ferrari drivers Phil Hill from America and Belgian Olivier Gendebien had to make sure they did not succeed.

With a British champion assured, Fleet Street and a hard core of British fans descended on the Ain Diab circuit, built only two years before along the Atlantic coast on the outskirts of Casablanca. King Mohammed occupied the royal box, he and his entourage in traditional dress. Rodney Walkerley of *Motor* magazine thought many of the spectators looked like they 'might have stepped out of some biblical illustration' as they mingled with European 'women clad in the elegance of Paris'.

Although Hawthorn was on pole, Moss led the race from the start and had no trouble keeping away from the Ferrari running second. All the decisive action was going to be down the field. Tony Brooks did get ahead of Hawthorn on lap nineteen, but his Vanwall's engine blew up, leaving a pool of oil on the track. Two laps later, Lewis-Evans suffered the same fate, but he skidded on his own oil and hit some trees. The impact severed a fuel pipe and the car was engulfed in flames. He managed to escape, his overalls ablaze. Unable to see in the smoke and confusion, he actually ran in the opposite direction to the marshals rushing to help him.

Moss never lost the lead, won the race and made the fastest lap. But Hawthorn was second; the championship was his. Although Moss had won four races he had also retired four times, while Hawthorn's Ferrari finished in the points in nine out of the ten races. Moss had now been runner-up in the Drivers' Championship four times.

For Hawthorn, the first ever British world champion, it was another tainted victory. His best friend Peter Collins was gone and now the Vanwall driver Lewis-Evans, with 70 per cent burns, was in hospital, fighting for his life. Hawthorn shunned the press, went back to his hotel room and cabled Collins's wife, who was playing at the National Theatre in Washington, DC. 'We did it,' he wrote.

Then he made his decision to retire.

'It's better to get out when you are at the top,' he explained later, 'after all it's good to be able to retire when Britain leads the world in motor racing.'

As indeed it did. The Constructor's Championship prize went to Vanwall, an extraordinary achievement for a team that five years before had not even existed. GAV's decision to abandon the British Racing Motors project and strike out on his own, using the combined skills of Cooper, Chapman, Costin and Moss to beat the Italians at what they considered to be their own game, was a milestone for Britain's motor industry.

Six days later, Stuart Lewis-Evans succumbed to his burns. Vandervell was devastated. The tragedy took away any sense of achievement for what he would later refer to as his 'stupid hobby' of building racing cars. On 29 October, the World Championship awards were presented at the Royal Automobile Club in Pall Mall. It was a very British affair. Vandervell collected the Formula 1 Constructors' Cup; Hawthorn the Drivers' Cup; and the Formula 2 Constructors' prize went to Cooper, father and son.

24

DUEL ON THE HOG'S BACK

Hawthorn had no idea what to expect from being Britain's first ever world champion racing driver. He wrote that when he got back to the TT Garage: 'My office was submerged beneath sacks of mail, the telephone rang unceasingly. Invitations poured in asking me to speak at this dinner, be the guest of honour at that function, endorse the products of Messrs So-and-So, open fetes, close bazaars, appear here there and everywhere.' In one week, he had twenty-seven engagements and still no manager or agent to help organise his life.

He planned to go into business with fellow Jaguar Le Mans winner Duncan Hamilton and change the habit of a lifetime by marrying his girlfriend, Jean Howarth, a Hardy Amies model from Huddersfield. She had said yes and Hawthorn had asked her father for her hand. But, on 22 January 1959, she had gone home to Huddersfield to clear up one outstanding matter with her parents – before the press got there first: the fact that her future husband had discovered he had an illegitimate son in France. It would turn out to be a wasted journey.

At 3pm on that same day, Mike was due to meet Peter Collins's widow Louise at the Westbury Hotel in Mayfair. After Peter's death, Louise had joined the cast of Peter Ustinov's Cold War comedy *Romanoff and Juliet* when it toured North America. This was her first time back in Europe.

That lunchtime, Hawthorn set off from the TT Garage in Farnham in his 'special-equipment' British racing green Jaguar 3.4 saloon. Heading along the A3 where it straddles the Hog's Back before it meets the Guildford bypass, he spotted a Mercedes 300 SL up ahead. It belonged to Rob Walker, the man who had straightened him out after the Le Mans crash. A formidable machine with spectacular gull-wing doors, the 'kraut car' was a red rag to the fiercely patriotic Hawthorn. The retired champion had not lost his competitive zeal.

Undaunted by the heavy rain, he caught Walker up and flashed the obligatory V-sign. Hawthorn was known to be good for a ton-up on a fast public road, and for a few hundred yards they drove neck and neck before Walker let up and the Jaguar pulled ahead. Walker didn't look to see what speed he was doing in the Mercedes, but recalled that he had just changed into fifth, which he only ever did once he was well over 100mph. As Hawthorn came into the first of two fast bends, the tail of the Jaguar slid wide. Walker expected him to correct it, but instead the Jag mounted a kerb, spun 180 degrees, hit a bollard which tore off the front bumper and clipped the tailgate of a lorry coming the other way before it 'disappeared into a huge cloud of mud and water'.

When Walker approached the Jaguar, he found it had been almost cut in half by the tree it had hit side on. Thrown into the back seat by the impact, Hawthorn was dead. The surgeon who had operated on his kidneys in 1954 later commented that it was a mercy; his judgement was that within a few years the world champion's condition would have caused him a slow and painful death.

Mike Hawthorn's World Championship and Vanwall's constructor win in 1958 marked a watershed for British motor sport, proving to all the doubters that there was the know-how and the talent to compete on the world stage at a level it had never before achieved. It seemed to promise the beginning of something. But these victories also represented the end of an era as well.

Both Hawthorn and his great friend Peter Collins, sons of the motor trade, were upstarts, enjoying international fame at the top of an exotic and glamorous sport that had previously been the preserve of the well-off. But they embraced the codes of the old Brooklands fast set, sustained by Hamilton and Rolt, of hard racing and hard partying, posing as amateurs in a world where it didn't do to look like you were actually trying. Hawthorn, with the bow tie and battered brogues he wore as part of his racing kit, paid no heed to the world changing around him. But having bagged the championship, he got out.

Tony Vandervell, an industrialist and a patriot, had been determined to right a wrong, to show those red cars a thing or two. But he was no Enzo Ferrari, for whom winning was his life, whatever the cost. For GAV, Vanwall was always a sideline, albeit a very engrossing one. And having won the Grand Prix constructor's prize, he withdrew, just like Hawthorn, because beyond the win, there was no plan.

For now, with Vanwall gone and BRM still struggling for traction, it looked like the British victory was a one-off and that the Italians would soon be back in front. Enzo Ferrari could continue to build his cars as he had done for decades past, producing tough, sturdy machines with fantastic power and traditional engineering as only the Italians knew how, that did not pay too much heed to weight or wind-cheating.

But revolution was just round the corner. Having finally elbowed their way to the front of the sport, Britain's designers and engineers were not about to give up. What's more, the revolution would not happen just on the track, but on the high street as well.

25

BURSTING THE BUBBLE

A decade after the end of the Second World War, the British economy was still struggling to recover as Churchill finally gave up the premiership to the forever PM-in-waiting Anthony Eden. Britain's influence in the world was weaker than it was, but along with France still controlled the strategically crucial Suez Canal.

Being the main shipping route for the supply of oil, the waterway was absolutely vital to British interests. But in July 1956, as part of his campaign to throw off the colonial yoke, Egypt's President Nasser abruptly nationalised it.

Caught unawares, Eden – aided by France and Israel – launched a military takeover of the whole zone, only to find he'd made the wrong call. Britain was cast as a pariah, condemned by the United Nations and several key countries including the United States. For Britain, it was a turning point in its status as a world power. For Eden, it meant resignation. For the British motorist, it was very bad news indeed: petrol rationing, which had only been lifted in 1950, was back.

The sales of new cars ground to a halt. Such was the severity of the panic that Leonard Lord took the unprecedented decision to sack six thousand workers overnight. And in the midst of the crisis came an unexpected – and most unlikely – new threat to the

British motor industry from a recent adversary. The appearance on British roads of German-made bubble cars with names like Heinkel and Messerschmitt was doubly galling for Midlands car makers, whose factories, little more than a decade before, had been flattened by aircraft of the same names.

Banned from building aircraft by the Allies after Germany's defeat, to survive, both firms cast around for other products, including miniature vehicles. The Heinkel Cabin Cruiser promised 'Travel in style for a penny a mile'. With three wheels and powered by a fuel-sipping 200cc scooter engine, the defining feature of this egg-shaped machine was that the whole of its front end, including the windscreen, and with steering wheel and dashboard attached, hinged open to form a solitary door.

Messerschmitt's Cabin Scooter, designed by former Luftwaffe technical officer Fritz Fend, was equally tiny and equally unusual, with two seats, one behind the other. Access to this cockpit was via a side-opening Perspex canopy, which gave it the unnerving look of an aircraft shorn of its wings and tail, a rolling metaphor for the fate of the company. In the British market, the size and number of wheels of these interlopers meant they enjoyed the same cut-price road tax as motorcycles. *Autocar*, in its 1957 road test of the Cabin Scooter, expressed tongue-in-cheek admiration: 'The KR200 has two and a half seats; the driver has a central one to himself and at the back there is a bench which will hold a small wife and child, or a larger wife and a shopping basket.'

No one was more incensed by this invasion than Leonard Lord, boss of Britain's biggest motor manufacturer, the British Motor Corporation (BMC), formed from the merger of previously deadly rivals Austin and Morris. Lord ruled over his empire with the same steely bluntness he had from his days as a production engineer. In his imposing new headquarters at Longbridge, on the floor below his large austere office, worked a vast engineering team. But Lord knew there was a gap in the ranks. BMC was not known for its engineering prowess. A new range of big Rileys and Wolseleys designed by former Morris engineer Gerald Palmer had been criticised in the press for its poor road-holding; his Riley Pathfinder had been cruelly nicknamed 'the ditchfinder'.

The car that stood out as by far the best-engineered machine in the whole BMC portfolio was the Morris Minor. And although approaching its seventh year, it easily outsold the Ricardo Burzi-styled Austin A30. The unique feature of the Minor's design was that it was all the work of one man, 'right down to the little knob on the dashboard glove box'. Unfortunately, he had left Morris before the merger took place.

Born in 1906, Alexander Arnold Constantine Issigonis, son of a Greek railway engineer, had arrived in London with his widowed mother in 1923. Through his work on the British-built Smyrna-Aydin Railway, his father had contrived to acquire British nationality for the family. It was an astute move, for when the Turks captured Smyrna in 1922, the Royal Marines evacuated the British expatriate community, including the Issigonis family. But Alec's father died en route. The bereaved mother and son arrived in England and found lodgings in a boarding house in Clapham, south London. Alec enrolled in the nearby Battersea Polytechnic to study engineering. He failed the maths exam three times but managed to find work in Victoria with Edward Gillet, who was developing a free-wheel device for car gearboxes.

Alec's mother Hulda, the daughter of a Bavarian brewer, doted on her only child and even sold her valuables – her rings – so that he could buy himself an Austin 7. The car gave him an entrée into the exotic world of the Brooklands motor circuit. Despite his unusual parentage, in Smyrna the precocious and somewhat effete youth had been schooled at home by British tutors. As a result, he spoke like a toff and moved with relative ease among the rich playboys of the Brooklands fast set. The connections of one new friend, Jeremy Fry, the Fry's chocolate heir, would one day play a pivotal role in Issigonis's rise to prominence.

A job of draughtsman at Humber was his way into the Midlands motor industry heartland, where he moved with his mother (he lived with Hulda for the rest of her long life). But it was low-level work on minor components and the industry in the 1930s was a hard world in which to progress. What helped him expand his engineering horizons was the decision to build a small racing car from scratch, entirely of his own design.

With the help of his friend George Dowson, and without power tools, he cut, drilled and filed every part by hand. It would take them five years. Although the engine came from his Austin 7, inspiration for Issigonis's revolutionary design owed more to intelligence he had gathered on a 1935 holiday to Germany, where he had observed at first-hand the advanced and all-conquering Mercedes W25 Grand Prix machine. But his own design was in fact far more radical.

The Issigonis Lightweight Special had no chassis, just a stiff, aluminium-faced plywood hull. All four wheels were independently suspended and used rubber instead of metal springs – just as on the Mini two decades later. And like the German Grand Prix cars of the time, it was left unpainted – a further weight-saving ploy. This little machine, while incorporating so many of the features of his later gems, also displayed the first signs of Issigonis's wilful – even exasperating – single-mindedness.

Fellow 'special' builder John Bolster wrote admiringly of it: 'The whole layout was designed on engineering principles, with no compromise whatsoever on account of finance, time or availability of parts. It has the appearance of having been built regardless of cost in the racing department of some great factory, whereas it is the result of sheer hard labour in a little shed with no proper equipment whatsoever.'

By 1938, Issigonis was at Cowley working for Morris, and it

was about then that he started making sketches on Arclight note-pads. These pads, dating from 1938 to 1957, and only recently discovered down the back of a plan chest by Issigonis's biographer Gillian Bardsley, are the automotive equivalent of the Dead Sea Scrolls. They are stuffed with notes, thoughts and drawings. Never a good technical draughtsman, despite his training, Issigonis's fertile imagination took flight in three-dimensional, free-hand sketches, renderings so astonishingly complete and detailed it is as if he were drawing them not from his imagination but from life.

Vic Oak, his manager at Morris in the late 1930s, had been the first to recognise his peculiar genius, and, teamed him with an experienced draughtsman to help transform his flights of engineering fancy into viable technical drawings from which parts – and ultimately cars – could be made. Another champion was Miles Thomas, who by 1940 was in charge of the day-to-day running of Morris. Thomas may have had no time for MG's Cecil Kimber, but he recognised Issigonis as the sort of forward thinker needed to deliver the new small car on which he imagined the company would have to depend after the war. He named the car the Mosquito, after the radical new de Havilland fighter-bomber, and backed Issigonis's desire to think the unthinkable, dispense with a separate chassis and 'make the body take the reaction stresses'.

In effect, what Issigonis was proposing was to abandon half a century's worth of automotive tradition in which chassis and bodies came from different teams in different departments and combine the development of the whole package as one.

It was now that Issigonis's perfectionism started to emerge. As he got to work, each decision on the design of the little Morris became his. Apart from the engine, which he was forced to accept from an existing vehicle, every single component sprang from his fertile mind. And Issigonis was not the type to compromise.

Less than a year before the launch of the Mosquito, he suddenly decided, purely on aesthetic grounds, that the car was too narrow. He ordered the prototype to be sawn in two and had the two halves moved apart until they looked right; he wanted four inches added to the width. This was so late in the pre-production schedule that the first batch of bumpers had already been ordered, but he got his way. Early models are distinguished by a small plate across the centre of the bumper disguising where it was cut in half.

Having backed Issigonis, Miles Thomas also served another useful purpose – shielding him from the suspicious gaze of the boss, William Morris, now ennobled as Viscount Nuffield. No fan of innovation, or foreigners, or men with airs and graces, Morris referred to his star designer as 'Issy-wassi-what's his bloody name'. It wasn't until 1947, a year before launch, that he was finally shown the prototype. According to Issigonis, the old man was furious when he saw it. He said it looked like a 'poached egg' and tried to have it killed off.

Fed up with his boss's refusal to give him a free hand to manage the business, an exasperated Thomas resigned a few months later, but only after ensuring the Mosquito was committed to production. There was just one last-minute change in deference to the founder: it was renamed the Minor, after a previous, though unsuccessful, small Morris.

Despite the Minor's universally rapturous reception at its launch in 1948, the turbulence in Cowley after Thomas's departure and uncertainty about the future of Morris prompted Issigonis to look for an escape. He found it in Coventry, at Alvis, a small specialist builder of upmarket touring cars. They offered him a safe haven and a clean sheet to design a whole new car – a V8 sports saloon. On the face of it, the new position was a dream job.

Over the next three years, Issigonis, true to form, produced another masterpiece, the TA/350. It too was stuffed with innovative ideas not seen before on upmarket British cars, like monocoque construction and all-round independent suspension.

But Alvis was a fraction of the size of Morris, and when the board were presented with this ambitious new design, they balked at the cost of putting it into production. It was a big blow for Issigonis: three precious years' work for nothing.

But for Leonard Lord, the timing of Alvis's failure of nerve could not have been better. In the seven years since its launch, the Morris Minor's stature had grown, its friendly curves as much a part of the British landscape as the red telephone box and the thatched cottage. And its all-round driving characteristics attracted several admirers. Stirling Moss had been an early adopter, as was W. O. Bentley, who praised its excellent handling. It was cheap, economical and reliable. Nothing on Britain's roads surpassed it. In fact, it rather put the rest of BMC's line-up to shame.

As soon as Lord heard that Issigonis might be available, he summoned him to 'the Kremlin' at Longbridge and offered him the position of deputy technical director for the whole of BMC, with the task of designing a complete new range of cars. Gerald Palmer, he of the 'ditchfinding' Riley, was unceremoniously dispatched to make room. Austin's own chief designer, Jim Stanfield, was also bypassed. Ruthless as he was, Lord had the wisdom to recognise that Issigonis, with his unique approach, could not simply be parachuted onto an existing team; he needed his own ecosystem in which his ideas could germinate. Ron Unsworth, who worked with him, said: 'Issigonis would be the first to admit he wasn't an administrator: he liked to build up "The Cell", a compact unit he could control. He would say that the purpose of the small group was "to make as many mistakes as possible, as quickly and cheaply as possible."'

Soon after his arrival at Longbridge, at the end of 1955, he made his first appointment, Jack Daniels, the draughtsman who had helped him realise the Minor. Although he shunned office politics, it was not lost on Issigonis that he was given an office on the first floor opposite Lord's deputy George Harriman and just down the corridor from the boss himself.

His brief was to develop an entire range of new designs, a three-car line-up, starting with the largest, the XC/9001. Within six months, a road-going prototype was being put through its paces. But events several thousand miles away, the biggest crisis Britain had faced since the Second World War, brought the XC/9001 to a sudden halt.

Lord summoned Issigonis and instructed him to shelve development on the two larger cars and go all out on the smallest, the XC/9003 – the 'charwoman's car' as Issigonis had characterised it. The BMC chairman was enraged by the German invasion; they needed to fight back and 'drive those bloody bubble cars off the road'. His only stipulation was that it be done as soon as humanly possible – within two years – and it should therefore use an existing BMC engine. Jack Daniels recalled Issigonis returning to their office, grinning ear to ear.

The small motor car would never be the same again.

26

SPUTNIK

My father's 1922 copy of the *Boys' Book of Motors* never filled me with much excitement when it was originally handed down to me. The fine colour plates showed ponderous machines with wooden-spoked wheels and pram-like hoods. But a second look several decades later revealed an extremely prescient observation made by its engineer-author, Wilfred Gordon Aston, in a paragraph headed 'A peep into the future': 'In the old days one could say that a motor car was a thing which was nearly all mechanism, upon which passengers managed to seat themselves. It will not be long before it will be possible to describe a motor car as a vehicle full of passengers, only room has managed to be found for an engine and transmission mechanism.'

It would take at least thirty years for Aston's premonition to come true. History does not record whether the young Issigonis had this book. Since it was one of very few general studies of cars available at the start of the 1920s, there is quite a high chance that he did, but if any words can be said to encapsulate Issigonis's genius, it is those of Wilfred Gordon Aston in 1922.

These are Issigonis's own words:

You know many people assume, quite incorrectly, that the first thing a car designer does when thinking of a new car is to sit down and doodle on a pad of paper until he has arrived at a pretty shape, and only then to start thinking of it seriously. This of course is totally wrong. What you do first is to lay out or sketch out how the people in the car are going to sit down. You must do this before you can start – only then do you sketch out and try to estimate how much room the mechanical parts are going to take. When you've done all this, which takes quite a long time, then you begin to think of the appearance . . . In fact you build the car around the people and the engine.

To Issigonis, this may have seemed obvious. To us looking back at it now, it may seem hardly worth mentioning. But what he was describing here was a unique approach: to work from the inside out. It sounds like common sense, but at the time it was revolutionary.

By the mid-1950s, the bodywork and mechanical engineering, the two core strands of car making, had grown closer. But still the mechanical engineers and those who created the bodies inhabited different worlds in different spaces. Although giant presses and jigs were increasingly used for the shaping and welding of bodies, this process was still done in different factories from where the rest of the car was made and where final assembly took place. The two processes required different engineering skills which operated in tandem but not always in unison. The move to 'unibody' construction, dispensing with the chassis frame, took years. And on many designs, body engineers had to work around what the mechanical engineers decided.

Issigonis never thought like this. For him the car was a single piece of engineering, in which the only given was the size of the occupants. His new car had to be no more than 10ft long. Maximising space for four passengers meant minimising the space taken up by the moving parts – the engine transmission and wheels. The whole package took shape in his head and in a never-ending stream of free-hand sketches, the only way he could express his engineering genius.

John Cooper, who befriended him when they raced their homemade specials on Brighton seafront in 1946, recalled how one animated design discussion evolved over dinner: 'He was a very good artist and began expressing his idea with a pencil on the tablecloth. By the time we finished that meal, there were so many drawings on it that Issigonis sent for the restaurant manager. "Sorry about this" – he smiled – "but I'm taking the tablecloth with me. Just put it on my bill."' Nor was this merely a gesture. The tablecloth duly ended up pinned to a wall in the experimental department where Issigonis pointed out the sketches he liked best to his team and told them to go ahead and make some mock-ups.

The conventional car layout, the 'Système Panhard', which dated back to the turn of the century, dictated that the engine sat longitudinally between the front wheels with the gearbox protruding into the passenger compartment and an underfloor drive shaft sending power to a rear axle. For the XC/9003, Issigonis turned the engine 90 degrees. He tucked the gearbox underneath and made it drive the front wheels. The radiator, which traditionally sat in the nose of the car, he moved to one side, and made a grille in the inner-wheel arch to let in fresh air. To save yet more space, he made the wheels smaller than on any previous British car – 10-inch rims, where the Morris Minor's were fourteen inches. For the suspension, compressed rubber was deployed instead of metal springs – another space- and weight-saver. And there was more.

To maximise elbow room, he gave the doors sliding windows, which dispensed with winding mechanisms that took up door space. He also added spacious bin-like door pockets, wide enough to take a bottle of gin, as he was fond of saying. The dashboard became a shelf with a single pod for the speedometer. The body weld seams, which were normally folded inside the shell, were pinched outward so as not to intrude into the interior. The whole concept was 100 per cent functional, the opposite philosophy to that of Jaguar's William Lyons, whose obsession with line and style frequently compromised headroom.

On 9 February 1957, barely five months after work had begun, a prototype was on the road, painted bright orange. This coincided with the surprise launch of the Soviet space satellite, so the strange-looking orange box got the nickname Sputnik.

As soon as he was satisfied with it, Issigonis took his boss out for a test run, making several laps of the inner roads of the Longbridge works at high speed, then slamming on the brakes outside the Kremlin entrance. A dazed Lord unfolded himself from the Sputnik passenger seat and uttered two words: 'Build it.'

Issigonis was caught completely off guard: 'When Len Lord told me to go ahead I was horrified. I even told him he was mad to build a car on what we had been able to demonstrate at that stage.'

Sputnik had done its job, but the process of moving the XC/9003 into mass production was even more daunting. Assembling such a radical configuration of drive train required new techniques and new machinery. The body shell demanded a more sophisticated welding process.

Issigonis kept an iron grip on the pre-production process, fending off all suggestions for compromise which so often crept in. Like the Morris Minor, the appearance of the Mini, with all its revolutionary underpinnings, was all from inside his head. Though not a theorist when it came to design, he was a minimalist by inclination and believed that form followed function. Even though British Motor Corporation (BMC) still had the Austin stylist Ricardo Burzi on the payroll, as well as a contract with the Italian design house Pininfarina, the final Mini appeared almost exactly as it had been sketched in those Arclight notebooks.

Happily for Issigonis, when the prototype was revealed to Batista Pininfarina himself, responsible for the most breathtaking Ferraris, the great stylist said: 'Keep it absolutely the same. It's unique.'

Less enthused was BMC's marketing department. The director of sales and his immediate team were all old hands who had started in the motor industry in the 1930s and bridled both at the car's wilful unconventionality and its designer's refusal to add any supposedly desirable styling flourishes. A visitor from a component maker was present when Len Lord's deputy George Harriman saw the finished car. According to him, Harriman said: 'When we get the chromium plate on it and the styling done its going to look quite nice,' to which a horrified Issigonis replied: 'If you do anything to that car I'm leaving. It's finished.' His only concession was to agree to cover the weld seam that stretched along the bottom of the car and round the wheel arches with a thin strip of bright metal. For the publicity material at its launch in the autumn of 1959, the press department used the words of Lord Nelson summing up his triumphant battle plan for Trafalgar: 'It was new, it was singular, it was simple.'

Given the place it has long occupied in the nation's iconography, it is surprising to discover how mystified the British public were on first encountering the Mini in 1959. Although the price was a mere £495 including purchase tax, as cheap as the wilfully old-fashioned Ford Popular, sales at first were sluggish.

The Suez Crisis and petrol rationing were forgotten – a mere blip. Eden's successor, Harold Macmillan, had only the previous year made his famous claim that 'we've never had it so good.' The cult of austerity and utility was finally over. Those who had frowned upon American excess were being overtaken by a generation reared on Elvis, Sinatra and Marilyn Monroe. It had become acceptable to show off a bit. Full employment, a massive house-building programme, commercial television, rock and roll were all raising expectations of how life could be.

On the face of it, nothing about the Mini appeared to chime with this new age of aspiration. Had Leonard Lord made the biggest mistake of his long career by giving the eccentric, autocratic refugee so much freedom?

Issigonis's world was an eccentric one. Until her death, he lived all his bachelor life with his Bavarian mother, to whom he was devoted. His free time was indistinguishable from his working life. He was always musing, doodling and fiddling either with his lightweight special, his Meccano set which he had had as a child in Smyrna or the model railway that ran around his bungalow and through specially cut holes into the garden.

But he was also something of a bon viveur, who enjoyed a Martini every evening and skiing trips to Davos, with a circle of influential friends who were charmed by his eccentricity and wit. Unlike his boss Leonard Lord, who became awkward and tongue-tied in the presence of royalty, Issigonis was thoroughly at ease among celebrities like Peter Ustinov and Noël Coward, whom he counted as friends. Also among his admirers was a fashionable young photographer whom he had met through his Brooklands friend Jeremy Fry, the chocolate heir.

As Issigonis returned home one evening shortly after the launch of the Mini, his mother reported that she had just seen on the television that 'your nice friend is engaged to Princess Margaret.'

Tony Armstrong-Jones and the queen's sister were the Posh and Becks of their day, A-listers who went their own way and were not afraid of thumbing their noses at the establishment with their fashion choices and the company they kept.

Issigonis was a guest at the wedding and Armstrong-Jones, now Lord Snowdon, wrote to him from the Royal Yacht *Britannia*, on which the couple were honeymooning, thanking him for his wedding present – an electric drill. The choice says everything about Issigonis's unworldliness. Snowdon's new life was unlikely to require him ever to need such a thing. But the letter went on to discuss some modifications he wanted made to the newlyweds' new car.

Snowdon and Margaret were determined not to submit to the conventions of royal behaviour, no more so than in their choice of transport. For the ultimate 'It' couple of their day were soon to be seen darting about London not in a chauffeured Rolls or a pre-Lady Docker Daimler from the royal mews, but in one of Issigonis's 'charwoman's cars'.

This was worth more than a thousand pages of advertising. Soon, more of the famous – and the about-to-be infamous – were adopting the Mini as their car of choice. Peter Sellers, the Beatles, Marianne Faithfull, John Profumo and Christine Keeler were all early adopters. The austere, functional little box on wheels was being seen as a cheeky, iconoclastic device that eschewed tradition. Though the word wasn't in common use yet, it was *cool*. The Mini's refusal to conform to automotive convention chimed exactly with the rebellious mood that would sweep the nation. Whether Mary Quant really invented the once-notorious miniskirt is still a matter of debate, but her naming of the controversial garment after Issigonis's car was a perfect fit.

The Mini was now a style statement. The lack of adornment that had so upset the BMC marketers became a virtue in the eyes of a generation that was embracing clean, egalitarian design. Ever the purist, Issigonis tried to keep an iron grip on his baby's minimalism, as Lord Snowdon himself discovered when he decided to change the utilitarian sliding windows in the Mini doors. 'I found someone who would put in wind down windows in a mews in London as I thought they would be much nicer than those slide windows. I sent it back to Alec for something else and it was promptly returned with the slide windows put back in. He didn't like that at all – he loathed gimmicks.'

But while the Mini was being adored as the new must-have item in Swinging London, admiration was coming from another quite different direction and for quite different reasons. The source was the man who had beaten Issigonis's Lightweight Special on Brighton seafront in 1946, the Surbiton *garagista*, John Cooper.

27

THINGS TO DO
WITH A FIRE PUMP

For John Cooper, there was no science to the development of his cars. He was driven by his own infectious enthusiasm, mechanical aptitude and willingness to experiment. Colin Chapman's fascination with aero-engineering meant that he absorbed all he could from his friends from de Havilland; the high technology fascinated him. Whereas in 1958, Cooper was carrying on much as he had a decade before, with designs sketched out on the garage wall then whitewashed over once they had served their purpose.

His father Charles Cooper wouldn't have wanted it any other way. Ever watchful of the overheads, he had only been lured into racing-car production by the clamour of demand for replicas of his son John's 500cc marvel. But the third person who came aboard the father–son operation in Surbiton would take Cooper to a whole other level. The results would turn motor racing upside down, or more precisely, back to front.

Owen Maddock's name does not loom very large in the motor-racing hall of fame. Where he does get some attention is in the memoirs of George Melly, the celebrated jazz singer and critic. The pair were both members of Mick Mulligan's Magnolia Jazz

Band. Maddock played the sax, bass clarinet and sousaphone and appeared as part of the line-up for the Royal Festival Hall's inaugural concert at the Festival of Britain in 1951. Melly's memoir alludes only obliquely to his fellow bandsman's engineering prowess.

> In his bedroom was an old-fashioned wind-up gramophone above which was suspended a weight through a pulley so adjusted as to lighten the pressure of the sound-arm on the record. On this antique machine he played Sidney Bechet records even while copulating. In fact the rather faded blonde with whom he was having an affair at that time told me she found it very disconcerting that, no matter what point they had reached, if the record finished, Owen would leap off and put on another.

Born in 1925, down the road from the Coopers in Epsom, Surrey, Maddock's life was divided between his twin passions – music and engineering. He attended Kingston Technical College, but his studies were interrupted by the war. Once he was demobbed, he resumed them but couldn't complete his course without a stint in a workshop. After several rejections, in September 1948 he discovered a vacancy in Cooper's garage for a general dogsbody. Being capable of technical drawing was merely a bonus.

When Maddock arrived he was dismayed to find that many of the parts were just made by eye. 'Technical' drawing went no further than those chalk marks on the garage wall. He campaigned for his own drawing board and was eventually given one in a space beneath the storeroom. Known around the garage as 'The Beard' on account of his unusual (for the time) prodigious facial hair, he had a volatile temper and frequently exasperated his employers. In fact, Charlie Cooper is reputed to have had a candidate for another job sent away merely because he too sported

facial hair. But Maddock did not just bring proper draughtsman-
ship to Cooper; by 1953 he was influencing the initial designs as
well. When Tony Vandervell approached them to build a chassis
for the first Vanwall, it was Maddock who was given the task of
shaping it.

Compared to the moonlighting aero-engineers at Lotus, the
technical expertise in the garage in Surbiton was more modest.
It was essentially the sum total of what was inside Cooper's and
Maddock's heads powered by John's infectious enthusiasm. Where
Colin Chapman came with a degree in engineering, had learned
stress engineering and understood the principles of aerodynamicists, John Cooper was more down to earth and intuitive.

> Fortunately I was trained as a toolmaker during my apprentice-
> ship and this came in very useful when we started making jigs
> for our tubular chassis, wishbones and other components which
> had to be fabricated on the spot. The routine was always pretty
> much the same. After Owen Maddock and I had come up with a
> new chassis, my next step would be to design the jigs that would
> enable us to build it. I personally would machine the necessary jig
> and I remember how I enjoyed working our old shaper to fashion
> the metal into the required patterns. That was a lot of fun.

Where the Lotus Mark VIII frame was constructed according
to best practice – with triangulated straight tubes – the curved
tubes of Maddock's Cooper chassis broke all the rules. To him
it was common sense to follow the shape of the body, thereby
eliminating the need for further framework to support the exterior
panels. Another telling difference of philosophy was that, where
Lotus's mathematically calculated triangulations made the engine
almost impossible for mechanics to reach, Cooper's tubes were
more sensibly arranged to make sure the moving parts could be
easily accessed.

By the mid-1950s, Maddock's designs were keeping Coopers on the leader boards of numerous Formula 2 and 3 races. He also designed the sports-car equivalent of Cooper's by-now-legendary 500, affectionately known as the Bobtail because of its sharply cut-off rear end. It too had the engine behind the driver. There was another ingredient, no less unlikely than the sousaphone-playing Maddock, behind Cooper's surprising success – the fruits of a government Civil Defence tender for a small portable fire pump.

~

In 1950, aged forty-five, having helped bring into the world Britain's most exciting new car engine, Walter Hassan felt the time had come to move on from Jaguar. So far, he had led a charmed life. At fifteen he had been taken on as a shop boy by W. O. Bentley and worked on his Le Mans-conquering machines. After Bentley folded in 1931, he gravitated towards Brooklands, like John Cooper's father Charles, and worked on numerous racing cars before being headhunted by William Lyons. But now, at Jaguar he was one of three top engineers, all of whom were about the same age, each of whom could have become chief engineer. But after Bentley, Brooklands and Jaguar, where was there to go?

Coventry Climax's roots dated back to 1903, having started life as one of the many component suppliers feeding the city's burgeoning car and commercial-vehicle businesses. Climax concentrated on building engines for road, rail and marine use, including for the tractors used on Ernest Shackleton's ill-fated Antarctic venture. During the First World War, they supplied generators for searchlights and until the 1930s built engines for several of the smaller car builders like Swift and Clyno. But the Depression picked off their clients, so the father-and-son owners Henry and Leonard Pelham Lee, finding themselves with a consignment of unsold engines, diversified into portable fire pumps.

With the outbreak of war, they won a 1,000-unit fire-pump contract from the government, with a design they named the Godiva
(after Coventry's most famous lady), which helped put out the fires
of the city's dreadful Blitz. By the end of the war their payroll had
swollen to five hundred and the Lees decided to branch out again,
this time with Britain's first forklift truck. But there was a problem
with the transmission. They needed a skilled engineer to come to
their rescue and sort it out.

Leonard invited Hassan to his plush offices in what had been
the old Riley car factory on Widdrington Road. If Hassan could
fix the forklift transmission, the job of chief engineer of Coventry
Climax was his. After the glory days of Le Mans and Brooklands,
not to mention his co-creation of the XK, it is hard to imagine a
more prosaic role. But with his racing days behind him, the chance
to run his own show seemed like a prudent choice. Lee also tabled
an offer that was hard to refuse, a salary of £2,500, double what
he was getting at Jaguar.

By 1950, the imperative to export had been overtaken by the
need to rearm. The Cold War had boiled over into an East–West
confrontation in Korea, spreading fear of how to cope with a
nuclear attack. One result was the Civil Defence Corps (CDC),
a volunteer force armed with emergency fire-fighting equipment.
One of the tenders put out for equipping the CDC was for a
new fire pump, twice as powerful as the old side-valve, cast-iron
Godiva, and half the weight, so it could be easily carried by two
people. Having sorted out the forklift transmission problems
over a weekend, Hassan turned his attention to trying to win
this tender.

He had brought with him a fellow engine specialist, Harry
Mundy, and together they developed what they called the 'Feather
Weight', or FW pump engine. As well as being light, it had to work
effectively and at continuous high revs since the job of pumping
water for a fire hose was a task that needed maximum force. It was

quite literally all hands to the pump and the job was done in seven months. The Saturday afternoon the engine was fired up for the first time it produced the power Hassan expected. Pelham's wife appeared with tea on a silver tray. The Lees, Hassan and Mundy toasted the new engine, sitting around it on packing cases.

The FWP (feather weight pump) came in a frame with handles like a miniature sedan chair. It was all aluminium, with an overhead camshaft, just over 1 litre and could pump 300 gallons of water a minute at a pressure of 100lbs per square inch. Hassan's and Mundy's lightweight little engine won the tender and an initial order for five thousand units, an undreamed-of figure for this modest company. Buoyed by this success, Leonard took a stand at the Earl's Court motor show, in the marine section, hoping to get the attention of boat builders. Instead, they got the attention of Colin Chapman and John Cooper.

Lotus and Cooper had been struggling to get the best out of Austin 7 and Ford engines that dated back to the '20s and '30s. Here was a lightweight overhead camshaft 1-litre engine. Not an experimental one-off but a fully developed production machine, unmatched by anything else available.

Hassan and Mundy claimed they didn't set out to build a racing engine; they were only doing what came naturally to them. The pump's requirements simply coincided with those of a racing car. Pelham Lee was amused by the idea of his engine being used in competition, 'a fire pump that wins races'. But in 1951, he had taken Coventry Climax public. There were bankers sitting on his new board, none of whom were likely to take kindly to the notion of resources being diverted to a racing engine. BRM had just shown very graphically the consequences of well-publicised failure. So they gave this initiative a very low profile. When a version was adapted for racing, it showed up on the balance sheet under the innocuous designation, FPF, or Fire Pump Four, after the number of cylinders it had, with any additional costs concealed in the general overheads of the company. Even when the cat was out of the bag, they stuck with the designations – the V8 version they would eventually build was called the FPE, though it's doubtful anyone was fooled by the notion of an eight-cylinder fire pump.

But for the likes of Cooper and Lotus, in the mid-1950s, Formula 1 still remained way beyond reach. BRM and Vanwall, with their deep-pocketed benefactors, had sunk huge sums into the quest for Grand Prix glory and the still-dominant red cars, Maserati and Ferrari, were backed by road-car businesses. John Cooper's operation was little more than a petrol station that happened to build racing cars round the back, presided over by his famously tight-fisted father.

Cooper's race-car building faced other challenges. The 1955 Le Mans disaster, combined with the fuel shortages prompted by the Suez Crisis a year later, caused a lull in enthusiasm for motor sport – and a drop in demand for bespoke racing cars.

For a few years after the end of the war, several other small outfits building racing cars had come into being, propelled by amateur passion, rapidly consuming life savings and goodwill as they burned brightly but too briefly. And for a time it looked like Cooper might have become one of those, but for the appearance on the garage forecourt one day of a new customer – one whose passport listed his occupation as 'gentleman'.

28

WHEN THE OX
PUSHES THE CART

Born in 1917, Rob Walker was just too late to join the Brooklands fast set of wealthy young men with money to burn on racing and fun. Nevertheless, he could have stepped straight out of a story by P. G. Wodehouse. Being an heir to the Johnnie Walker fortune could have been a poisoned chalice – literally. His grandfather's fondness for the family product killed him at thirty-three; Rob's father died of it at thirty-two. Shortly before his death in 1921, he warned Rob's mother that they were running out of money and had better give up the chauffeur. As it turned out, there was still £50,000 in the bank.

Not at all academic, Walker never even mastered joined-up writing, but that did not stop him getting to Cambridge, where he concentrated on driving the French Delahaye that had once belonged to the racing prince, Birabongse of Siam.

He entered it in the last Le Mans before the war, wearing a pin-stripe suit for the evening stint, as that was what a gentleman wore at that time of day, and changing into a Prince of Wales check for the morning. Shortly before the end of the race, the pit crew, running low on champagne, flagged him in to share a last glass before the chequered flag. He came eighth.

Also a qualified pilot, Walker earned a lifetime ban from the Air Ministry after an incident during lunch at the Cottenham National Hunt when he provided entertainment by 'jumping' the fences in a Tiger Moth biplane. But with the outbreak of war he got his licence back and as a pilot in the Fleet Air Arm took part in the liberation of Sicily. Of the 260 of those who enlisted at the same time, only twenty-five survived.

Having come this far unscathed, he accepted his fiancée's pre-condition for marriage that he give up driving. So he started his own privateer racing team, painted not in British racing green but the Scottish colours – dark blue with a white stripe – and became a regular customer of small racing-car builders like Connaught, Hersham and Walton Motors and then Cooper.

Walker nursed ambitions to break into Formula 1. He had watched British Racing Motor's (BRM) and Vanwall's uphill battle with traditional machinery and he also liked how the nimble little Coopers handled in Formula 2. On a visit to Surbiton he made the Cooper father and son an offer they couldn't refuse. He would pay for all the development costs of a Coventry Climax Formula 1 engine if he could have first use of it, plus a Maddock-designed chassis. He also wanted the services of another of the Cooper recruits, a promising young mechanic-cum-driver who had recently arrived from Australia, who also happened to be his lodger. His name was Jack Brabham.

Walker entered his new Cooper in the 1957 Monaco Grand Prix. With the exception of the notoriously unwieldy Auto Unions of the 1930s, Grand Prix cars since the dawn of motor sport had their engines in front of the driver. No one had seen any reason to deviate from this practice. Enzo Ferrari, the grand old man of Grand Prix, dismissed the back-to-front Cooper. The ox, he proclaimed, does not push the cart.

Of all the fixtures in the international motor-racing calendar, Monaco was the most high-profile. The Cooper would be up against the big Italian beasts, the 2-litre, four-cylinder back-to-front machine taking on V12 and V8 2.5-litre Ferraris and Maseratis as well as Vanwall. But what did Cooper have to lose? Unlike BRM, the Surbiton *garagisti* had never over-promised. Besides, Rob Walker was paying the bills and he didn't care about reputation; he just wanted to go racing.

The race weekend was a nail-biter even before the event got going. Brabham arrived in the principality a day late, having missed the first practice. He had never been to Monaco before and in his first time out in the car, he locked the brakes coming down to the hard left at the Hôtel de Paris and went straight on, ploughing into the sand bag barrier which protected the casino's side entrance and knocking over a post which came smashing down on the engine cowl just behind his head.

The machine was a write-off. The only option was to cannibalise the Coopers' Formula 2 car, which had been brought along for the support race. In a frantic eight-hour overnight operation, John Cooper and Walker's mechanic Alf Francis transplanted the bigger engine from the crashed machine, just in time for the race.

Brabham qualified thirteenth out of sixteen starters. But the drama had only just begun. The engine sprang an oil leak which had to be fixed and then just before the start the oil gauge showed a terminal drop in pressure. Time had run out; the only thing to do was attempt the start.

Brabham managed to get off the grid and to everyone's amazement battled his way up to fourth place. But at a fuel stop on lap sixty-two, the car refused to restart. All the pit crew could do was lift the rear wheels off the ground and spin them to get the engine to fire. In desperation, Charles shouted at them to push – a move that could have disqualified them – and Brabham got away. He carved his way through the field to third place but on the penultimate lap disaster struck again.

As he was making the descent from the casino towards the

harbour, the fuel pump failed and the little Cooper rolled to a halt just at the mouth of the tunnel. So Brabham climbed out and pushed the dead machine, with cars passing him in the semi-darkness at over 100mph, all the way to the finish line. He had dropped three places to sixth, just out of the points. Fangio in his Maserati cruised to first place, but there was no question as to who was the hero of the race.

For Maserati and Ferrari, still the big beasts of Formula 1, the Rob Walker Cooper's performance was of little account, an amusing adventure by the plucky but always accident-prone British. In any case, Monaco's twisty, round-the-houses track was kinder to smaller, less powerful machines. And anyway, who'd ever heard of Jack Brabham?

At the end of the year, Walker was skiing in Switzerland when he got a telegram from Stirling Moss. The 1958 season had been expected to start at Monaco in May and Moss was contracted to drive for Vanwall. But at short notice, the sport's governing body, the Commission Sportive Internationale, added a further competition in Argentina in January. Vanwall were not ready; and nor were BRM, who were also still struggling to become competitive.

For Moss, focused on that elusive championship win, this was a disaster. He had to race; he needed those points. Even for the wealthy Walker, the matter of flying his team out and back to Buenos Aires was a consideration, but Moss, a smart operator, already had that sorted. Without any British entrants the Argentine race organisers faced the prospect of an entirely Italian field of red cars. Moss was wise to this and offered to find a car if the Argentineans picked up the £3,000 bill for airfreighting both car and team to Buenos Aires. Moss had even got the race organisers to pick up the tab for his and his wife Katie's accommodation, a big bonus since this was a time when drivers were still expected to pay their own travel expenses.

What the organisers hadn't bargained for was that Moss would show up with a ridiculous, hump-backed, wrong-way-round machine that looked like a toy beside the Italian racers. They suspected that the Englishman might be having a laugh at their expense and even considered barring his entry.

The night before practice, Katie accidentally poked Moss in the eye, scratching his cornea. He now had to drive with an eye patch. Another challenge was that, unlike the Italian cars, whose wire wheels could be changed by undoing a single central 'knock-off' hub or 'spinner', the Cooper's lightweight cast wheels were attached by four separate nuts and were not intended for long-distance races that demanded quick pit-stop tyre changes. Swapping the Cooper's wheels would eat up two laps' worth of racing. At that time in Formula 1, tyres were expected to last forty laps, but the races ran for at least eighty.

On a ten-car grid, Moss qualified seventh, but he made a good start and worked his way up the field through the heavier cars, knowing that there would come a point when they would all have to come in for a change of tyres. Rob Walker's team put the fresh set out on the pit counter while Moss pressed on, nursing the car through the corners and avoiding sharp braking to minimise wear. Moss found the little Cooper's controls very communicative, helping him to precisely judge his own input and minimise tyre and brake wear. On lap thirty-five, five-time world champion Juan Manuel Fangio pulled into the pits, which put Moss in the lead.

Just past the forty-lap mark the Cooper pit crew noticed a white spot on one of the front tyres, then two. The spots gradually grew into stripes, broadening with each lap; the rubber was wearing right down, exposing the canvas inner case of the tyre. Moss's lead was growing but a change of tyres would put him back down the field. Lap after lap he refused to stop until gradually it dawned on the Italian teams that they had been bluffed. Moss had planned all along to go the full distance without stopping at all.

The little car came home first, 2.7 seconds ahead of the pack.

Walker wasn't in Argentina for this historic moment, having decided that his seat on the plane was better taken up with a mechanic and, besides, his son Robbie's first 'half' at Eton was about to start.

To the motor-racing grandees like Ferrari, the Cooper still looked like an eccentric British one-off. Stirling got lucky with his tyres; the circuit was comparatively slow, with sharp corners that favoured the nippy little machine. But the truth was out there – Stirling had been easy on the car to preserve the tyres – and still won. Imagine if he had been going all out. Ferrari driver Phil Hill witnessed the effect on the hitherto vastly superior team: 'After the race, our team manager was wandering around the paddock, with his hands palm upwards, fingers interlocked and waggling in the air – a sign like a bug on its back wiggling its legs. He couldn't believe his masterpieces had been beaten by this horrible iddybiddy thing with its engine in the wrong end.'

The position of the Cooper's engine gave it several advantages that were not at first apparent to the competition. It meant that with no propeller shaft beneath the seat, the driver sat lower, which made it more aerodynamic. The lack of propeller shaft also saved weight, and the engine, gearbox and differential all being bolted together needed fewer load-bearing structures to hold them, which made it even lighter. The Cooper came in at 458kg, while the BRM of the time weighted a mighty 673kg. As well as a greater power-to-weight ratio, the lighter car was kinder to tyres and brakes. Far from being the result of scientific analysis, the Cooper magic was a succession of improvisations that had all started with the motorcycle-engined 500 just a decade before.

The Cooper was unbeatable. For the next two seasons, 1959 and 1960, powered by Wally Hassan's Coventry Climax fire-pump engine, they took the Formula 1 World Constructors' Championship. The writing was on the pit wall. Even Enzo Ferrari had to swallow his pride, break the habit of a lifetime and follow Surbiton's best practice with his own rear-engined car. By the end of the 1961 season, the entire Formula 1 field had followed suit. Not only had the British arrived – and won – they had completely rewritten the rules of the game.

Cooper's supremacy did not last. Having risen to such dizzy heights, the Surbiton *garagisti* never had the resources to defend their position long-term. It was almost as if success had taken them by surprise, but that was the spirit of the age. For the father-and-son team, nothing much had really changed in the fifteen years it had taken to reach the top of their game. John Cooper, who liked to turn somersaults in the pit lane when his cars won, was always quick to dismiss any claims about what lay behind his success, making it sound like a series of happy accidents, as in this conversation with motor-sports commentator Timothy Collings: 'When we came to make our first 500 racer, it was just a hell of a lot more convenient to have the engine in the back driving a chain. We certainly had no feeling that we were creating some kind of scientific breakthrough ... And it wasn't until we built the bob-tailed sports car in the mid-1950s that we really began to think that we may be on to something.'

For a short time, Surbiton became the centre of the Formula 1 motor-racing world, a magnet for all the hopefuls in search of some of that race-winning Cooper magic. But even at the peak of its success, the amateur-enthusiast culture still prevailed. When the American Ferrari driver and future champion Phil Hill paid a visit, the place seemed to be deserted. Eventually he opened the door to the design office where he found Owen Maddock and a mechanic. They were playing conkers.

No sooner had John Cooper's Formula 1 career peaked than he hit on another idea that – even more than his relatively brief Grand Prix career – would ensure that his name still resonates today. And, like his first 500, it would be another case of taking some existing bits, putting them together and finding the combination worked rather well.

29

SCORCHED EARTH

Colin Chapman was always a man in a hurry. By the time his engineering team had fulfilled his latest demands, he had moved on to the next exciting thing. By the end of the 1950s, he was not far behind the Surbiton *garagisti*, but where John Cooper and his pennywise father Charles had been content to build just enough racing cars to fund their motor sport, Chapman had bigger plans. He wanted to be more like Enzo Ferrari or even William Lyons and become a credible builder of cars for the road as well as the track.

Like Lyons, Chapman was a great salesman, and like Ferrari he was obsessed with winning for its own sake, whatever the risks. Unlike Tony Vandervell, he did not have an industrial combine to lean on, though he did manage to acquire his own plane and fly to races. And unlike *any* of them, he was a qualified engineer.

Chapman saw motor racing as a technological joust. He was going up against the greatest names in the history of the sport using clever engineering. He loved new technology and wanted to be first with it, even if that meant being the first to fail. Aeronautical engineering – not only in aerodynamics but the battle against weight – fascinated him in a way that separated him from his peers. 'Just add lightness' was his motto – which created a new set of problems.

His first foray into serious road-car building was the 1958 Lotus Elite, a truly stunning coupe that worked equally well on the track. Powered by Coventry Climax's fire-pump engine, the whole structure was made out of fibreglass, a revolutionary composite of plastic and threads of glass. It was strong and didn't corrode, but came with its own peculiar challenges. Other fibreglass cars, like Chevrolet's Corvette, relied on a traditional steel chassis.

Chapman wanted what Jaguar, MG and Austin-Healey had – a piece of America's burgeoning sports-car market. At the Sebring Raceway in Florida in 1956, Chapman befriended a well-connected, west-coast racing enthusiast, Jay Chamberlain. He lured Chamberlain over to Britain and showed him the Elite. It was love at first sight. And when Chamberlain departed he went home as the official importer of Lotus cars to California. Chamberlain recruited a wealthy backer and arranged a line of credit that helped Chapman fund his move out of the Hornsey pub stable block to new premises in Cheshunt. But the honeymoon was soon over.

In 1959, only four Elites reached California, all of them right-hand drive and all needing rectification. Some of the next batch arrived bearing the message 'engine to follow'. Worse, in the hot California sun, the paint refused to remain on the fibreglass. They all had to be resprayed. By the time a further fifty were on their way, Chamberlain was done with Lotus.

The Elite was a car in Chapman's own image – dashing, beguiling but hurried and somewhat unreliable. It excelled on the track but in the marketplace alongside MGs and Jaguars, built in proper factories, it was like all Lotuses before it – a home-made special. And, at £1,300, it was expensive. Few sold and every one that did lost money. Having had to outsource the complicated fibreglass body, Chapman racked up debts to sub-contractors of £100,000. Fortunately, at the same time he was dreaming up the Elite, he had listened to his wife Hazel, who told him he should also make a simple basic kit car – the Lotus Seven, which owners assembled themselves, thus avoiding the 50 per cent purchase tax. The Seven ensured a steady income and kept Lotus afloat – just.

For now, any further road-car ambitions were on hold. He had other worlds to conquer. His input into Tony Vandervell's Vanwall had convinced him that he should make a play for a seat at the top table of motor sport. But John Cooper's rear-engined machines were on the cusp of changing the way racing cars were built. Chapman was on the back foot and needed to catch up. Help came from an entirely unexpected source.

~

Giovanni Cemuschl Lurani was the Count of Calvenzane, but to his friends he was Johnny. Before the war he had raced MGs at Brooklands, but at heart he was a great Italian patriot. A *dottore* of engineering, he had built his own cars, edited two Italian motor magazines and by the late '50s had become a powerful voice in the nation's motor sport.

And he was troubled. Although Ferrari had become a formidable racing stable, Alfa Romeo had withdrawn from Formula 1, Lancia had come and gone and Maserati was also fading. Just as worrying, Italy's star drivers, Farina, Ascari, Villoresi, Taruffi and Castellotti, had all either retired or died and there were no replacements on the horizon.

Lurani had seen what Formula 500 had done for Britain since the war, stimulating a whole new generation of constructors and inspiring a new generation of internationally successful British drivers. What Italy needed, he believed, was an entry-level formula of its own to do the same. He proposed a Formula Junior championship to the Automobile Club d'Italia. The machines would be cheap to build, powered by production-car engines of up to 1,100cc and use only road-car gearboxes and other moving parts. To keep the playing field level, overhead cam engines were banned and ordinary petrol-pump fuel had to be used. For decades, car-obsessed Italy had its own thriving community of *garagisti* converting small Fiats into sports cars; a move to open-wheeled racers using the same off-the-shelf parts was a small step.

The club agreed to Lurani's proposal and announced a trial national series. First to seize this opportunity was Stanguellini, a family engineering business that dated back to the nineteenth century. Their first Formula Junior car was a perfect poster child to raise excitement for the series. It looked almost exactly like a scaled-down version of Maserati's legendary 250F – the dream machine of every aspiring Italian racer. Underneath was a simple ladder chassis and a Fiat engine. Close behind came Volpini, Taraschi, Oscar, Wainer, De Sanctis and Foglietti, all of them stirred by the promise of a national auto-sport renaissance. And just as Lurani dreamed, a new generation of Italian drivers appeared, among them Bandini, Scarfiotti and Baghetti. Lurani's dream looked all set to come true.

The first full Italian race series in 1958 was so successful that the sport's international governing body, the Commission Sportive Internationale, decided to replace the old 500cc Formula with Formula Junior and make it an international series. The result was an explosion of interest from all over Europe and America. More than fifty constructors entered the fray. There was even an entrant with a Soviet-Russian Moskvitch engine. The series got a further boost when Monaco decided to run a Junior event as a support race to their Grand Prix.

As these tender young hopefuls gambolled around the streets of Monte Carlo, watching them from the pits were John Cooper and Colin Chapman, competing in the weekend's other events.

Both realised straight away what they were looking at: here was a potential new market for what they were already good at – selling racing cars to privateers.

Chapman had already realised that to catch up with Cooper, his next racer, the Lotus 18, would have to have its engine behind the driver. But what he now envisaged was a single basic design that could work just as well for Formula 2 and Formula 1 *and* Formula Junior.

And he had another ace up his sleeve. Through his contacts at Ford, he had discovered they were about to launch a new small car – with a new engine. All through the 1950s, British Ford's small cars had been powered by a sturdy but low-revving side-valve engine that dated back to 1933. Chapman had used them in his early trials days. But Ford's brand-new 1-litre engine, the 105E, with a high rev limit of 5,000rpm, was a breakthrough.

For Count Johnny Lurani, 1960 was the year his dream turned into a nightmare. Lotus burst into Formula Junior like a fox in a hen house. Cooper also plunged in with a Mini-engined car. Technically, the Stanguellinis and all the other budding Formula Juniors were completely outclassed. Cooper and Chapman each brought a decade's worth of small-capacity racing to the party. Lighter, nimbler, they could lap up to ten seconds faster than the competition. At £1,250, only a few hundred pounds more than an average family car, even less if bought as a kit, the Lotus was also cheaper to buy than the wildly inferior Italian machines. For new drivers wanting to make their mark, there was no question where to go for a winning machine.

Italy's nascent Formula Junior industry was left for dead. The French fought a last-ditch campaign by dividing races into two classes, for French only and 'foreign' cars. And at Monza the vengeful Italians disqualified Lotus on the flimsy pretext of having 'dangerously low suspension'. But Chapman was now on a roll. The lightweight, multipurpose Lotus 18's success in Formula

Junior gave Chapman his entrée into Formula 1 – albeit with the help of two of British motor-sport's grandees.

Stirling Moss's surprise 1958 Argentine Grand Prix win had been his first drive for Rob Walker. After the demise of Vanwall at the end of the season, leaving the serial runner-up yet again without a car, he and Walker formed a partnership that would last for the rest of his racing career. Walker fielded both Cooper and Lotus cars. Moss now had the pick of Britain's most competitive cars. Surely nothing now could stand in the way of his championship?

Any irritation Chapman felt about his works team being beaten by a privateer Lotus was cancelled out by the fact that it was thanks to the man who was now the world's best driver. But going to the next level brought him the first of many of the controversies that shadowed his mercurial rise.

The 1960 Belgian Grand Prix was a bleak event for Chapman and the ascendant British racers. In practice, Stirling Moss's Lotus 18 shed a wheel at 135mph. He broke his legs and nose and cracked vertebrae. The machining of the rear hub was discovered to be substandard. And in the race itself, Mike Taylor's Lotus 18 crashed after a weld on the steering fractured. Taylor broke his neck but survived and later successfully sued Lotus.

Chapman's quest for speed by 'adding' lightness prompted questions about the strength of his cars. The failures were down to negligence. His team had not been scrupulous enough about checking the quality and finish of components.

In the same race, another Lotus driver, Alan Stacey, a privateer, was killed when a bird struck his face. Although there was no real dispute about the cause of the accident, the whiff of suspicion hung around it. And doubts about the new rear-engined cars from Britain were deepened by the fate of a Cooper driver, Chris Bristow, who also suffered a fatal accident that day. The revolutionary, lightweight cars riled the opposition. The Italians, smarting from the British invasion of what had been *their* Formula

Junior, saw a chance to get back at them. For the Italian Grand Prix at Monza, the organisers were persuaded to include the old banked section of the circuit that dated back to before the war. It was fast – and bumpy. Seeing this for what it was, an attempt to strike back at the lighter and more delicate cars, the British teams withdrew. Ferrari, still racing their old front-engined machines, triumphed, taking first, second, third and fifth places. It was a hollow victory and the last time a front-engined car would ever win a Formula 1 race.

The French were also piqued by the resurgent British. During the 1950s they had virtually abandoned Le Mans to the duelling Jaguars, Aston Martins and Ferraris, but one part of the race they considered for ever theirs was the Index of Performance category, which favoured smaller cars with engines under 1 litre.

When Chapman arrived at the 1962 event with a pair of Ford Anglia-engined Lotus 23s, he was invading that last bastion of French motor-racing prowess. The scrutineers got to work. They combed through the cars, in search of any breach of regulations. A new rule stipulated that all four wheels had to be fixed to the car in the same way. This had been to stop a practice the previous year of some teams fitting wire wheels with centre-fixing spinners at one end of the car and bolt-on wheels at the other. Lotus's cars duly arrived at the circuit with bolt-on wheels all round. But the front wheels were held on by four nuts, the rears by six. The cars were disqualified.

Dismayed, Chapman asked if the cars could be modified. The scrutineers shrugged – the race was only twenty-four hours away. He had arrived at the circuit in his own plane. He called the works and ordered a new set of stub axles with four nuts to replace the rear six-bolt units, flew back to England, picked them up and had them fitted to his cars with twenty minutes to spare. The scrutineers zeroed in on the replacement hubs and shrugged again. Since the car had originally been fitted with *six* bolts at the rear, replacing them with *four* bolts, they said, could compromise safety. The disqualification stood.

Chapman was apoplectic. He vowed there and then never to race at Le Mans again as long as he lived. No one, not even Ferrari, had ever boycotted this world-renowned event. It was considered too important. Not to Chapman. The French won the Index of Performance, but a privately entered Lotus Elite won the 1,300cc class.

Chapman thrived on adversity. Setbacks just seemed to harden his resolve. But as he made the leap to Formula 1, the stakes were now even higher.

~

Stirling Moss had had a glittering racing career, except that after a decade of trying he still had yet to win a World Championship. He had yearned to win in a British car, but for most of his racing life they had been uncompetitive. He had also been up against motor sport's all-time great – Fangio. Now, in 1962, there was no one to touch him, and with team owner Rob Walker fielding more than one make, he had a choice of machine. All the stars were aligned. Even so, it was not to be. Moss's career came to a spectacular end – at the wheel of a Lotus.

The season promised to be a walkover for the British. BRM had finally become championship material, as had their star driver Graham Hill, a recent arrival to Formula 1 even though he was a few months older than Moss.

The crash at Goodwood on Easter Sunday in a non-championship race remains a mystery, because few people witnessed it. Moss himself remembers nothing about it. One theory is that he was bearing down on Graham Hill so fast that Hill hadn't seen him soon enough to move over, forcing Moss to take to the grass and hit a protrusion left over from the track's days as an RAF airbase. Another is that he was having gearbox problems. In the previous crash at Spa when he lost a wheel, he had brilliantly spun the car to scrub off enough speed and minimise impact. This time he went straight into a bank at full tilt.

The accident sharpened the debate about Lotus's reputation, but there is nothing definitive to suggest the car was at fault. Moreover, the fact that the fuel tanks were not ruptured and the driver's compartment had not completely collapsed on impact says something for the structural integrity of Chapman's design.

It is a miracle that he survived at all. The emergency services took forty minutes to extract Moss from the wreckage. A month would pass before he fully regained consciousness, only to discover that he was partially paralysed, and it was more than a year before he stepped back into a racing car.

Back at Goodwood, in secret, on 1 May 1963, Moss tried out a Lotus 19 that had been brought to the track for him. After one lap he knew it was all over. The almost supernatural competitive edge was gone. As he ruefully noted afterwards: 'I'm cursed with being a perfectionist. As long as my powers aren't perfect, I won't race. I won't drive again until I know I have a chance to beat the other fellows.'

At thirty-three years old – younger than newcomer and future double world champion Graham Hill – Stirling Moss retired. The British cars having finally become worthy of his talents, he was out of the game. Although the championship eluded him, as did Le Mans, of the 494 competitions he entered he won 222 of them. It is a record no driver has ever matched.

30

COMETH THE ICE MEN

John Cooper had dramatically disrupted motor racing. Largely self-taught, unconstrained by the disciplines of an engineer, he applied what he had absorbed from his father – a mechanic's facility for improvisation – and in the process changed the racing world.

Although he was seventeen years younger than Alec Issigonis and their backgrounds could not have been more different, the genial mechanic's son and the urbane, idiosyncratic refugee respected each other's disinclination to stick to the rules.

Since their first meeting at the 1946 Brighton Speed Trials, where they had observed each other's handiwork, they had remained in touch, although Issigonis claimed he couldn't see the point of motor racing since in his view it contributed little to road-car development, which was his passion.

But racing was what brought Cooper back into Issigonis's orbit. When he decided to enter the Formula Junior fray, he needed a supply of British Motor Corporation A-series engines, those which served the Morris Minor and now the Mini. But the Longbridge bureaucrats were disinclined to make any engines available at a discount. Issigonis, whose clout there was now formidable, came to his old friend's rescue with a briskly worded memo to the engine department, reminding them of the advertising value of a BMC-engined winner.

It was during this time that Cooper got to hear about 'ADO 15', soon to become the Mini. Issigonis let him have a spin round the works and Cooper was immediately impressed by its handling. 'You haven't built a people's car; you've built a racing car,' he told the designer. Amused, Issigonis lent Cooper two for him and his Formula 2 driver Roy Salvadori to take to the Italian Grand Prix at Monza in 1958.

Across France they travelled in convoy with Aston Martin's team manager Reg Parnell, in a DB3. The Aston Martin was very much in the lead as they sped through France and approached the first of the Alpine passes, but this formation didn't last long, as Cooper remembered. 'Salvadori with an engine of only 850cc got ahead of the 3-litre Aston, and on the twisty mountain roads he completely lost Parnell. Finally Roy and I both stopped at a little Alpine cafe and waited for Reg to show up with his very costly Aston Martin of infinitely greater power.' Parnell was flabbergasted; the Aston just could not match the Mini's road-holding around corners.

Cooper's entire career had been one long David-versus-Goliath battle, beating the more powerful opposition with lighter, nimbler designs. As they waited for Parnell to catch them up, Cooper was already imagining a Mini with more power and stronger brakes. Back in Longbridge, Cooper broached the idea with Issigonis, telling him it would be 'one for the boys'. Issigonis was not enthusiastic. 'You know, John, this is only a people's car. It was never intended for what you have in mind.' But he also knew that the Mini was struggling in the showroom. Although he had an extremely high opinion of his own engineering skills, he had not forgotten that it was Cooper – and no one else – who had seen him off on their blast up Brighton seafront twelve years before. And now that same young man was making history in Formula 1.

Together they cornered George Harriman, Len Lord's more emollient successor. So excited was the irrepressible Cooper by his idea, he told Harriman to make a thousand so they would qualify as a production car in competition. Bemused, Harriman told him to take one away and develop it.

Back in Surbiton, Cooper bored out the engine to 1,000cc, added a new manifold to take a second carburettor and upgraded the gear-lever linkage. Having made it go faster, the next challenge was to stop it. The Mini's drum brakes would be no match for the high speeds he had in mind.

Disc brakes pioneered by Jaguar at Le Mans just a few years before were still a novelty. And for a Mini they would have to be specially made extra small. Luckily for Cooper, component makers Lockheed had been experimenting with a miniature 7-inch-diameter disc brake. Two weeks later, Cooper was back at Longbridge with his 'hot' disc-braked Mini parked outside the Kremlin, ready for Harriman to try. It worked. 'We never did get that car back from Harriman,' Cooper said later. 'He simply refused to part with it.'

But Cooper wanted to race it. He needed that minimum build of a thousand to qualify it as a production car rather than a racing special. Harriman was doubtful there was a market for that many. The man from Surbiton was not to be deterred. What if they carried the Cooper name? For only an extra £100, buyers would get a 90mph car with the latest disc front brakes. Cooper didn't have the resources to convert the cars himself; they would have to be made in-house by BMC. Harriman relented and agreed a royalty of £2 for Cooper for every car sold. In the first year alone, seven thousand were sold.

But not before a last battle with Issigonis. Harriman thought the Mini Cooper should be 'tarted up' to give it a more upmarket image to go with the price. The utilitarian Issigonis was having none of it and only after much persuasion grudgingly allowed a different colour roof and some chrome trim round the front-door frames.

Cooper's ambition for the Mini was in saloon-car circuit racing, but its launch coincided with the arrival at BMC of a new competitions manager, who had other plans.

After National Service, Stuart Turner intended to take up accountancy, but was diverted by what began as a weekend hobby navigating for rally drivers and writing for the motoring press. He developed a reputation for methodical preparation, wherever possible doing a recce of routes beforehand so that as well as map reading, he could supply his driver with details about upcoming bends. He also demonstrated a cool head in the seat beside the fearsome Saab-driving Swedish rally legend Erik Carlsson, whose nickname, 'På Taket' – Swedish for 'on the roof' – spoke for itself. Turner was only twenty-eight when he was offered the job of competitions manager for BMC, based in the old MG works in Abingdon.

When he arrived, he was dismayed to find the sprawling multi-marque corporation's strategy at the time was to field as many of its models as possible. 'Apart from two Mini-Coopers, there was an 850 Mini, an Austin Healey 3000, an MGA 1600 Coupe, a Riley 1.5 and an Austin A110. Actually looking at the list again, "experimental" isn't quite the right word. "Deranged" seems more fitting – for instance, would you care to load a service car with spares for all that lot?'

The Austin-Healey was the odd one out, powerful but challeng-ing to drive, and since it was a comparative exotic in the BMC line-up, any successes did not translate into sales of the more mainstream models. But with the formidable Healey came a driver who knew how to tame it.

After a successful career as a showjumper, Pat Moss, Stirling's younger sister, had followed her mother, father and brother into motor sport. Adept at mastering the Healey, she was already one of BMC's leading drivers, having become the first ever woman to win an international rally, the 1960 Liège-Rome-Liège. Despite the line-up of talent, Turner faced a daunting challenge. Mini sales needed help, but with those tiny wheels, how could it too have rally potential? In 1962, Pat Moss gave the Mini Cooper its first outright win in the Dutch Tulip Rally, though she found the car 'twitchy and difficult', preferring bigger, more powerful cars.

Ulsterman Paddy Hopkirk had been rallying Triumphs and Rootes Group Sunbeams without much success. In 1962, aged twenty-nine, he approached Turner looking for a Healey drive to give him a chance of winning something. But Turner steered him towards the Mini Cooper, where he excelled, thanks in part to the peculiar way he had honed his skills. Like many successful drivers, Hopkirk had learned his craft as a child, in his case at the controls of a bath chair invalid carriage that belonged to an elderly clergyman in his native Belfast. Powered by a JAP motorcycle engine (by the same manufacturers as the engine in the original 500 Cooper), it had one-wheel drive and tiller steering. Hopkirk remembered it affectionately in his autobiography: 'It was highly unstable, I learned to drive it flat out sideways ... The brakes only worked at the back, so when you tried to slow it down, it was like doing a handbrake turn.' This particular technique turned out to be critical to his – and the Mini Cooper's – rise to stardom.

Unlike conventional rear-drive cars, the Mini could be steered 'on the throttle'. The trick was to approach a bend keeping the power on the driven front wheels to maintain traction, apply the brakes and simultaneously flick the steering. This would make the rear end step out. If it was done right, by the time the car arrived at the apex of the bend it would be facing in the direction of the exit line. A more extreme version for hairpin bends was the handbrake turn, a similar procedure but with a tug of the handbrake, which operated only on the rear wheels to bring the rear end right round 180 degrees.

With Hopkirk behind the wheel, Turner now saw the Mini's surprising potential, especially in situations which involved slippery conditions. To seasoned rally campaigners, the idea of a 1-litre car with 10-inch wheels and next to no ground clearance surviving the snowy mountain passes was laughable. But since this was the BMC car most in need of a marketing push, Turner decided to go for broke and enter it in all the major European events, starting with the season opener, the Monte Carlo Rally.

The event dated back to 1911, eighteen years before the first Monaco Grand Prix, and was a means of publicising the principality as a winter tourist destination. To spread the word as widely as possible, the promoters came up with the inspired idea of having entrants start simultaneously from several cities all over Europe – as far away as Athens, Oslo and Minsk. And as it was always staged in January, survival was the challenge rather than speed. Winners were judged on how well presented their cars were at the end of the run and how many passengers – or potential tourists – they had managed to bring with them.

Over the decades, speeds crept up. By the 1950s, manufacturers started to field their own teams. In 1961, the event was taken over by Monégasque former racing champion Louis Chiron. He introduced special timed stages on closed roads up in the spectacular Alpes-Maritimes that surrounded the principality. They were littered with steep hills and hairpin bends, which needed a mix of raw power, strong brakes and nimble road-holding. Run at night, on snow and ice and often in fog, these competitive dashes placed huge demands on drivers. By the 1960s, regular campaigners were mostly ice masters, like Erik Carlsson, from Scandinavian countries in Saabs, Volvos, Citroëns and Mercedes-Benzes.

A fanatic for detail, Turner brought an unprecedented level of preparation to the task. He introduced 'Turner Bibles', thick files of information about every stage of every event; what surface to expect, what tyres to use. For cold-weather events he added 'ice notes', intelligence gathered at the last minute before the special stages were closed to traffic. A works-team crew would drive the stage and mark on a map with a red pen wherever the most treacherous ice was to be found.

It could have been to no avail. Ford of America had decided that the Monte Carlo Rally was just the event to revive the fortunes of their lacklustre bottom-of-the-range Falcon model. Much modified, with 4.7-litre V8 engines, stronger brakes and bigger wheels, they arrived expecting to win against more modest European machinery. Their team of eight cars were driven by a crack team of European drivers including Britain's Graham Hill. Entrants all had to be production cars to qualify, but all the teams tried to read the regulations as creatively as possible. As if 4.7-litre V8s were not enough, these Falcons sported limited slip differentials, stronger brakes, bigger wheels and fibreglass body panels.

With a keen eye for publicity, Turner decided to have Hopkirk start from Minsk, the first time in fifty-two years that the rally had included a Soviet city. Surely that would attract press interest. But the 18 January start time was half past midnight. And the temperature was below -20°C, which froze Hopkirk's starter motor. The Mini had to be tow-started, much to the amusement of the hardy locals who had turned out to wave off the supposedly superior Western machines.

After breakfast in Frankfurt, they motored on through icy fog in the Ardennes and Luxembourg, arriving in Rheims just after 8pm, where the entrants from all the other cities converged at a large Elf garage on the outskirts of the city. After fifty-six hours on the road, it was their first opportunity for the teams to get some proper sleep. From there it was a long but quick run south, where the serious competition began.

The first of the five special stages came after midnight: fourteen miles over the Col du Festre with a slow grind up and a very fast downhill. Here the Swedish rally ace Bo Ljungfeldt's Ford Falcon V8 was the fastest.

The next, which included three cols between La Madeleine and Pelleautier, was the longest, over twenty-eight miles and a mixture of fast sections interspersed with series of sharp corners. Ljungfeldt again had the fastest recorded time. But Hopkirk was only nineteen seconds slower on scratch. Hopkirk then equalled Ljungfeldt's time on the ice-slicked Chorges-to-Savines stage. A handicap system designed to level the playing field and give smaller cars a better chance put the Mini forty-four points ahead. But Hopkirk did not yet know this as he was being sent off ahead of the pack. He just assumed he had to go as fast as he could and hope for the best.

All the remaining entrants who had started at Minsk faced the last two stages above Nice first. On St-Martin-Vésubie, the leading Falcon was nearly half a minute faster than the Cooper, but with the handicap that still put the Ulsterman ahead and, in the last stage, the notoriously twisty Col de Turini, the Mini's agile handling outpaced the lumbering Ford.

The scoring was so fiendishly complicated that neither drivers nor teams could ever be quite sure how they were doing. A 'factor of comparison' was used. First a number was obtained by taking the cylinder capacity, dividing it by eight times itself plus one, then taking the square root. Then a constant was added to this, o for Group One, 1.04 for Group Two and 1.05 for Group Three. This gave each entrant a 'factor'. Then the times achieved over each of the final five special stages were added together and multiplied by the 'factor'.

The last section was a series of four-lap races around the streets of Monte Carlo, following the Monaco Grand Prix route – in daylight. Each car's scratch time in these races was then added to the adjusted stage times to give the final result. It's doubtful that anyone understood it thoroughly enough to declare who had won with any confidence before the final reckoning.

Hopkirk thought he had done all right on the stages. Not only had the Mini delivered on the tight, icy mountain bends, it had outperformed the other front-wheel-drive Citroëns and Saabs. But the ice-free dry tarmac street sprints counted as the same points, regardless of engine size, which surely meant that the big, fast Fords would prevail. Ljungfeldt could gain considerably and the gap to Hopkirk was only sixty-four points. Exhausted, Hopkirk went to bed, only to be woken at 4am by a phone call,

'It was Bernard Cahier, the French journalist. He wanted to know how it felt to be the winner. I thought he was kidding and told him it was a bad joke.'

It wasn't. The Falcons had set the fastest times on the street race, followed by a Porsche and a couple of Mercedes 300 SEs. But Hopkirk had made the most of the Cooper's abilities round the tight circuit and lost only thirty-three seconds to Ljungfeldt. Hopkirk had won convincingly. And to prove it was not just a fluke, Mini Coopers also came in fourth and seventh. Even though all eight Falcons finished, BMC also bagged the team prize.

It was a sensational result. Tony Dawson, BMC's PR man, went into overdrive. He had already pulled off one coup in Paris the week before when, having discovered that Beatles drummer Ringo Starr had arrived at the airport late for a concert, he had arranged for a Mini Cooper rally car to pick him up and get him to the venue. But there was more, as Stuart Turner recalled: 'Tony's final stroke of genius was to get the winning car, together with Paddy and Henry, flown back by the Channel air ferry so that it could appear live on Sunday Night at the London Palladium, which was at the time by far the most-watched programme on TV.'

The triumph at Monte Carlo took interest in the Mini Cooper to another level. The American press corps, who had flown in to follow the fortunes of the Ford Falcon team, instead all wrote up the David and Goliath tale and the triumph of the strange little red-and-white car. From then on, rallying entered a twenty-year-long growth spurt, with ancient events given new vigour and ever more ambitious ones devised, culminating in the London–Sydney Marathon in 1968 and the London–Mexico event in 1970.

But Stuart Turner was not about to rest on Paddy Hopkirk's laurels. Having proved that the Mini Cooper was not only competitive but a winner, he set about repeating the victory. Inevitably the competition stiffened. In 1965, the Monte rally organisers abandoned the handicap coefficients that had helped compensate for the Mini's small engine size, but the Mini Cooper S engine had grown to 1,275cc. It triumphed again at Monte Carlo and won eight more international rallies that year.

The opposition grew restive. In early January 1966, when the BMC Competitions Department press officer Wilson McComb arrived in Monte Carlo ahead of the team, he found the rumour mill working overtime. The Coopers, it was being said, could not be allowed a hat-trick: this year the winner had to be French.

To reduce the Minis' chances, there were more rule changes. The organisers required that BMC's Mini Coopers had to conform to the Group One category specification for all production cars with minimal modifications. Now they were going up against the big Citroën DS, which also had the same advantage of front-wheel drive.

Turner was bent on securing another Monte win. He hired new talent, Finnish ice aces Rauno Aaltonen and Timo Mäkinen, who had learned their craft racing on frozen lakes. A voracious collector of detail, Turner even arranged for garden thermostats to be placed on the mountain stages days before the event to better gauge ice conditions during the night. And conducting a last check on the Mont Ventoux stage, noting that there had been a fresh fall of powdery snow that wasn't too deep, he waited for all the other recce cars to go through and, with the floor mats of his Austin Westminster service car, he and his crew swept the snow off the corners and instructed the team not to bother with fitting slower snow tyres. Again the Mini Coopers triumphed, coming first, second and third.

Unhappy with the outcome, the scrutineers insisted on the cars being stripped down and searched for rule-bending modifications. A fresh rumour was circulating that Turner's team had swapped the cars with more powerful versions before the special stages. Eight hours passed as, in a wearisome replay of what had happened to Chapman at Le Mans, the officials combed through the cars. Eventually they found an irregularity. Two of the Minis' four lights were fitted with single filament quartz halogen bulbs, which only worked on main beam, so when the lights were dipped those two went out, leaving the two to function as driving lights. And voila: all the Minis were disqualified, as was a British Ford Cortina.

Turner protested. A connoisseur of small print, he had checked the regulations in advance with the Paris-based motor-sport governing body, who had confirmed the bulbs were acceptable. They were, after all, primarily safety assets. But the organisers were immovable. The French works Citroën of Finland's Pauli Toivonen was declared the winner.

But the disqualification turned into a brilliant PR coup. Just as the world's press were getting very used to Mini Cooper victories – and therefore giving them *fewer* column inches – they now went into overdrive. The story was splashed across the front pages of Europe's papers. Once again, the British and their cheeky little cars were the plucky underdogs up against scheming French–Monégasque bureaucracy. Even worse for the French, Citroën's Toivonen, appalled at his fellow Finns' disqualification, refused to accept his prize, and a furious Prince Rainier, who was due to present it, also boycotted the celebrations. And for good measure, Bruce Forsyth had the whole Monte Mini team back on his Sunday-night show.

31

SEX ON WHEELS

The Mini phenomenon mystified the rest of the motor industry. Here was a machine of wilful functionalism which had achieved a chic status that made stylish cars look dull. No amount of optional extras or other bolt-on goodies could bring everyday competitors anywhere near the Mini's position as a fashion icon. Only the Volkswagen Beetle in the USA attained a similar counter-intuitive cult status, but with nothing like the Mini's performance.

Issigonis's creation was a piece of pure engineering that sprang fully formed from the mind of someone who had no time for embellishment. Form followed function; it was all about the job it had to do and yet it was loved in Britain and beyond like no other car of that century or this.

The Mini was the antithesis of Britain's other automotive fashion icon – Jaguar. For William Lyons, style was something he held dear, and even into his sixties he kept it tightly under his control. As both chief stylist and boss of his own company, Lyons had no one above him to enforce any compromise.

Only when it came to the requirements of his racing department did Lyons delegate shape. Ironically, the most revered Jaguar design of them all was one that Britain's greatest auto stylist did not dream up himself.

By the second half of the 1950s, Jaguar had achieved everything Lyons had set out to do. Having made his name with attention-grabbing designs, he then produced an engine that powered his big saloons and won Le Mans – four times, which gave the marque global recognition.

Lyons decided to withdraw from racing while Jaguar were at the top of their game. The business had expanded dramatically through the '50s. The road-car range now included two saloons. The flagship 100mph saloon, which had grown into the Mark IX, was joined by a smaller, smoother model, which, after an early makeover, became known to all as the Mark II. But for all the racing success, road-going sports-car development had remained almost static. The 1958 XK150 was merely a mildly updated version of the XK120 show car of ten years before, and it was not actually capable of the 150mph that its name implied.

The success of the D-Type on the track and the need to homologate it for certain races as a standard production car meant that a limited production run was commissioned for sale to privateers, many of them in the USA, where sports-car racing, thanks to the post-war influx of British sports cars, was booming. But orders were scarce. The Sports Car Club of America (SCCA), perhaps weary of the Jaguar's supremacy, now demanded that cars eligible for their races have more everyday equipment, like hoods and windscreen wipers.

Jaguar's answer to this was simply to fit those additions to the run of mildly modified D-Types and rename the car the XKSS, which was announced in January 1957. Only partially domesticated, it was a formidable machine, strictly for the enthusiast. Inevitably, and just as with the original XK120 show car, this very niche, limited-edition model was showing every sign of grabbing far more attention than Lyons intended – so much so that it was in danger of stealing the thunder of the decade-old XK's forthcoming facelift.

But it was not to be. On the night of 12 February 1957, a massive fire swept through the assembly hall of Jaguar's Browns Lane plant. No one was injured but one fatality was the XKSS – all the remaining bodies were destroyed as well as the jigs on which they were built. Only seventeen ever reached their customers, one of whom was Hollywood star and racer Steve McQueen.

Despite Jaguar's withdrawal from racing, the competition department did not close. The same team remained and there was a general assumption that the halt to competition was only a pause. A replacement for the D-Type was already being explored with aerodynamicist Malcolm Sayer.

For the C-Type, Sayer had had to reconcile pure aerodynamic efficiency with the need for the car to be recognisably a Jaguar. Lyons never lost sight of the fact that the racing car's primary purpose was to attract publicity for his road cars. But once Jaguar's racing credentials had been firmly established with the C-Type, Sayer was given a freer hand.

The D-Type not only looked nothing like its predecessor, it looked nothing like any other car at all. Its ellipse-shaped radiator air intake owed more to a jet-engine pod than any car, as did the tail fin that grew out of the driver's head rest and stretched all the way to the rear. The wheel arches were kept low, enveloping the tops of the tyres and rims with the body shell, which together with its heavily curved sides made it look even more like a fuselage. The D-Type was also a true monocoque. There was no frame underneath holding all the moving parts. The body *was* the frame, which made the D-Type both smaller and lighter.

But adopting more aircraft-like characteristics posed new challenges. Aerodynamics in aircraft was all about maximising lift; cars needed the opposite. Sayer was acutely conscious of the need to keep the car on the road at speed and resist the tendency of air to flow under the car and cause the nose of the car to rise. On one occasion, an early D-Type was about to be sent off for a high-speed test when Sayer noticed that the Perspex head lamp covers had yet to be fitted. When he warned that this could lift the car off the ground at high speed, no one thought he was being serious. Test driver Norman Dewis set out for the run, only to return very slowly. On the first fast corner he had discovered that he didn't have enough grip to steer.

There was nothing about Sayer's life to suggest he was a great designer; he was very much a back-room boy who shunned attention. His lifestyle suggests that he was paid as modestly as Jaguar's other engineers. He drove a Bedford van that had belonged to a chimney sweep, which he fitted with homemade seats for his children. He designed and made candelabras, and artificial plants – because they lasted longer than the real thing. These were unlikely products from the designer of what Enzo Ferrari – the last man to credit competitors – would call 'the most beautiful car ever made'.

Although Jaguar's racing programme was suspended at the end of the 1956 season, in the hands of private teams like Scotland's Ecurie Ecosse, in 1957 the D-Type had its best year, taking five of the top six places at Le Mans. But with no works team to build cars for, it made sense for the competition department to think of their next project as a road car that could be used on the track rather than the other way round. It was a prudent move as no one would dare suggest it could replace the ageing XK, the master-work of the boss who had shaped all of his own cars since the SS days. So what Sayer came up with was essentially an evolution of the racing D-Type with a more spacious cockpit.

When Lyons first saw the prototype, designated E1A, he didn't like it. This was the first Jaguar for the road he had not designed himself and it was not his style at all. For a start, it had no Jaguar 'face'. One of Lyons's design rules was that all mechanical parts of a car should be concealed, but the E-Type's exhaust silencers, bolted to the rising rear under-tray, were visible when viewed from behind, and from behind was how other road users most often viewed a Jaguar. Lyons also believed that wheel arches should hug a car's wheels, with only the minimum gap between the metal and the tyre. As on the racing D-Type, E1A's wheel arches partly shrouded the wheels, which meant they had to stand proud of the tyres to allow room for the front wheels to steer.

In an effort to give the project some momentum, the first running prototype E1A was entrusted to the editor of *Motor*, Christopher Jennings, and his wife Margaret, who had also raced at Brooklands before the war. On the understanding that it remained top secret, they were allowed to take it on a weekend trip to Wales. The pair were smitten. Jennings reported that it had 'sensational potential'.

Sayer's initial designs had only been for an open car. He delegated the hardtop version to his team's panel beater, Bob Blake, an American who, as a GI in Britain during the war, met and married an Englishwoman. He had worked with American millionaire racer Briggs Cunningham, who sank a fortune in the attempt to build his own European-style sports racing cars. When Cunningham gave up the chase and decided to race Jaguars instead, Blake returned to Britain and joined the firm.

Singlehanded, without a drawing and by just working the metal, he created a striking 'fastback' with a sloping rear that stretched all the way down to the rear bumpers. He also gave it an opening rear door – it would be called a hatchback today. When Lyons happened on the mock-up, he was taken aback. Blake virtually stood to attention while the 'Old Man' moved slowly round the car, silently examining it from every angle. After several silent minutes, Lyons spoke.

'Did you do this, Blake?'

Blake was terrified. He knew how fanatical Lyons was about the shape of his cars.

He said he had.

Lyons nodded.

'It's good. We'll make that.'

Having been won over by Blake's fastback, Lyons began to get involved. Key details, such as the slimline, nail-paring-like bumpers and the single bar bearing the Jaguar emblem that dissected the otherwise empty elliptical air intake, helped the design make the transition from a pure, austere aerodynamic creation into an attention-grabbing road car. Yet, not unlike the Mini, the E-Type very much projected its engineering credentials. Even on the world's sexiest car, form followed function.

As well as aerodynamic design and racing pedigree, Lyons felt the new car, now called the E-Type, or the XKE in America, needed a further USP. He had conceived his first post-war saloon as a 100mph saloon. The E-Type, he decided, would be the 150mph sports car. Getting there was another matter. They knew the motoring press would conduct their own top-speed tests, so the car had to deliver. Test driver Norman Dewis was charged with persuading pre-production prototypes to meet the magic figure, a challenge as the engine had also to be tuned so it would as happily crawl along in traffic.

When the XK120 was revealed at the London motor show in 1948, the amount of international attention had taken Lyons completely by surprise. But 1961 was a different world. The sports-car market had exploded worldwide. The XK's successor would be given a truly international launch at the 1961 *Salon International de l'Automobile* in Geneva, the first motor show of the year and one where European *carrozzerie* liked to show off their latest creations. Although the car had yet to be scooped (the press back then were scrupulous about observing embargoes), word of mouth had dramatically swollen the press numbers for the event. Two hundred-plus journalists and photographers descended on Geneva, poised for what promised to be a front-page story.

A single show car had been dispatched by transporter. Another, registered 9600HP, had been given to *Motor* and *Autocar* for testing, having been specially prepared to ensure that it did hit the magic 150mph mark. But, at the last minute, Lyons decided he wanted to reveal the car himself *outside* the show, in Geneva's Parc des Eaux-Vives, the day before the show opened. It was too late to have the show car moved out of the exhibition hall, so with forty-eight hours to go, he ordered the test car 9600HP to be delivered to Geneva ASAP. It was too late to send it by lorry and there was no means of sending it by air.

In the summer of 1951, Bob Berry, a car enthusiast and Cambridge undergraduate studying modern languages, had been on a summer course in Grenoble. Seeing that Jaguar were intending to compete in Le Mans, he wrote to Lofty England, the team manager, offering himself and his language skills. Much to his surprise, he got a reply, and spent an unforgettable week helping the team at the race track. Completely smitten, as soon as he graduated he joined the Jaguar press office.

Someone had to get that car to Geneva in time for the launch. Berry was about to make the drive of a lifetime. At 7pm on a cold March night, armed with two bottles of milk and a bag of apples for sustenance, he set off from Coventry, reaching Dover in time for the midnight ferry. The launch was scheduled for noon the next day, with the boss on hand to personally unveil it.

Berry was an accomplished driver who knew his way round Europe, but the weather was brutal. It rained continuously and the fog in Rheims was so thick in the main square that Berry missed several turns before he found his way out of the city. He said later: 'I simply drove it as if it was a race ... It was simply a case of balancing speed with getting there in one piece. I was going as fast as I possibly dared – torn between being late and shunting it.'

Wherever there were straights clear of traffic he regularly touched 140mph and more. Wary of the more direct mountain roads that might be blocked by snow, he took the roundabout route via Nantua and Bellegarde, only to find it clogged with trucks. Weaving his way between them was a true test of the E-Type's powers of acceleration and braking.

In Geneva he went straight to the service department of Marcel Fleury, the Swiss Jaguar agency, which was in the basement of a block of flats. He got there at 11.40, where a waiting crew descended on the car to clean off all the road grime. The engine cover was still hot from its Continental dash when Berry drove into the park. William Lyons was waiting, stone-faced. 'Good God, Berry, I thought you weren't going to get here.' A lecture followed on leaving things to the last minute.

As Lyons pulled the dust sheet off the hastily polished machine, there was an audible gasp among the seasoned hacks. The headline to Basil Cardew's *Daily Express* report was unequivocal: 'NEW JAGUAR CAN BEAT THE WORLD'. The *Telegraph*'s John Langley said driving the E-Type would be 'more like flying than motoring'. The *Mail* article was titled 'THE PEDIGREE OF POWER'. And there was consternation at the price. At a shade under £2,000, it was a third of the price of a Ferrari. And it was faster.

The subsequent press reception in America confirmed it: Jaguar was back on top. French journalist Bernard Cahier was one of the first to cover it for the US press in *Sports Car Graphic*: 'The E-Type Jaguar GT is very striking indeed because it is very different from all its direct competitors and because it looks so fast just standing still. Its style is not Italian or German nor, in a way even English. It has its own Jaguar style.'

Frank Sinatra summed his feelings up this way: 'I want that car and I want it *now*!'

The pure aerodynamic shape that emerged from Malcolm Sayer's calculations followed no tradition or heritage. It spurned all design convention and it is to Lyons's great credit that he was prepared to put his own prejudices aside and embrace the wholly new look that the E-Type gave Jaguar.

It is easy to fall for generalisations about a car becoming an icon of its time, but it is worth reflecting that in 1961, the year the E-Type arrived on British streets, the Beatles had just started playing at the Cavern Club in Liverpool, *Private Eye* was launched and *The Avengers* was first aired on ITV. Each of them in their own way was rebellious, subversive, flaunting their determination to be different – they were shocking and new.

Britain in the '50s had struggled to dig its way out of the rubble of post-war austerity. For a nation that had been exhorted to make do and mend, showing off was frowned upon and even as the country prospered, producers trod carefully, for example when Rover's Wilks brothers rebuked the keen, young David Bache for his attention-seeking designs and Lady Norah Docker's out-rageous Daimlers caused uproar with their insolent rejection of pervasive utilitarianism.

But Jaguar's timing could not have been better. Heralding so much of what the '60s would promise, the E-Type's brash, uncen-sored sexiness was a cause for celebration. Later, when Herbert Muschamp, architecture critic of the *New York Times*, opined that the Jaguar was 'blatantly phallic', it was unclear whether this was a criticism or a compliment. Either way, the curators of his city's Museum of Modern Art considered it such a landmark design that they bought one for their permanent collection.

From the time of his first motorcycle sidecars, William Lyons's mission was to make the special affordable. His philosophy ran counter to the prevailing view that exclusivity was a necessary condition of excellence. Unlike almost all his competitors, rather than try to make money by charging a premium for style, his mission had more in common with Henry Ford's – to create some-thing must-have and keep the price down to bring it within reach of as many people as possible.

In the post-war West, where an economic miracle had brought many more people within reach of things they could only have dreamed of before, William Lyons in his own way was part of that mission, as rebellious as what was happening in the Cavern Club that year, or Carnaby Street. And it worked for him. In Britain, his was the most profitable manufacturer, per car.

But Lyons didn't quite have it all his way. Elbowing its way into the limelight was another British sports-car maker – one which had almost never made a profit.

32

FOR SALE: HIGH-CLASS
MOTOR BUSINESS

When James Bond stepped into the secret-service motor pool in the 1959 novel *Goldfinger,* he made a choice that would change automotive history. It was between a 3.4 Jaguar and a battleship-grey Aston Martin DB2/4 MkIII. Bond did not take long to make up his mind. The Jaguar, at half the price of the Aston, had become just too familiar. For his next mission, he needed something truly exclusive, out of reach of mere mortals. The Aston fitted the secret agent's cover as 'a well-to-do rather adventurous young man with a taste for the good, the fast things in life'. Bond found himself so at home in it that his author entitled Chapter 7 of *Goldfinger,* 'Thoughts In A DB III', and gave the reader a tantalising sense of what driving such a machine could be like – through Kent.

'James Bond flung the DBIII through the last mile of straight, did a racing change down into third and then into second for the short hill before the inevitable crawl through Rochester. Leashed in by the velvet claw of the front discs, the engine muttered its protest with a mild back-popple from the twin exhausts . . .'

Aston Martin specialists will be quick to point out that there was no such road car as a DB III, and we can be fairly certain that author Ian Fleming was not referring to the DB3 racing car. Almost certainly, Fleming was thinking of the DB2/4, of the mid-'50s. One such example belonged to a man who can only be described as a central casting Aston Martin owner – and a model for James Bond.

DB 2/4 Mark I Vantage, chassis number LML-819, was delivered new on 4 July 1955 to the Honourable Squadron Leader Phillip Ingram Cunliffe-Lister, DSO.

During the war, Cunliffe-Lister had flown Spitfires with Fighter Command and later joined 1409 Flight to gather meteorological information for Bomber Command and the USAAF in a twin-engined Mosquito, based at RAF Oakington. On one such mission, in July 1943, he ran out of fuel over occupied Holland.

He managed to bring the aircraft down, but after evading the enemy for four days he was captured and remained as an inmate of Stalag Luft III until the end of the war. Restless in peacetime, he abandoned his new wife and young child and took part in international car rallies and other high-adrenalin pursuits, culminating in the purchase of a gunmetal-grey Aston Martin.

Although there is no evidence that Fleming and Cunliffe-Lister ever met, the squadron leader's father, Lord Swinton, was head of MI5 during the war and is thought to be one of the many possible inspirations for M. There can be little doubt, however, that Fleming met this car. For this was no ordinary DB.

It had reinforced steel bumpers, concealed lockers, a heavy-duty, anti-interference ignition system, a two-way radio and a Halda Speed Pilot competition timing kit – features strongly resembling some of those on Bond's car in the *Goldfinger* novel:

> These included switches to alter the type and colour of Bond's front and rear lights if he was following or being followed at night, reinforced steel bumpers, fore and aft, in case he needed to ram, a long-barrelled Colt .45 in a trick compartment under

the driver's seat, a radio pick-up tuned to receive an apparatus called the Homer, and plenty of concealed space that would fox most Customs men.

Cars, exotic cars especially, always fascinated Fleming. In July 1932, as a junior reporter for Reuters, after several months' hard labour updating obituaries, he landed a dream assignment reporting on the Alpine Trial from the passenger seat of Monte Carlo winner Donald Healey's 4.5-litre Invicta.

Originally an Austrian event, this high-altitude jaunt had grown to a challenging competition across the Alpine passes of Germany, Italy and France. It had all the ingredients to excite and inspire the young Fleming – fast cars, fancy hotels, exotic locations and a duel with dastardly foreigners.

Healey and Fleming drove the 700 miles to the start in Munich, which began with a 4am torchlight procession through the streets. Into the first mountains, and despite torrential rain, Healey's Invicta was soon up among the front runners – German Mercedes, Italian Lancias and French Bugattis. Over five days they covered 1,500 miles of tortuous Alpine passes. Healey set the fastest time for climbing the notorious Stelvio Pass and celebrated with a glass of Krug at the Grand Hotel in St Moritz, all good material for the future creator of 007.

Healey didn't repeat his outright win of the previous year, but he and Fleming were awarded the Coupe des Glaciers for finishing without a single penalty point. With it came a free flight in the Graf Zeppelin airship, which required a ground crew of 250 hands to launch and land it. For Fleming, the whole occasion was a defining experience as, Healey noted in his autobiography: 'It started in him an interest in cars that lasted right through his life, always prompting him to buy the most exotic he could find.'

Since it opened for business in 1913, Aston Martin had made few cars and even fewer profits. Like Bond, it was never far from sudden death. In fact, the vehicle in the *Goldfinger* novel would not have existed at all had the company not been rescued from oblivion by a passionate and wealthy Yorkshireman. His name was Brown, David Brown.

In several ways, David Brown would have made a good model for Fleming's Bond – amateur racing driver, joint master of the South Oxfordshire Hunt, sailor, pilot, polo player, water skier and racehorse owner. Born in 1904, he had inherited the Huddersfield family's engineering business at the unexpectedly young age of twenty-eight. In the '30s, he expanded into foundries and tractor manufacture and, like William Lyons, Tony Vandervell and Rover's Wilks brothers, he had a profitable war.

One morning in 1946, Brown opened his *Times* and spotted a classified advert for a 'High-class motor business'. Intrigued, he made enquiries. The business turned out to be Aston Martin, based then in Feltham, so he made an appointment to go down south and have a look.

When he got there, there wasn't much to see. Most of the staff had gone and there was little sign of anything being made. But there was a pre-war prototype under a dust sheet called the Atom. He borrowed the car and drove it home to Yorkshire. Its stunted, beetle-backed, four-door saloon body was ugly and the engine underpowered, but he was impressed by the chassis and its superb road-holding. So he bought the company for a mere £20,500 and instructed its few remaining engineers to turn the Atom into an open sports car.

Word got round, and within a few weeks Brown was asked by a friend to look at another ailing pedigree marque. It was Lagonda.

'I told him: "Not on your life – it's far too large a company for me."' But a few days later Brown had a call from Lagonda's official receiver, who persuaded him to fly down and look over the factory in Staines.

Brown was met at the aerodrome by none other than W. O.

Bentley, the hero of Le Mans. After his own bankrupt company was sold from under him to Rolls-Royce in 1931, Bentley had found an outlet for his design skills at Lagonda; he arrived in their latest prototype, powered by a new twin-cam, six-cylinder engine designed by his team.

Brown was impressed with the performance of Bentley's engine, but on discovering that there were already three offers for Lagonda on the table, the highest of which was £250,000, he made a token offer of £50,000, went back to Huddersfield and thought no more about it.

A few months later, in the summer of 1947, the already fragile British economy plunged further into the red; the other offers for Lagonda evaporated. For the weary Bentley, this meant another liquidation and the end of another of his brilliant designs.

The receiver called Brown again, the deal was done and Lagonda joined the David Brown stable for a mere £52,000.

Brown's rescue of Aston Martin was by no means its first. Ever since Lionel Martin founded the company and won the Aston Hill Climb in 1914 – where he got the other half of the name – the firm had a reputation for making a very small number of interesting sports cars with racing potential. But, like many others of that era, it survived mainly on enthusiasm rather than investment – or profit. Bankrupt in 1924 and again in 1926, sold off in 1928, rescued in 1932, then sold again in 1933, the tiny company then enjoyed a period of relative calm up to the war, thanks to a succession of benefactors and gifted engineers. Nothing was ordinary about Aston Martin's fraught history, not even the names of some of its key pre-war patrons and designers, émigrés Count Louis Zborowski and Augustus Bertelli. Brown would continue the tradition, hiring two more fugitives from Europe: Professor Robert Eberan von Eberhorst and Tadeusz 'Tadek' Marek.

Brown ordered Bentley's new engine to be dropped into the Atom chassis. Body stylist Frank Feeley, who had joined Lagonda in the 1920s aged fourteen, gave it a modern sports-car body with clean, purposeful lines, just the right level of understated glamour to catch the eye of Ian Fleming's James Bond.

The DB2 was the first car to wear David Brown's initials, and it would see Aston Martin through the best part of the 1950s. But despite its racing pedigree, the company lacked profile. Kjell Qvale, the American who had discovered the MG TC and pioneered sales of British sports cars to Californians, told Brown he wouldn't take on Aston Martin until they had won Le Mans.

Cushioned by his successful engineering business, Brown threw Aston Martin into a frenzy of racing development: a win at Le Mans was the goal. He hired John Wyer from Monaco Motors, a company that had specialised in preparing privateer racing cars for rich enthusiasts. Like Raymond Mays at BRM, Brown had also been impressed with the all-conquering German racing teams of the 1930s and recruited one of their foremost designers, Professor Robert Eberan von Eberhorst.

An Austrian from an aristocratic family, Eberan von Eberhorst had worked alongside Ferdinand Porsche to create the legendary V12 supercharged Auto Union racing cars. In 1940, he turned to academia as professor of engineering at Dresden's technical college, but found time to consult on the Tiger tank and the V2 rockets. He fled the city just before the Allied bombing and escaped from the Russian Zone in just the clothes he was wearing. He survived on bits of consulting work, which eventually brought him to England. Ted Cutting, a draughtsman at the time, remembered his arrival at Aston Martin: 'When he came to Feltham, he wore an old pair of tennis shoes and a pair of trousers I would have used for gardening.'

With Le Mans the priority, Brown put the professor to work designing their first pure sports racing car – the DB3. Having such an eminent engineer on the premises impressed a young Harold Beach, newly recruited to the Aston Martin drawing office. The first thing Beach did was invest in a 20-inch slide rule to keep up with his new master's demands for precision.

Adjusting to life in Feltham was not easy for the refugee. He found that, compared to Auto Union, a conglomerate of five different car makes with a racing team bankrolled by the Third Reich, Aston's racing budget was in his opinion 'very small'.

Eberhorst's comments about Aston's racing manager, John Wyer, reveal a yawning difference of approach: 'He was very much in favour of improvisation and felt that I was too cautious, but you can't be cautious enough as an engineer engaged in racing. I'd much rather miss a race and break an engine on the test-bed.'

Wyer, whose motto was 'when in doubt, do something', believed that only the rough and tumble of competition was a true test of a car. These opposing philosophies typified the differences between the British and Teutonic automotive cultures at the time. The Austrian even managed to wind up Doreen Green, Wyer's secretary. 'He would dictate in his broken English and got annoyed when I typed it up and corrected it.'

At races, where the mechanics and drivers played tricks on each other, even the professor was a target, according to Green: 'At one Continental race the Prof had an attractive lady in his room – but the mechanics had attached the bell wire to the mattress so all evening chambermaids kept knocking at the door.'

As it turned out, Eberan von Eberhorst's DB3 arrived a year late and proved too heavy to be competitive. He left Aston Martin in the summer of 1953, with a parting shot at David Brown, who had given him his first decent job after the war: 'Aston Martin was a very nice hobby for him and he was fortunate enough to find in me and John Wyer and others, men who were prepared to work day and night for success, but the manner of spending and preparing things properly was not up to the task.'

Wyer ordered the remaining engineers to sort the problematic DB3 into the more promising DB3S, clothed in Frank Feeley's far more exciting bodywork. He then picked 28-year-old engineer Ted Cutting to design a new car – the DBR1. Work began in August 1955 and it raced at Le Mans the following summer.

David Brown was impatient for success. Like Enzo Ferrari, he saw the road-car business as a means to finance his racing, and fans were thrilled to have Aston Martin as well as Jaguar to cheer on. David Brown's claim that racing success enhanced his tractor and gear business involved a degree of wishful thinking as the spending on racing grew.

Brown feared the Bentley-designed six-cylinder was always going to be at a disadvantage against Ferrari, so he sanctioned the creation of his own V12 engine and badged the car a Lagonda. For such a small company, developing two quite distinct engines was too much. The V12 failed to deliver the promised extra power and drivers found it an unruly beast. In the 1954 Le Mans, five cars – three Astons and two Lagondas – started; none finished. Jaguar would win Le Mans no less than five times in the 1950s. John Wyer would call the great race 'the graveyard of our hopes' and noted ruefully that what Jaguar had going for them was 'years of development and nothing too new about the car and the drivers'.

In spite of this, Aston Martin had no trouble attracting drivers, and not just the gentleman amateurs. Peter Collins became a regular and the very earnings-conscious Stirling Moss, who, after a £1,000 bonus from Jaguar for winning the Tourist Trophy, found himself being offered a paltry £50 retainer by John Wyer – but Moss accepted.

At races, the team got to stay at the best hotels and eat at the best restaurants. Aston Martin was a long way from a household name, but within the small world of motor sport it had a pedigree that went back four decades, which only added to its charisma. American hopefuls who had discovered road racing at the wheel of MG TCs came to Europe in search of drives. Texan roughneck and failed chicken farmer Carroll Shelby appeared in Feltham claiming to have backers ready to buy a DB3 for him to race. The backers never came through but Wyer absorbed him into the team, put him in a car and sent him to the debut race at Aintree, where in a torrential downpour he came second.

Wyer was a steely tactician of few words. His nickname was 'Death Ray' because of the cold, silent look he gave drivers when they had gone off the road or mechanics who had made a mistake. But he created momentum, and soon Aston Martin was winning regularly – except the one place it really mattered: Le Mans.

By 1959, the golden age of British sports-car racing looked like it was drawing to a close. Hawthorn and Collins were gone, Jaguar had withdrawn. Aston Martin were now the only British contenders, with a car that was starting to show its age. Brown and Wyer decided to put all their resources into the 24-hour spectacular. The DBR1, with two seasons' worth of racing behind it, had become a favourite with drivers because of its superbly balanced handling. But it lacked the sheer grunt of the V12 Ferrari Testa Rossas, so named for having their cylinder heads painted red, a reminder to anyone who cared to look under the bonnet of their superiority in cylinder numbers.

But then Stirling Moss made an offer Wyer couldn't refuse. The previous year, 1958, he had taken a DBR1 to Nürburgring and won the 1,000 kilometres. He wanted to try to repeat his victory, even if it meant funding the excursion out of his own pocket. It was a huge personal risk, financially, but a great vote of confidence in the car.

Nürburgring was like no other track. It had been conceived in the 1920s as a public works project to bring work to the severely depressed area around Cologne, a venue where Germany could match Le Mans and the Mille Miglia, only on a dedicated circuit. Twenty thousand men built it. A vast closed circuit, it threaded through the forests of the Eifel Mountains and circled the medieval castle of Nürburg. Full of thrilling swoops and curves, the difference in elevation between the lowest to the highest point was 1,000 feet. There were over seventy corners, several straights nearly two miles long and gradients of one in six. It also boasted a luxury hotel with stunning views of the track.

The Ferraris had the power, but on the twisty, multi-cornered Nürburgring it was all about handling, and Moss loved how the Aston cornered. Race rules dictated there had to be two drivers, but did not specify how long they should each race. Moss chose 46-year-old Jack Fairman as his co-driver. He needed someone steady, who wouldn't cut up rough about driving the bare minimum. This was going to be Moss's show.

In the Le Mans-style start, Moss got away first and in his opening seventeen-lap stint broke the lap record sixteen times. Fairman took over just as the sky was darkening, and as the rain started to fall, so did the Aston's lead. After six laps he braked too hard to avoid a slower car and spun off the road at Brünnchen corner, into a ditch. He attempted to lever the Aston out with a piece of discarded fence: no luck. With the leading Ferraris and Porsches flying past him, Fairman, in a last act of desperation, put his back against the aluminium rump of the car and attempted to bodily heave it back onto the road.

In the pits, as the minutes ticked away, Moss was staring at an expensive humiliation. He had bankrolled this stunt on the expectation of bagging the prize money. Now he would come away empty-handed. There was nothing for it but to pack up and get going. He put away his helmet and gloves and was about to pull off his overalls when Fairman roared into the pits, a sizeable dent in the Aston's rump to show for his herculean effort.

Moss roared off in pursuit, first of Umberto Maglioli's Porsche, then the two Testa Rossas in first and second place. Thirty-three laps later, having built up almost a three-minute lead, Moss handed back to Fairman. America's Phil Hill in his Ferrari clawed his way past Fairman, who stopped and gave the car back to Moss for the final ten laps. Moss tore after Hill and caught him up. By the time the chequered flag fell, Moss had built up a shattering 41-second lead.

But then came Le Mans, where raw power really mattered. And despite Moss's brilliant performance against the Ferraris in Germany, the DBR1 was actually no faster than it had been two years before. This was definitely going to be its last year of competition. But over the years the bugs that had dogged earlier Astons had been ironed out. All they had to do was stay out of trouble. Moss's task, as it had been in his first Le Mans for Jaguar, was to be the hare and try to break the Ferraris. But after eight attempts, he was also after that elusive Le Mans win.

As usual, he made an electrifying getaway. But Jean Behra, having stalled his Testa Rossa at the start, showed the spectators what the Ferrari was made of, slicing through the field and taking the lead from Moss after only an hour. A few hours later, Moss's Aston expired. But then, one by one, all three Ferraris dropped out. Where, previously, no DBR1 had lasted the twenty-four hours, this time two of them came through. American Carroll Shelby and Essex-born Roy Salvadori won the race and Frenchman Maurice Trintignant and Belgian's Paul Frère were second.

Kjell Qvale, the Californian British sports-car dealer, had got what he demanded, a win at Le Mans – and with America's star driver, Carroll Shelby, at the wheel. It had taken ten years, but finally David Brown's dream had come true.

Aston Martin now faced a dilemma, however. Having originally planned to race only at Le Mans, Moss's one-off triumph at Nürburgring, combined with the triumph at Le Mans, put them in contention for the World Sportscar Championship. Since its inception in 1953, Ferrari had won it every year but one. This year they had racked up eighteen points, but Aston Martin had sixteen and Porsche fifteen. The last race in the calendar would decide it: the Tourist Trophy at Goodwood – the only British race.

The nine-hour TT was particularly tough on tyres. Fast pit stops could make or break the race. John Wyer introduced a secret weapon – on-board, quick-action hydraulic jacks, a device unknown in Europe but common practice on Indianapolis cars. Precious seconds could be shaved off tyre changes.

Again, Moss led the race from the start, and his co-driver Salvadori kept the position until the second pit stop. The speedy tyre change dismayed the competition, but as the Aston was being refuelled some spilled onto the exhaust and immediately ignited. Although Salvadori escaped with minor burns and singed eyebrows, the car was a write-off, as was much of the wooden pits.

Team orders were deployed. Moss and a bandaged Salvadori took over the Shelby–Fairman car, which was running fourth. Moss, at his absolute best when making up lost ground, delivered another virtuoso performance. He regained the lead just a few laps from the finish to take the chequered flag – and the Sportscar Championship for David Brown.

It was a very British coup. Having set out *not* to compete for the championship, Aston Martin walked away with it. They had ironed out all the bugs that bedevilled their previous cars and that gave them the reliability, if not the sheer power, to beat the Testa Rossas. The hydraulic jacks brought Aston tyre changes down to thirty seconds, whereas the Porsches – with four nuts per wheel and no on-board jacks – were taking anything up to two minutes fifteen seconds.

When his team boss, Romolo Tavoni, telephoned Enzo Ferrari in Maranello with the bad news, the furious boss demanded a minute's silence. The Formula 1 World Championship had already been snatched away from him by the rear-engined Coopers. Now more green cars had added insult to injury.

33

WE'VE BEEN EXPECTING YOU

Six weeks after claiming the Sportscar Championship, David Brown announced that he was withdrawing from sports-car racing. Later he confessed to author Chris Nixon that Eberan von Eberhorst had been right: the Aston's racing campaign had been a hobby, but why not?

'The racing years were a very special part of my life. It was a money-losing project, but the team had an atmosphere about it unlike any other. I worked with some very special people and enjoyed every minute of it. It was a great experience for me and everybody else concerned.'

Brown had raised Aston Martin's profile, at least in racing circles, but it was the cinema that would turn the marque into a household name – across the world.

When he joined Aston Martin in 1949, Brown gave John Wyer a one-year contract to manage the racing team. Six years later, he was elevated to works manager. He ordered a hasty update of the DB 2/4, the Mark III that had caught James Bond's attention in *Goldfinger*, but it was merely a stopgap model. The next would be Brown's signature car – not a hybrid created from the best bits of the two firms he had bought, but an entirely new model with a new engine, to see Aston Martin into the 1960s.

Jaguars were half the price of Aston Martins and in many ways just as good. But the DBs were hand-built in tiny numbers. There was no way they could compete on price. It was clear to Wyer that the company would never expand dramatically, so the best route was to head further up market, above and beyond Jaguar. Having taken on Ferrari in competition, it was time to take the fight to the showroom.

He envisaged a car that would cost £1,000 more than the current DB. Frank Feeley had produced very stylish functional bodies for both road and track Astons, but when Wyer saw the former Lagonda stylist's renderings for what was then called Project 114, Feeley got the 'death ray'. Wyer decided that, to take on the Italians, he needed Italian style. But what attracted him to Carrozzeria Touring of Milan was more than mere style.

Touring had pioneered a very effective if labour-intensive method of body building known as *Superleggera*. The shape of the car was built up with lightweight welded steel tubes rather like a birdcage, which followed the contours of the design, onto which the hand-beaten aluminium body panels were attached. The method had a lot in common with traditional coachbuilding but with thin-diameter steel tube replacing the wood frame. Aston bought a licence to use the *Superleggera* system and paid Touring a royalty of £9 per car, dropping to £5 after the first five hundred units.

The actual shape that Touring's stylists Carlo Felice, Bianchi Anderloni and Federico Formenti came up with for the DB4 was not so much a radical departure from Frank Feeley's clean, functional lines as a subtle update. They kept what had become the marque's trademark 'hump back bridge' grille and straight-through waist line that ran from headlamp to tail light. The results, however, were dramatic.

Polish émigré Tadek Marek created a new, light-alloy, twin-cam engine that could be up-rated to 4 litres. The DB4 was a labour of love by skilled craftsmen, an exclusive product for the few, a true *gran turismo* and, with a top speed of 140mph, for a moment Britain's fastest road car. With a price tag of £3,976, it was twice the price of a 3.8-litre Jaguar XK150.

When the first car, finished in primrose yellow, was unveiled at the 1958 Paris Motor Show, tears rolled down the cheeks of Marcel Blondeau, Aston's passionate French dealer. Even at that price, they could never make as many as he knew he could sell.

There was only one car ready for the show, so no one outside the factory had driven it, not even the press officer Alan Dakers, who needed something to write about. Wyer had the answer: 'You might say it will accelerate from a standing start to 100 and stop within thirty seconds.' Daker obliged, but on seeing the claim in print, Wyer worried if it were true. He sent a test driver to find out, who managed the feat in twenty-seven seconds.

For such a small company to launch an all-new model with nothing carried over from its predecessor was brave – and risky. After the Paris Motor Show, Blondeau did brisk business, but soon he was in trouble with owners returning their cars with engine-bearing failures, four in France, three in Italy.

Tadek Marek was dispatched to Paris to investigate. Wyer told him not to come back without a diagnosis. Two days later, he called Wyer: 'I can only find one common factor between the failures.' Full of relief, he asked Marek what it was. 'They all happened on Good Friday,' came the designer's answer.

There turned out to be some truth in Marek's frivolous observation. Good Friday was a public holiday, when Europe's roads were free of heavy-goods traffic, and that year it had been unseasonably warm. The ultra-straight 193-kilometre *route nationale* between Paris and Le Mans had long been a magnet for record breakers. Even in racing such speeds were never sustained that long. And in Italy, the Autostrada del Sole between Milan and Bologna had just opened and enthusiasts were keen to establish the first unofficial record.

The DB4 had not been tested at top speed for more than ten or twenty miles at most. Continuously flat out for over an hour, the engine temperature soared and bearing clearances expanded to a point where the oil pump could no longer cope. At full revs the entire oil supply was circulating the engine every eight seconds; the pump, gasping for more, sucked in air as well as oil, with disastrous consequences. Fitting an oil cooler solved the problem.

Back in Britain, in November 1959, the first leg of the new M1 was opened. Wyer ordered Aston's test driver Bobby Dickson to take the car on a sustained high-speed run. Newport Pagnell, Aston Martin's base, was almost midway between the north end of the new motorway at Crick and where it finished near Watford, about a 125-mile round trip. As Wyer recalled: 'I went in, made a few telephone calls and then looked out of the window and saw the test car at the pumps. So I went out and asked Bobby: "Why haven't you started your run?" and he gave me a hurt look and said: "I've been."' Dickson had completed the run in fifty-six minutes – at an *average* speed of 133mph – unimaginable before on British public roads. A new age of speed had begun.

~

In 1963, James Bond was still a relatively young film franchise, with *Dr. No* and *From Russia with Love* doing promising business. Bond's car, seen only fleetingly in *Dr. No*, was a vintage Rolls-built Bentley, and not a particularly distinguished one. Its only gadget was a cumbersome-looking built-in telephone. And in *From Russia with Love,* the only Bond gadgetry was his Swaine Adeney briefcase. But for the third film, *Goldfinger,* the producers planned to raise their game.

The budget of $3 million was double that of the previous two. Ken Adam, the designer, fresh from his triumph creating the war room for *Dr. Strangelove,* was a car fanatic. It was his vision to turn Bond's car into a secret weapon, festooned with gadgetry.

On their first visit to Aston Martin, Adam and special-effects creator John Stears were rebuffed. The fact that Adam showed up in his own E-Type Jaguar might not have helped. John Wyer's successor as general manager, Steve Heggie, listened to them in sombre silence, as Stears reeled off the dizzying list of proposed gadgets. In fact, they would need two cars, one for the gadgets, another for exterior filming. Heggie made only one comment: that the car was already packed with technology and therefore unlikely to have room for any more.

He also had other things on his mind. Aston Martin was going through a tough time financially. Every sale was needed. Promotions were a luxury they couldn't afford. Adam and Stears went away. They consulted Jaguar about borrowing an E-Type and got back a firm 'no'. As usual, they were struggling to fulfil demand. There weren't any other contenders, so co-producer Harry Saltzman was pressed to make direct contact with David Brown, who batted the matter back to Heggie, cabling him to 'do as he saw fit'.

Stears and Adam tried again, pointing out that James Bond films were growing an international following and their car on the screen would raise Aston Martin's profile overseas – and in front of people with the right sort of money to spend on such expensive cars. Heggie thought again, then relented once he realised he could get away with lending them what is known in the trade as a 'development mule': DP216/1, a prototype DB5 that had actually started out as the DB4 and served as the 1963 London motor show car.

On its arrival at Pinewood, there was an almost ceremonial moment as, like a trainee surgeon full of trepidation, Stears drilled the first hole in the roof to cut out the hatch for the ejector seat. Over the next five weeks, the car was loaded with technological wonders: a bulletproof rear shield that rose out of the boot lid, a pair of Browning machine guns hidden behind the front indicator lights, tyre shredders which extended from the wire wheels, and front bumper over-riders that transformed into extending rams. Each rear light cluster also had a surprise – one could spray oil into the path of pursuing vehicles while the other spat out tyre-bursting, multi-headed tacks. The twin exhaust pipes blasted out a smoke screen for a clean getaway.

Director Guy Hamilton, who was prone to racking up parking tickets, came up with the gloriously tongue-in-cheek notion of a revolving number plate. Given the scarcity of DB5s, only the very dimmest of parking wardens would have been fooled. But the coup de grâce was Adam's vision of the ejector seat, operated by a red button concealed inside the top of the gear-lever knob. Anticipation of the moment when the unwanted passenger was dispatched added a whole layer of tension to the film.

In fact, the Aston's floor could not have withstood the force of the detonation and the driver would have been at the very least severely scorched. So, to spare the car – and Sean Connery – Stears's team added a mock-up seat containing a compressed-air canister that would fire a dummy figure forty feet into the air.

Converting the car cost £15,000, and the additional gadgetry added 136kg to its weight. When Heggie visited Pinewood to view its progress, he was horrified.

'At first I couldn't believe that the car in front of me was ours. There were panels everywhere, cables and pipes protruding from all angles. It looked a right bloody mess. I pray that they know how to put it back together again.' They did, and before filming it returned to Newport Pagnell for its final coat of silver birch.

Once filming was under way, details began to leak out, creating a buzz about the car with its still-secret special features. Beatle Paul McCartney visited the set and immediately ordered a DB5. It had to be delivered to him in complete secrecy, quickly handed over behind a motorway services from which he could make a speedy exit.

Goldfinger premiered at the Odeon Leicester Square on 17 September 1964 and recouped its entire budget from UK takings alone. Bond's car featured on the BBC's *Tonight* show and *Blue Peter*, and for the *Today* radio programme, host Jack de Manio visited the Aston factory in Newport Pagnell to talk to the employees. For the following week, the car was exhibited in the menswear section of Rackhams department store in Birmingham, where the unprepared store staff had to take on extra help to manage as shoppers queued for over an hour to get a glimpse.

Even Eon, the production company, were caught off guard by the car's phenomenal appeal. For the film opening in the USA, the car was shipped on the liner SS *France*, along with Mike Ashley, the then 24-year-old Aston press officer, on the assignment of a lifetime. When the ship docked in New York, he saw the TV news crews from all the major networks on the quay and assumed they were waiting for a glimpse of the singer Lena Horne, who was also on board. But the cameras ignored her. The star they were there for was the Bond car. That night it featured on the evening news nationwide. At the New York World's Fair it was put on show, billed as 'The Most Famous Car in the World'.

Dudley Gershon was Aston's engineering director at the time the film came out:

> As soon as the film was shown, a massive wave of publicity hit us, the like of which no other car company in history had ever experienced. All of a sudden every ten-year-old boy knew the name of Aston Martin. It ran in an amused way right through every stratum of society, and if we had been able to produce fifty DB5s every week then we could have sold them. Unfortunately we were just able to do about eleven at the time and we were unable to really cash in on the main initial benefit that would have been so easily available.

Aspiring future Aston owners and junior spies did better. In a stunning flourish of miniaturised technology, Corgi Toys produced their own James Bond 007 DB5 complete with functioning ejector seat. Over 2.5 million were sold, making it the biggest-selling toy of 1964.

The *Goldfinger* DB5 was undoubtedly the greatest product placement triumph of all time, and the beginning of a relationship between Bond and Aston Martin that has lasted half a century. Across the world, Aston Martin became a byword for automotive exclusivity.

But it took some time for the enormity of this coup to be appreciated, especially in Newport Pagnell. Despite its celebrity status, at the end of its world tour DP216/1 was returned to Aston Martin, where all the gadgetry was stripped off, the development chassis plate removed and the car returned to the production line, where it was reborn as a brand-new, standard DB5 and sold to an eagerly waiting customer who had no idea of its stellar provenance.

There was no sudden ramping up of production. The waiting list got a little longer, but there were only so many people in the world with £5,000 to spend on a hand-built GT car. And, as with members of a gentlemen's club or customers of a bespoke Savile Row tailor, Aston Martin owners liked it that way.

34

THE SHEPHERD

Jim Clark's sights were set almost as far away from motor sport as it's possible to imagine. He was the polar opposite of the previous generation of British Grand Prix drivers – Moss, Hawthorn and Collins – with no petrol running in his family's veins. He started out as a shepherd.

The plan was to become a farmer like his father, in Berwickshire, just over the border in Scotland. Instead, he became the *world's* most successful racing driver of his time, who in his tragically short reign won more Grands Prix than Fangio.

Where the first post-war generation of winners were extroverts, Clark was notable for his reserve. Never outwardly comfortable with his fame and status, he was, perhaps partly because of this, universally liked. Some drivers succeeded through vaulting ambition, others by managed aggression or the fear of failure. In Clark's case, it was pure, untutored talent.

He also came in to Formula 1 at its tipping point, when the British had well and truly arrived and rewritten the rules of engagement. It was also the point when it was about to become a much more serious and dangerous business.

Collins had been killed on the track; Hawthorn died on the road, just weeks after his retirement; and Moss miraculously survived a near-death crash that ended his career. But they were a generation who accepted danger as part of the package. The possibility of death was always near but never discussed; danger was what made the sport serious and what got drivers their respect.

Clark was only in his second F1 race at the Belgian Spa-Francorchamps Circuit in 1960 when Chris Bristow, thrown onto the track from his cart-wheeling Cooper, died right in his path. Clark only just missed the mutilated body, but was splattered by the dying Bristow's blood. Minutes later, fellow Lotus driver Alan Stacey was also killed after being hit in the face by a bird. Later, Clark admitted that he was 'driving scared stiff pretty much all through the race'. Then, the following year, at Monza, the Ferrari of Wolfgang von Trips touched Clark's Lotus and catapulted off the track, killing the driver and fifteen spectators. It was Chapman who persuaded him to keep racing. The Lotus boss and Clark forged a bond – one of the most successful pairings in the history of sport; two men at the very top of their game.

Back at Spa three years later, Clark's performance showed how exceptional he was. The race went ahead, despite rain and fog. He started eighth on the grid. By lap seventeen, with the rain worsening, he had lapped the entire field and was five minutes ahead of Australian champion Bruce McLaren in a Cooper. It was the first of seven victories that year that would propel him to the championship – and the prize so longed for by his predecessors: to be British champion in a British car.

Born in 1936, he grew up with four sisters. It was on the way back from a cricket match at Jedburgh that he encountered the Ecurie Ecosse team of C-Type Jaguars. 'I just happened to be there as the drivers went into this tight hairpin, weaving about as they braked, and I remember thinking what a shower of madmen they were. But at the same time I felt a slight twinge of envy.'

His first taste of competition was in a Sunbeam-Talbot, which he entered in local rallies. He soon caught the attention of the

Border Reivers, a local group of amateur racers, mostly farmers, who shared a Jaguar D-Type. Behind the wheel of the Jag, Clark showed consistent success, winning twelve out of the twenty races he entered. In 1958, one of the Reivers, fellow local farmer Ian Scott-Watson, took Clark down to Brands Hatch in Kent for one of Colin Chapman's customer track days, where he tried out a Formula Junior Lotus.

Clark's lap times soon came close to those of Lotus works driver Graham Hill, who was there to show how it should be done. Scott-Watson pointed out to Chapman that this was Clark's first time ever in a single-seater. Horrified, Chapman went white and ordered the newcomer to stop before he killed himself. Clark had to be overreaching himself. But before the day was over, Clark was allowed to try a Lotus Elite sports car, which he liked very much, so Scott-Watson ordered one for the Reivers.

Clark was back at Brands Hatch the following Boxing Day, with the new Elite, this time to race. Chapman himself was competing, as was Lotus engineer Mike Costin. Clark recalled that before the race he had overheard the two Lotus men agreeing how they would carve the race up for themselves. The young Scot was having none of it, as Costin ruefully recalled: 'I could see as we approached Paddock [Corner] that Jim was determined not to lift off first and Colin was equally adamant. I didn't want to get mixed up in all that so I was the prat who backed off and that dropped me down to third. I then had a grandstand view of a real ding-dong between them for the rest of the race.'

What followed was a spectacular wheel-to-wheel tussle as Chapman fought a furious but losing battle against the Scottish nobody. The race would have been Clark's had he not had to avoid a spinning backmarker, which allowed Chapman through.

But it was a life-changing moment for both men. Chapman knew talent when he saw it and signed him up on the spot. So began a partnership that would take them both to the top of the world. For four seasons, Clark and his Lotus were only beaten when he suffered mechanical problems. He almost never made mistakes.

In 1963, he won seven out of ten Grands Prix. In 1964, he missed the championship due to an oil leak in the last race of the season and in 1965 won six of the ten races. In all he made thirty-three poles and won twenty-five Grands Prix out of seventy-five starts. His total number of wins eclipsed the previous record set by the great Fangio. His record seven wins in the 1963 ten-race season remained unbroken until 1988, when Ayrton Senna managed eight, though that was out of sixteen races. He was also unusually versatile, winning the 1964 Saloon Car Championship in a Lotus Cortina.

The shy but gifted Clark was dismayed by his own talent, but the ambitious showman Chapman recognised what he had and they formed an extraordinary bond. On race weekends the two often shared hotel rooms, for easier further discussion and reflection.

Clark was the least mechanically able of all the British drivers to date. Moss, Collins and Hawthorn had all got their hands dirty tuning and repairing cars, as did Graham Hill, Clark's main British opponent, who had started out as a Lotus mechanic.

Preparing a car for a race involves much intense testing to iron out any inconsistencies that are reported by the driver. Despite this lack of technical know-how, Clark could communicate his experience of a car to Chapman in such a detailed way that his engineers could make the necessary adjustments to get the absolute best out of car and driver. Decades before computers, Clark could download what his revs were in whatever corner, how each wheel behaved and what gear ratios worked best for each section of a circuit.

Chapman's cars were almost controversially light, highly strung machines, but Clark's smooth, sensitive, precision driving got the best out of them and got them to the finish line. Tyres used on Clark's cars could last up to four races and brake pads survived three times longer than those of any other driver. According to Lotus mechanic Derek Wilde, when he dismantled gearboxes post-race he could always tell which one had come out of Clark's car; they always had the least wear. The Lotus champion could also nurse a sick machine and remain competitive. Leading the 1964 Monaco Grand Prix, his speed started to dip, but he carried on and came home fourth. Only when the car was back in the pits did his team discover he had driven almost the whole race with a broken anti-roll bar. Whatever the problem, he simply managed to work around it.

Clark also had a sixth sense about the tactics of other drivers. In the 1964 Italian Grand Prix at Monza, Clark was in the lead, being chased by Dan Gurney in a Brabham and blocked by the stubborn Innes Ireland, a driver Chapman had dropped and replaced with Clark.

Clark told his biographer, Graham Gauld:

I went round the rest of the lap thinking what I was going to do. I had Dan right behind me. The next time we came into the corner I just sat right back and watched Innes and waited until I saw him glance in his mirrors. As soon as he glanced in them I just lifted off, and of course Dan shot right past me and went for the inside, and Innes saw a nosecone coming up the inside. He thought it was me and chopped across again, but of course nobody does that to Dan Gurney. And while both of them were wobbling I went round the outside.

There was no debate. Clark was in a class of his own.

35

INSIDE MAN

Watching Colin Chapman's progress from his office in Brentwood, Essex was a former newspaper man, Walter Hayes. In 1958, as editor of the *Sunday Dispatch*, he had asked Colin Chapman to write an occasional column. It was a foolish idea, as the workaholic Lotus boss was terrible at meeting deadlines. A few years later, in 1961, when his paper was merged with the *Sunday Express*, Hayes found himself out of a job.

Ever since he'd started as a copy boy and worked his way up through Fleet Street, his first love was journalism. But at thirty-six, with a young family and newspaper-editor openings thin on the ground, Hayes searched further afield. He was offered a job running public relations for Ford of Britain. It would be crossing over to the dark side. But Hayes liked challenges and saw that Ford's image was in dramatic need of attention.

Although the British outpost had some degree of autonomy, the fabled bean-counters inside 'the Glass House', Ford's monolithic World Headquarters in Detroit, kept a tight rein on investment. Every car was costed down to the last windscreen wiper. In 1945, when Henry Ford II found himself at the helm of his grandfather's corporation at just twenty-eight, he wrestled control from the founder's shady and thuggish minders and brought in a team.

Hired from the US Army's Office of Statistical Control, the original Whiz Kids were so named because of their youth and wizardry with numbers. They were led by Robert McNamara, one day to be Secretary of Defense, and together they transformed Ford's internal processes. Their mission: to make every cent count; no investment for anything left-field like motor racing or exotic versions of their resolutely middle-of-the-road model line-up.

Their only departure from this strategy left them badly burned. The Edsel, a flashier sub-brand based on a massive market-research operation, failed spectacularly. Overhyped and underdeveloped, it was also ugly. Its signature vertical grille was compared variously to a horse collar, a toilet seat and a vagina. Two years and $250 million later, it was axed and the designer of its infamous aperture, Roy Brown, was exiled to Ford in Britain. From then on, any diversion from the core business was anathema. Ford bosses even nixed a venture into front-wheel drive, on the grounds that it would be an extra expense.

To Hayes, Ford was a brand that shrank from distinction when that was just what it needed. The Mini Cooper had shown what a lightly modified car with race-winning potential had done for the British Motor Corporation's public image. With the Mini, Britain's biggest, most mainstream motor manufacturer had magically turned its cheapest car into a chic, must-have object of desire. An unforeseen consequence of the Mini's stardom was to make Ford products look even more bland and middle of the road.

One of Hayes's first acts was to campaign for Ford's new Cortina (designed by the exiled Roy Brown), a mildly sportier version with a GT badge. By Ford's standards it was an audacious move which raised a few eyebrows. Those hallowed letters, which stand for *gran turismo*, had been the preserve of Lancia, Ferrari and other exotica. Few were fooled by the GT Cortina; the car had none of the Mini Cooper's competition pedigree. To make any real impact, Hayes concluded that Ford would have to move a lot further out of its comfort zone.

Seeing what Chapman had done with Ford's engine in Formula Junior, Hayes decided to renew the acquaintance. At the very least, Ford of Britain should be benefitting from some of the reflected glory of Lotus's Formula Junior success, especially where it mattered most – in the showroom.

But Chapman's experience of road cars was decidedly patchy. The Lotus Elite had nearly sunk his company. As well as losing money on every sale, the car's mechanical parts were prone to detaching themselves from the fibreglass structure. Disgruntled owners regarded the Lotus name as an unflattering acronym: Loads Of Trouble, Usually Serious.

Chapman concentrated his energies on broadening his racing activities and selling car kits. But by the early 1960s the market for smaller sports cars was growing. BMC had the Austin-Healey Sprite and MG B; Triumph offered the TR4 and Spitfire. Chapman wanted a piece of that market, so he put his team to work on a completely new small two-seater, much more domesticated than the troublesome Elite and the spartan Seven. The Lotus Elan boasted such comforts as wind-down windows, and the added novelty of retractable headlamps, though being on a Lotus they didn't always follow orders. To get the right power unit, he commissioned two of his former protégées, Frank Costin and Keith Duckworth, who had started their own consultancy, Cosworth, to design a twin-cam version of the Ford engine that had worked so well for him in Formula Junior.

Like the Elite, its body was fibreglass, but underneath was a revolutionary steel backbone chassis. As with so many of Chapman's ideas, this was not exactly new.

The backbone chassis dated back to the 1920s, when it was pioneered by Austrian designer Hans Ledwinka, father of the legendary Tatra, and found its way into the original VW. But in

Chapman's hands it gained sophistication, being both extremely stiff and light. Each end splayed out like a tuning fork, to which were attached the wheels, suspension and drivetrain.

The Lotus Elan was a far more user-friendly machine than the Elite. It stayed together and drivers did not have to be amateur mechanics to own one. Lessons had been learned. It also performed better than any other two-seater sports car of its size. Finally, Chapman was a player in the road-car trade. He would sell over twelve thousand and a further five thousand of its bigger +2 sibling.

When Chapman showed Hayes the prototype Elan, with the Ford-based, Cosworth-designed, twin-cam engine under the bonnet, it gave him an idea. Enthusiasts were already tuning up Anglias; it was only a matter of time before they did the same with the Cortina. Why not beat them to it? Hayes made Chapman a dream offer – an order for one thousand Cortinas breathed on by Lotus. Ford would supply the body shells and do the sales and service; Lotus would do all the modifications. Unlike the Mini, the Cortina did not come with inbuilt racing potential. Where Cooper's Mini modifications were comparatively minor, the Cortina would need a much deeper makeover. Along with a twin-cam engine, Lotus gave it a new rear suspension using coil instead of cart springs, lightweight body panels, gearbox and differential casings. Inside was a new gear shift, a row of serious-looking dials across the lip of the dash and a wood-rimmed wheel as beloved of Italian sports cars. The suspension was lower, the wheels wider. And it came in one distinctive finish: white with a green flash. The car was recognisable as a Cortina but had a whole different look and feel. It could reach 108mph and accelerate from zero to 60 in 9.8 seconds – half the time of a standard Cortina. But at £1,100 it was a different proposition from the £700 Mini Cooper.

For Ford of Britain, sex appeal began in 1963.

It was an extraordinary coup for Chapman – his Lotus badges on a version of one of Britain's most popular cars. But for Ford, it was a huge reputational risk. How the affable, mild-mannered Hayes managed to get this idea past the risk-averse Ford brass was down to what his former colleague and automotive historian Karl Ludvigsen described as an 'intuitive guerrilla approach'. Hayes had a newspaperman's instinct for how to create a good story, combined with a good editor's skills at managing upward, able to convince wary management to go out on a limb. What Hayes also gained was access to Chapman's world champion driver. In Jim Clark's hands, the Lotus Cortina became the 1964 British Saloon Car champion.

For Hayes, the editor turned corporate guerrilla, the Lotus-badged Ford Cortina was just the beginning. With Chapman as his secret weapon and Clark his world champion star driver, Hayes embarked on what would become a global transformation of Ford's image. The former pressman also dreamed up a winning slogan: 'Total Performance'.

Chapman, still only thirty-five, appeared to be at the top of his game. Not only had he bagged the Formula 1 World Championship, he now had two road cars with which to exploit that reputation in the showroom. At the same age, Enzo Ferrari had yet to build his first car.

But for the man who less than a decade before had been operating out of a pub stable block, moonlighting from his aluminium salesman job, even this dizzying success was not enough. The debacle with the Elite in America still rankled. He had failed to gain a foothold in the world's most lucrative car market, where Jaguar, Austin-Healey and Triumph had all made it. America did not pay much attention to Formula 1, so across the Atlantic Lotus's achievements didn't count for much. But at the same time, another failure was not an option. He could only go where he thought he could win. So, with Hayes's gentle encouragement, Chapman decided to explore another way into America, one where foreigners feared to tread.

36

GASOLINE ALLEY

Detroit had taught the world how to make cars in vast numbers, but up until the 1960s it maintained an arm's-length relationship with motor sport. Henry Ford, having won the only race he entered at the start of his meteoric career, frowned upon any further association of his name with the sport. One consequence of this was that America's indigenous motor sport grew up in almost complete isolation from both Detroit and the rest of the motor-sport world, its peculiar characteristics evolving around the demands of that nation's first and foremost race track, the Indianapolis Motor Speedway, opened in 1909.

When Chapman went to Indianapolis to take a closer look, he was flabbergasted. The machines were hefty, lumbering, front-engined monsters known as roadsters, with solid axles, separate chassis and two-speed gearboxes, essentially vintage machines that had hardly developed since the 1930s. The Speedway is an elongated O-shaped bowl, with steeply banked corners for continuous high speed. For a time it was surfaced with over 3 million paving bricks from which it got its nickname, the Brickyard. Despite the simple format – a 500-mile charge – the races could be full of surprises. Midwestern spring weather can deliver everything from dense humidity to blazing sun to torrential rain.

It is said that, like sailors who can feel the wind on their face, old Indy hands had a sixth sense of how to get the best out of the conditions. The roadster community was also a closed shop. No foreigner had won the race since 1916.

For Chapman, it was just another summit to be conquered. What also appealed was that the race had become the world's biggest one-day sporting event, watched by a larger audience both at the venue and on TV than any other sporting fixture. And then there was the prize money – close on half a million dollars. Undaunted by neither the idiosyncratic engineering nor the strange track characteristics, Chapman decided to do an experiment. In 1962, Jim Clark won the US Grand Prix at Watkins Glen. After the race, Chapman arranged for Team Lotus to travel to Indiana so Clark could try the Lotus F1 car at the Brickyard. As Clark put in the laps, Chapman watched from Gasoline Alley, the Brickyard's pit lane, and did his sums. Even with the comparatively tiny 1.5-litre racing engine, Clark was only a few seconds off the pace of the 4.2-litre roadsters and faster round the banked corners. The heavy-duty roadsters were powered by gas-guzzling racing engines that ran on methanol. Chapman calculated that a less thirsty petrol engine would give more mileage, so the Lotus could carry a lighter fuel load than the competition, go for longer and spend less time filling up in the pits. Also, a lighter car would also mean less wear on the tyres. It soon dawned on him that he would not even need a racing-car engine. Based on his conclusions, an off-the-shelf standard stock V8 would be enough for Lotus to win the most famous motor race in America.

But how far could he take his new relationship with Ford? Not only had Detroit always given Indianapolis a wide berth, in 1957, the Automobile Manufacturers Association, chaired by Henry Ford II, had banned American car makers from giving direct support to racing teams or using race wins in advertising. Chapman, with respected American racing driver Dan Gurney in tow, travelled to Michigan and met the suits in Ford's Glass House.

Hayes primed his colleagues. Their response was typical of Ford – they decided to conduct a feasibility study. Was this just kicking the idea into the long grass? Indianapolis was as alien to them as it was to Lotus. But Chapman being Chapman, he decided to forge ahead. He obtained the drawings with all the dimensions of the Ford V8 and started building his Indianapolis car.

Behind the scenes, Hayes worked on his American bosses, pointing out that the Lotus Cortina was coming into its own. But that was niche; the Indianapolis 500 was prime time – no place to fail. They were still smarting from the high-profile Edsel debacle. Eventually Ford released a pair of V8s, to be fitted into the Lotus chassis at a Ford proving ground. When the engine arrived missing some key parts, not wishing to rock any boats, Chapman simply went to Hertz, hired a pair of Ford Fairlane V8s, removed the parts for the test and replaced them after. The tests worked; Ford decided to come aboard.

In May 1963, Lotus made its debut at the Brickyard, very much the outsider. Despite being Formula 1 World Championship runner-up the year before, Clark was required to take a rookie test, which involved driving several laps at lower speeds. Here, his international status counted for zero. There was no briefing on Indy 500 etiquette. Team Lotus had to learn the hard way, even when it came to finding accommodation, which was strangely unavailable. Clark, Chapman, a mechanic and the timekeeper all shared one room at the Speedway Motel.

At the track, the Ford V8-powered Lotus 29 was greeted with derision. The delicate British machine with its engine in the wrong place just looked way too flimsy for the rigours of the Brickyard, as did the slight-framed driver with the funny accent. Clark found the atmosphere uncomfortable. Shy and formal, he was thrown when people just came up and started talking to him without being introduced. Chapman was also infuriated at how Indianapolis proclaimed itself to be the 'World Capital of Auto Racing'.

Clark started fifth. From the off it was clear that he was a challenger. Although slower on the straights, his Lotus was faster round the corners and he led for twenty-eight laps. After 177 of 200 laps, Clark was five seconds behind Indy veteran Parnelli Jones when the race leader developed an oil leak. Rules stipulated that any car dropping oil had to be black-flagged. But clerk of the course Harlan Fengler was not doing anything about it. As J. C. Agajanian, Jones's team owner, recalled: 'Colin Chapman comes rushing up with his English accent and says: "Pull your car off there before it kills all the other drivers," and I yelled back: "Get your butt over that wall, Chapman, Fengler and I are talking. It's not your car's in trouble."' The problem was that Agajanian was also an event promoter and a member of the governing body which organised the Indy series. After a big show of peering at his car through binoculars, he announced to Fengler that it was water coming from Jones's car, not oil. Fengler did not beg to differ. Jones won the race.

Chapman, himself a master rule-bender, protested loudly. He wasn't alone. Another driver, Eddie Sachs, who skidded and crashed on Jones's oil, got into a post-race fight with him over it. But Clark won respect because he didn't make a fuss. Jones might have beaten him, but Clark had finished ahead of another Indy legend, A. J. Foyt. Coming second was an astonishing achievement for car and driver first time out. Clark congratulated the winner and never mentioned the oil that had spattered his goggles and slicked his tyres.

But the other side of Clark, the steely, determined race-winner, soon showed itself. Before the post-race celebrations were over, he told Chapman he wanted to enter another Indy car race as soon as possible; he had a point to prove. So, in August, Team Lotus pitched up at the Milwaukee Mile race. Clark put the Lotus on pole and won the race, having lapped everyone except A. J. Foyt, whom he decided to spare out of respect. Clark and Lotus had come and conquered.

Two years later, Clark would pull off another crushing win, this time at the Indianapolis 500, making him the first non-American winner since 1916. Still, the United States Auto Club (USAC), the sport's sanctioning body in America, were determined to make life hard for Lotus. They ruled the car's suspension out of order, so it had to be remade before the race, and then they queried the thickness of the wheels, so Chapman ordered them to be recast. He was not going to have a repeat of what had happened to him at Le Mans. These last-minute attempts to undermine Lotus merely underlined the level of Clark's faultless, virtuoso performance. He led the race for 190 laps and took the chequered flag two minutes ahead of runner-up, Parnelli Jones.

Chapman, the London publican's son, had gone where no other foreigner had dared. He had broken into the closed shop of Indianapolis, muscled his way past the most seasoned practitioners of the sport and the vested interests determined to see him fail, won their race and was now teaching them how to design their cars.

The era of the front-engined roadster that had been the mainstay of Indianapolis for half a century was over. From here on, all cars on the Brickyard would be built the British way. Chapman with Clark at the wheel achieved what no other driver–constructor partnership had done before or since – winning *both* Indianapolis and the Formula 1 World Championship in the same year. And still Chapman was not done.

37

THE JET SET

By 1964 Britain was in a state of revolution and pillars of Britain's establishment were crumbling. Harold Macmillan, the post-Suez prime minister who had told the nation 'we've never had it so good', was out, engulfed by the scandalous relationship between Secretary of State for War John Profumo, his Mini-driving mistress Christine Keeler and a Russian spy. Labour were swept back into power, with its energetic leader Harold Wilson promising Britain a bright new future forged in the 'white heat of technology'.

The certainties that had kept the fabric of society in order had unravelled. Fashion, interiors, graphics, haircuts and music were all being reinvented. The last traces of wholesome utilitarianism that had guided so much of Britain's post-war design ethic were disappearing fast. But one former car stylist who should have been claiming credit for helping start the revolution was aghast. 'Where has our world of elegance gone? What has happened to our virtues?' complained Lady Norah Docker.

Her misfortune was to have arrived too early, for much of the brash iconoclasm of her one-woman stand against austerity was to be found in the exuberant new style that pervaded popular culture. A generation that had been biding its time was finally in the driving seat; nothing would ever be the same. British auto-motive design was being led by extremes – with the Mini and the E-Type leading the charge from opposite ends of the automotive spectrum. Lotus was king of Grand Prix and its Elan starred in hit TV series *The Avengers,* driven by Emma Peel, a stunning martial-arts expert polymath played by Diana Rigg, who broke just about every convention going.

Possibly the last straw for Norah Docker was the appearance of Rover, that embodiment of establishment restraint, at Le Mans, with a jet-engined racing car.

Rover's designs had changed little in the previous ten years. Both of its staples, the P4 saloon and the Land Rover, launched before 1950, soldiered on with only the mildest of makeovers by the reined-in David Bache. In its last new model, the 1958 3-litre P5, stylist Bache had reconciled his own bold aspirations with the Wilks brothers' insistence on being masters of understatement.

Come the '60s, Rover looked like it could be on the wrong side of history. But at the 1963 London motor show, to the dismay of its regular clientele as well as its rivals, it introduced an entirely new car that ditched the company's decades-old ethos of cautious development.

The Rover 2000, or P6 as it was known around the former shadow factory in Solihull from which it sprang, shared not a single part with its predecessors. A compact, four-cylinder sports saloon with four individually sculpted bucket seats, it looked nothing like previous Rovers. Conventional wisdom about car styling is that it pays to show some family resemblance; all it shared with its predecessors was the badge, no longer mounted on a traditional radiator but between four headlamps in a horizontal grille.

The cabin was even more radical. Instead of a set of round dials mounted in solid wood, the dash consisted of a shelf with all the instruments combined in a single rectangular pod. Out of the high transmission tunnel that separated the front seats protruded a strikingly short gear leaver.

It looked like David Bache had finally got his way. The slap on the wrist he had got from Maurice Wilks for his 'head-turner' had actually been a useful lesson. In a memo dated December 1957, he laid out his vision for the new company design ethic. He called for 'a simple classical form devoid of all superfluous ornament ... a clean elegant form with all character lines expressed by the medium of sculpture in the basic panels, with no external rubbing strips. The general form flows forward creating vivid movement with a new and unused character.' No retrospection here; these principles had more in common with the modernist style manual of Terence Conran's Habitat store, opened in 1964, which revolutionised British interiors.

Rover's new design vision ran all through the car. The inner skeleton, developed by chassis engineer Gordon Bashford, formed a strong, safe cage around the passengers. On to it were attached the body panels, the whole drive train and an advanced new independent suspension.

But this radical new Rover was not a knee-jerk response to events, as the Mini had been to Suez. The P6's engineering gestation was under way more than a decade before its launch. What started it all was a top-secret project for the war effort handed to Rover by the government back in 1940.

~

Frank Whittle, the father of the jet engine, was renowned for his genius and his awkwardness. At the start of the war it was unknown whether his invention, patented in 1930 but still in need of serious development, was the miracle machine that would transform Britain's air war or turn out to be just another harebrained notion.

To find out – and quickly – the Air Ministry paired Whittle up with Rover's Wilks brothers. Maurice Wilks's team rose to the occasion, set up their own jet-propulsion laboratory in a disused mill in Clitheroe and pressed on with the job. From the start, Whittle, who jealously guarded his intellectual property, was hostile. He thought his own company, Power Jets Ltd, should control all development, but their resources were limited, and since there was a war on there was no room for umbrage. To break the ice, Maurice, having discovered they shared an enthusiasm for fencing, challenged Whittle to a match. Relations were not improved, however, when Wilks beat the inventor soundly.

Relations worsened when Whittle discovered that the Rover men were making their own modifications to *his* design – they were, in fact, solving some of the problems that had dogged his early prototypes. He accused them of altering his plans to get round patent fees and claim the designs for themselves. In desperation, Maurice's brother Spencer confided in his friend, Ernest Hives, boss of Rolls-Royce. Late in 1942, Hives and his chief engineer, Stanley Hooker, travelled to Clitheroe for a secret lunch at the Swan and Royal Hotel. According to Hooker, Wilks, normally known for his calm restraint, did not hold back. 'We can't get on with the fellow at all and I would like to be shot of the whole business,' he told the Rolls men. Hives, who had already got wind of the discord, made Wilks an an offer. 'You give us this jet engine job and I'll give you our tank factory in Nottingham.' The deal had all the speed and finesse of a playground conker swap, but its impact was seismic. Rover's version eventually became the Rolls-Royce Derwent, which powered the Gloster Meteor, Britain's first jet fighter, and secured Rolls's future as the leader in jet-engine manufacture, a position that it still holds nearly eighty years on.

That could have been the end of Rover's interest in jet propulsion, but for the arrival in 1945 of a young Wilks nephew, Charles Spencer 'Spen' King. As an apprentice at Rolls, he'd had a ringside seat at the birth of the jet engine. He said: 'Everyone there was so bright and agreeable, it was far better than a university engineering course. They were all brilliant people, working very hard on very exciting things but willing to communicate to an eighteen- or nineteen-year-old.' King was convinced that at Rolls he had seen the future and how it would work – not just in the air but on the ground as well.

Like many of his generation, he was unimpressed by the pre-war notion of time-serving and waiting your turn. Perhaps it helped being part of the Wilks family, but when the twenty-year-old King announced that he wanted to build the world's first jet-powered car, the idea got a cautious welcome from his uncle Maurice.

Having expended so much time and energy on helping sort out Whittle's engine, Wilks felt they might as well try and get something out of it for Rover. So, in 1946, in a wooden shed, Department C was established, headed by King and another Rolls-Royce apprentice, Frank Bell. That this happened at all, at a time of severe rationing and anxiety about the future course of the company, speaks volumes about the mix of forces at work among Britain's motor engineers in the late 1940s – struggling to rebuild and survive, but also fired up by all the technological leaps brought on by the war.

It took King and his team just four years to produce the world's first jet-powered car. Appropriately registered JET 1, it managed an astonishing 150mph on its first high-speed run. The timing could not have been better. A new set of national heroes had just emerged. Test pilots John Derry, Bill Waterton and Neville Duke were breaking records and sound barriers with thrilling new jet planes which they showed off at the Farnborough Airshow. And here was a record-breaking jet *car*.

King's Jet 1 brought Rover worldwide publicity, so the Wilks brothers indulged him. Over the next decade, more jet cars emerged, each one a little more domesticated but still some way from something that could be sold to the public. There was a limit to how far this made economic sense. In 1957, King was diverted onto the P6 development programme. Still obsessed with jet cars, he merely saw this as a chance to develop a proper four-door saloon car that could be petrol *or* jet-powered.

And he had an ally. Gordon Bashford, who had joined Rover at fourteen in 1933, was now responsible for developing the radical new skeleton on which all the car's body panels and mechanical parts would be hung. As part of the secret Clitheroe lab team during the war, he too had contracted jet fever. So Bashford and King designed the new car's front suspension and unusually wide, square-shaped engine bay specifically so it would accept a jet engine. They also gave it a high transmission tunnel between the front passenger seats, which could double as a giant duct to help cool and disperse the jet's considerable exhaust gasses. In 1961, two years before the launch of the petrol-engine P6, their jet-turbine saloon, with Bache's bodywork, was revealed. It was so futuristic-looking and so different from Rovers before, none of the press twigged that what they were looking at was also the next Rover production car.

The free hand that King, Bashford and Bache were given was unheard of anywhere in the rest of the motor industry. King put this down to 'a case of the older generation at Rover backing the youngsters' enthusiasm'. Sales and marketing hardly got a look-in. For a start, they would have liked more than four seats and more than four cylinders. The whole car exuded engineering enthusiasm and a level of innovation that took competitors completely by surprise. But rather like the Land Rover, the 2000 created its own niche, previously unknown to marketers: the 'executive saloon'; compact, fast and innovative. Expected to be produced at a rate of three hundred a week, Rover soon had to double output demand. Beating the Rolls-challenging Mercedes 600, it won the first ever COTY, the new European Car of the Year Award, chosen by a panel of motoring journalists from across Europe.

~

William Martin-Hurst arrived at Rover in the late 1950s from a company called British Thermostat, with no previous experience of the motor industry. But his sister having married yet another Wilks, he almost counted as family and brought with him the pragmatism needed to balance the free-thinkers like King and Bache.

But even before the 2000's launch, he identified a problem. While the sales team's plea for a six-cylinder version had been ignored, cost and fuel consumption ruled out production of a jet version. Rover's only six-cylinder engine was almost twenty years old and the square dimensions of the P6 engine bay meant it was too short to accept a longer engine without major re-engineering of the whole front end. But serendipity had often played its part in Rover's fate, and so it would again.

Martin-Hurst, or MH as he became known around the works, won over King by agreeing a partnership with BRM to produce a jet car for Le Mans. But he badly needed to try to get something back for all the jet-programme investment.

This mission took him to Mercury Marine, a powerboat builder at Fond du Lac, Wisconsin, on the shores of Lake Winnebago, where he hoped to interest its founder, Carl Kiekhaefer, in Rover jet turbines for his power boats. As it turned out, the Mercury boss was more interested in Land Rover diesel engines for a project involving Chinese fishing junks. During this somewhat surreal conversation, which took place in the Mercury workshops, MH's attention was caught by a compact aluminium V8 power plant. It had come out of a General Motors (GM) Buick Skylark, but was no longer being made; GM accountants had axed it for a cheaper iron V6. MH asked for a tape measure. The V8 was only an inch longer than the P6's four-cylinder and, although twice as wide, would slot neatly into the engine bay, thanks to the extra space allowed for the jet version. He persuaded Kiekhaefer to crate it up and ship it back to Solihull.

But MH faced a battle royal to even get his idea looked at. GM would not take his approach seriously; they were not in the habit of selling the rights to their designs. And Rover's proud engineers refused to consider using someone else's cast-off engine. Peter Wilks – yet another Wilks cousin – who had just taken Maurice's place as technical director, also said his team were too busy to look into it. Undeterred, MH enlisted the recently formed competition department, which happened to have some down time between preparing Rovers for rallying. They willingly slotted the V8 into the P6 engine bay. MH drove the car down to London for a board meeting and without telling him what was under the bonnet, offered Spencer Wilks, soon to retire as chairman of the board, a drive back.

The elder Wilks was flabbergasted, pronouncing it the first Rover he had driven that was not underpowered. MH won the day. Peter Wilks was overruled and General Motors were persuaded to sell the design outright, with no royalty. Not only did the former Buick engine transform the P6 into a 125mph express cruiser; fitted to the ageing P5, the V8, at more than 200 pounds lighter than its old six-cylinder, gave Rover's flagship another five years of active life. But that was only the beginning.

Having had to accept the bought-in engine, Rover engineers started thinking more creatively about its potential. The consequence would have an impact on the company far more significant than any of Rover's products, jet-powered or otherwise, that had gone before, and would keep the lights on in Solihull through the dark decades that were looming and well into the next century.

38

GRACE, SPACE AND PACE

For the first time in his long career, William Lyons was caught off guard. Beside Rover's new 2000, Jaguar's Mark II looked like a dinosaur – albeit a charismatic one, its wood and leather old-world charm for now alarmingly out of step with David Bache's modernism.

The E-Type had secured Jaguar's place as creator of the world's sexiest sports car, but to Sir William Lyons sports cars had always been a niche business, a means of publicising his staple saloons. But the 1961 Jaguar Mark X, replacement for his original 100mph saloon, failed to live up to expectations. Imposing to some eyes, *Motor Sport* magazine's editor considered it 'portly', a devastating comment for Lyons to swallow. William Towns, a David Bache understudy at Rover and future Aston Martin stylist, called the Mark X a 'great fat pudding'.

Had Lyons, now in his sixties, had his day and taken his eye off the ball? His business had grown dramatically. He had bought Daimler, truck and bus builder Guy Motors, and Coventry Climax, the power behind Cooper's first Grand Prix championship. Knighted in 1956, Sir William was now a considerable figure in the motor industry, but he still ran his empire like a true autocrat; no detail was too trivial. He berated John Morgan in

Jaguar's London office for ordering a new chair for his secretary and told him to go round the office and see if there was a spare one first. Lyons was also disturbed to find what looked like new carpets, but this changed to delight when Morgan explained that the old ones had been re-laid so that worn areas were concealed by strategically placed filing cabinets.

In 1961, Lyons had turned sixty, but since the tragic death of his son John days before the Le Mans carnage in 1955, he had blanked out any thoughts of succession. Another looming distraction was the pressure to join forces with other manufacturers. Jaguar was his creation. Since parting with Walmsley in the 1930s, he hated any interference. But he was realistic enough to accept that the next car he designed would probably be his last. If the reception of the Mark X had dented his confidence, he did not let on.

His 100mph saloon, when it was launched in 1950, had no real competition. By 1965, the prestige saloon market was becoming crowded. Mercedes and BMW now produced big, spacious saloons that were chipping away at Jaguar's clientele. But Lyons still went his own way.

There was no market research or product plan; it was all instinct. Fred Gardner, keeper of the sawmill, who turned seventy in 1966, was still attending to his needs. 'Sir William would throw his coat on a bench, roll up his sleeves and set to with a rasp, or have me holding nails while he banged them in. Every day he was in there, sometimes with sketches drawn in the middle of the night which he threw on my desk saying: "What about this, Fred?" It was still all done by eye, with the full-size mock-ups erected outside his mansion, the engineering department struggling to adapt to the co-ordinates of the evolving shape. This was where Lyons, even in his mid-sixties, a captain of industry, was happiest.

Project XJ4 began as a four-seater coupe that handled like an E-Type. Then it grew two more doors. Lyons sliced off the rear end but retained the tapering curve of the E-Type's rear wings and 'hips' where the rear roof pillars met the boot lid above the wheel arch. He had never liked how the E-Type's wheel arches sat proud of the wheels, so he minimised the gap between tyre and metal. The front gained an extra pair of headlights and a square grille replaced the E-Type's aero-derived intake. The shape evolved and grew; XJ4 gradually lost its sports-car proportions but retained the signature feline form. It had all of Lyons's favourite details: a low roofline; long bonnet; tall wheels that filled the wheel arches; and a crouching, muscular look – of a jaguar about to pounce.

The result was a shape that looked unmistakably Jaguar yet absolutely of the moment. On 26 September 1968, Lyons revealed his new car at the Lancaster Hotel in London's West End. Only at the last minute was any thought given to the name, so XJ4 simply became XJ6 as an indication of how many cylinders it had.

As a mark of how confident he felt about his latest design, Lyons opted to be photographed with the car for the full-page newspaper advertisements that appeared the following day. In one fell swoop, the XJ superseded all the Jaguar saloons – the 240, 340, 420, 430G and S-Type. The 'old man' had staked everything on one design. He believed it was his career best, 'closer than any other to my idea of an ideal car' – a fast, capable saloon that turned heads. It was such a confident design that it would see Jaguar into the 1990s.

At a little over £2,000, it was at least £1,000 cheaper than the equivalent Mercedes or BMW. According to *Motor*, it was 'Unbelievable value. If Jaguar were to double the price of the XJ6 and bill it as the best car in the world, we would be right behind them ... As it stands at the moment, dynamically, it has no equal regardless of price, which explains those twelve-month delivery quotes from dealers ... We set it as a new yardstick, a tremendous advance guaranteed to put it ahead for several years at least.'

One teenage admirer, Ian McCallum, was also smitten. 'The wheels were enormous. Nobody had seen anything like them before. They filled the whole body. I remember collecting a brochure from the local dealer and going back the next day for another. I still have them both.' It was a defining moment for the teenager who would one day be Jaguar's design director.

39

WORLD DOMINATION

By 1966, after Clark's triumphs at Indianapolis and in Formula 1, it was hard to see what Colin Chapman had left to conquer. The Lotus Cortina and the Elan had finally earned him some credibility as a road-car builder. He had moved to new premises at Hethel in Norfolk, once home to the US Air Force 2nd Air Division, so he could keep his aeroplane by the office.

Like David Brown and Tony Vandervell before him, he had reached a level where he could commute to races in his own plane. All this and he was still only thirty-eight years old, younger even than two of the other F1 drivers, Graham Hill and Jack Brabham, and thirty years younger than his great rival Enzo Ferrari.

But, as ever, there was trouble ahead for Chapman. Since the 1950s, for their Formula 1 campaigns both he and Cooper had depended almost exclusively on engines supplied by Coventry Climax, but in 1964, they announced that they were pulling out of racing-engine construction. Lotus would be high and dry without a power unit just as the rules were about to change permitting 3-litre engines. The only options were to try to muddle through with the existing Climax 2-litre or source or use another complicated sixteen-cylinder that BRM had built. He needed a new engine good enough to keep his drivers on the podium. As always, he was over extended and in no position to finance the development of a new racing engine. But he knew who he wanted to design it.

~

Keith Duckworth was trouble. A bluff and direct Lancastrian who always shot from the hip and was always convinced he was right, he had started out by getting it famously wrong. Born in 1933, at eighteen, when training to be an RAF pilot during his National Service, he fell asleep at the controls while circling an airfield, was judged incompetent and banned from flying. Retraining to be a navigator, he fell out with his instructor. He just couldn't help himself, or, as he explained it: 'I simply won't accept theories that are wrong. I can spot bullshit at 100 yards, and I have to say so.' Discharged early, he fared only slightly better at Imperial College, where he scraped a pass in his engineering degree, with a dissertation that consisted of a withering critique of the course and its methodology.

In the mid-'50s, an interest in motor racing had drawn him to Colin Chapman's Hornsey stable block, where he helped out. It was an intoxicating atmosphere for a young engineer, being around Chapman with his inexhaustible well of new ideas. And Chapman, for as long he could get away with it, was still using volunteers, bartering their time for spare parts or promises of drives. But Duckworth was too much his own man to put up with this for long. Tasked with sorting out Lotus's first gearbox, he was soon giving Chapman a piece of his mind: 'I'm not prepared to waste my life developing something that will never work.'

Duckworth and fellow Lotus exile Mike Costin founded Cosworth Engineering in 1958, based in a rat-infested premises in the north London suburb of Friern Barnet, famous only for its psychiatric hospital. But far from being a loss to Chapman, the arm's-length relationship on a proper business footing worked a lot better as they developed the Ford Anglia engine for Lotus's all conquering Formula Junior, followed by the units for the Cortina and Elan.

Chapman now asked Duckworth – hypothetically – what it would cost for him to design and build a couple of trial engines. *A hundred grand would cover it*, Duckworth thought. Armed with that figure, Chapman did the rounds of possible funders.

In 1966, £100,000 sounded like a huge sum of money to risk on an entirely new engine which offered no guarantee of success. Formula 1 was a sport full of trial and error, mostly error. But for Ford, Walter Hayes's pairing of the blue oval with Lotus had reaped rewards, so he agreed to try the idea on his masters in Detroit. He knew that this decision was one that would have to come not from the head but the heart, a place from which very few of Ford's decisions sprang. Their people would want to see a full cost-benefit analysis. That was impossible with a Grand Prix engine, which seldom worked first time (indeed, some never worked at all). And even when they did, there was no guarantee that the rest of the car would match up, nor the driver.

At least Lotus was currently building the world's best Grand Prix cars and had the world's best driver. Before he got near Detroit, Hayes's first hurdle was the Ford of Britain Policy Committee, which met in their Brentwood headquarters. At the last minute, he decided not to put the matter on the agenda. There, it would just draw attention to itself and alert hostile bean counters to prepare their arguments against it. Instead, he raised it in 'Any other business'.

It was an astute move. Minutes before, a decision had just been taken to put synchromesh on the first gear of the Ford Anglia gearbox – at a cost of £1 million. So when Hayes raised his hand and said he wanted to make a Grand Prix engine, at one-tenth of the price of the Anglia's first gear, suddenly it did not seem like such a big ask. It was nodded through.

Even Hayes, a perennial optimist, could not have envisaged quite what Ford would get for its hundred grand.

Back at his home in the village of Harpole, Northamptonshire, Keith Duckworth set up a drawing board and got to work with his slide rule, while Ford's legal department drew up a contract. When Duckworth received the contract, he did what came naturally – and ignored it. When Hayes gently reminded him about it he got a characteristic response: 'Do you want me to read the contract or design the engine? Because I don't have time to do both.'

From the first pencil line to launch took a shade under two years. Duckworth regularly worked sixteen-hour days through the nine-month design period, losing 40lbs in weight in the process, just hunched over his drawing board. Never mind the contract, Duckworth knew this was the project of a lifetime – a Grand Prix engine from a clean sheet of paper, all of his own.

On 4 June 1967, for the Dutch GP at Zandvoort, with the Ford name modestly displayed on its cam covers, the Duckworth-designed V8 DFV – for double four valves – made its first competitive appearance. It was the first time in the history of Grand Prix that the Ford logo had appeared on a racing car, and not since Mercedes-Benz over a decade before had a major motor manufacturer got involved with Formula 1.

Apart from that, there was not much more about it that the press could say. In an age of V12s and even H-16s, a V8 was hardly news. Four valves per cylinder was something that W. O. Bentley had applied to his first car in 1919. But as geniuses go, Duckworth was on the practical end of the spectrum. He wanted the engine to be rugged and predictable, but light and easy to work on. A V8 had fewer moving parts, fewer to go wrong.

The car itself was new, too. Chapman's Lotus 49 was another leap in the dark. There was no frame holding the engine; the engine block itself was bolted to the cockpit hull; and the rear suspension bolted onto the engine, which doubled as an integral part of the car structure. In the pits before the race, Walter Hayes forewarned the press that Ford expected it might be several races before it won. When Jim Clark arrived at Zandvoort, he had not even seen the car before. Graham Hill was also driving for Lotus and put his car on pole; Clark qualified sixth. Hill charged into the lead and stayed there until his engine broke. Clark, always kind to his machinery, nursed the Lotus Ford to a smooth and stunning debut victory.

Lighter, more powerful and more reliable than any of the competition, by the end of the season, Duckworth's design seemed to be in a class of its own. Domination might have suited Chapman, but Hayes feared Ford's reputation might suffer if Lotus appeared to be winning against only inferior machinery.

His solution, though not to Chapman's taste, was inspired – Ford would offer to sell the engine to other teams. It would be a win-win for Ford – quite literally. It ushered in another golden age for Formula 1, as smaller, poorer teams were able to access the world's best engine. Ford's worldwide reputation was dramatically enhanced as the power behind the cars that were beating Ferrari, even though the engine had sprung from the mind of a man with a slide rule in Harpole.

By the time of the DFV's last Grand Prix victory in 1983, it had notched up 155 Grand Prix wins and powered twenty-three World Championships, a record that is unlikely ever to be bettered. It was a great return on Ford of Britain's hundred-grand investment.

40

LIVING IN PARADISE

Jim Clark had warned Chapman when he signed him up that he would not take any risks, telling him: 'If I'm driving the car and I don't think it feels right, I'm not going to push it, I'm just going to drive it.'

Concerned about safety, Clark shunned the drive-on-the-limit approach of his predecessors. And yet he was also capable of shattering pace when it was called for. At Monza for the 1967 Italian Grand Prix, Clark was on pole and was in the lead when his Lotus 49 got a puncture. Changing the wheel put him sixteen places down the field but he worked his way back up to the lead, progressively shortening his lap times, only to run out of fuel on the last lap and coast to third.

The youngest driver to have won a Grand Prix, he would beat Fangio's historic record of wins. He became the world's most highly paid sportsman, yet for all this glory he shied away from attention. Pat Mennem, who ghosted a column under the driver's name for the *Daily Mirror*, remembered accompanying him to a farmers' market in Edinburgh: 'He'd won both his World Championships, but nobody ever mentioned motor racing at all. All they talked about was sheep. He told me that was what he wanted to go back to.'

As well as being famously shy, bizarrely for a racing driver he was also indecisive, reportedly often unable to make a decision about which restaurant to dine in. Although he had a long-term girlfriend, Sally Stokes, he refused to commit to marriage while he was racing.

Despite his success and wealth, there was no let-up. Grand Prix drivers today only compete in Formula 1 Championship races, but Clark campaigned at all levels, including saloon cars and Formula 2. And it was in April 1968 at Hockenheim in a Formula 2 race where his Lotus careered off the track and into one of the many trees that lined the circuit. He was killed instantly.

All racing fatalities are tragic, but Clark's death unnerved the motor-racing community more than any other. Here was a driver known for his smooth efficiency behind the wheel, who had never been injured in a race. 'We all thought the same thing,' said fellow driver Chris Amon. 'If it could happen to Jimmy, what chance did the rest of us have?'

A deflated tyre caused Clark to swerve but it was the trees lining the track that had killed him. Growing concern about motor-racing safety, championed by his fellow Scot Jackie Stewart, stepped up a level. After Clark's death, attempts to justify danger as an integral component of the sport's gladiatorial drama stopped. From then on a campaign gathered momentum that would change the design of cars and circuits until motor racing became safer than everyday motoring.

Clark's death was the end of one of the greatest partnerships in the history of the sport. The brilliant, introverted Clark, whose precision and lightness of touch fitted perfectly with Lotus's ultra-light, highly strung machines, also complemented the brash, extrovert, hard-charging Chapman. From his first outing in the Lotus Elite, Clark never considered driving for anyone else. They formed an exceptional bond and Chapman, although he would have many more years of success ahead of him, was never quite the same after the loss of his protégé. An era was drawing to a close, which Clark's loss seemed to hasten. As Lotus team manager Andrew Ferguson observed: 'After he'd gone, you realised that you'd been living in paradise.'

It was the end of the line for the gifted amateur; no more shepherds would be champions. The sport was becoming a business. Ford's arrival in the sport and a change in regulations that permitted more overt sponsorship took the money involved in the sport to a new level. Chapman, inevitably, was the first to really exploit the opportunities of the new order. He painted the cars in the livery of the tobacco company that sponsored him, even going so far as to change the name of the car from Lotus to John Player Special, thereby forcing all reporting to namecheck his sponsor – whether the BBC liked it or not. And never again would one man sit at a drawing board and draw a race-winning engine with just a pencil and slide rule.

The coming changes were not confined to motor sport. The days of gifted auteurs like William Lyons and Alec Issigonis were numbered. All Britain's motor makers were being subjected to new forces that would shape their futures in ways few of them liked and even fewer of them could control. But the can-do, right-here-in-this-shed spirit of the fire-watchers had one more flourish, with an impact that rolls on half a century later.

41

HOME ON THE RANGE

Market research barely gets a look-in in this story of stubborn visionaries. The chances are that if any heed had been paid to it, many of the most innovative and transformative designs examined here would never have seen the light of day.

In Britain, the twenty-five years that followed the Second World War produced an automotive engineering renaissance which spawned a host of inspired, radical, game-changing, trail-blazing machines that made British automotive engineering a world leader. Instinctive designers fiercely guarded their creations from the deadening hand of compromise. But one of the most ground-breaking designs of the time was born out of a piece of analysis produced by an economist.

In 1962, Graham Bannock, a London School of Economics graduate, was in Paris, working for the Organisation for European Economic Co-operation, when he got a call from Rover's William Martin-Hurst. Exactly what made Bannock abandon his desk in the Château de la Muette in the Bois de Boulogne for one of the wooden sheds in Solihull remains unclear. One reason could have been what Bannock describes as MH's 'overpowering' energy; another was the prospect of travelling all over the world. Because MH's preoccupation at the time was the future of Land Rover.

Once the Land Rover turned out not to be the anticipated stopgap model but an enduring cash cow, Solihull's designers had tried to think laterally about how to develop its new off-road product – and failed. An early attempt, awkwardly known as the Road Rover, fell very neatly between two stools. The added weight of a more car-like body compromised the Land Rover's agility, and on the road the 4 × 4's cart-sprung live axles made the ride more like that of a truck. So, for twenty years, the Land Rover had soldiered on with barely any development. But what was there not to like? The order books were full – for now.

Bannock's research took him all over the world to the far-flung places where Land Rovers were sold. There were few countries the ubiquitous 4 × 4 hadn't reached and some were places where only a Land Rover could get. In economic parlance, this was impressive market penetration. In July 1965, Bannock put his findings into a memo addressed to the Rover management board simply titled 'Land Rover'. In it he noted that almost twenty years after its introduction, it had captured 20 per cent of the 'light 4 × 4 market'.

That was the good news.

What Bannock also discovered was that the worldwide growth of the whole 4 × 4 market had slowed to just 1 per cent. Even if Land Rover got a makeover or expanded its range, there was no new market share to be gained and, 'to make matters worse, that market had split into three distinct classes – workhorse 4 × 4s, military and "fun" vehicles'. Only in this last sector did Bannock detect any growth.

Bannock was influenced by what he had seen and heard in America, where Land Rover had failed to gain any traction in the market. There the only comparable vehicle was the Willys Jeep Wagoneer, a sturdy four-wheel-drive station wagon from the maker of the Land Rover's original inspiration. But the Wagoneer was a far more domesticated beast, with wind-up windows and softer springs, air conditioning and a sturdy 3.8-litre V6 engine. It was popular among people who enjoyed outdoor pursuits, who towed boats or went hunting, but also capable of doing the school run.

Bannock's prescription had as much to do with inspiration as research: 'If we are to make the best uses of our massive reputation in the 4 × 4 market and fulfil the criteria above it seems to me that we can only do so by developing a radically different vehicle for the leisure market and not allowing its design to be compromised too much by the requirements of either workhorse or military vehicles.' He added that it would have to set high standards of styling, appeal and quality, passenger comfort, ride and performance on-as well as off-road. He had seen the future, though it was a few years before anyone put together the letters SUV.

Bannock already knew what his idea would be up against. Inside the company, over the years the Land Rover had acquired zealous guardians of its utilitarian reputation, bent on fending off any attempt to debase its character with such car-like fripperies as wind-up windows or softer suspension. Tom Barton, a former railway apprentice who had worked on the development of the original Land Rover in the 1940s, opposed the notion of coil springs, warning that greater comfort would actually encourage people to drive too fast and risk damaging the vehicle. And in 1965, this so-called 'fun, leisure market' was completely unheard of – except perhaps when applied to sports cars. 'Fun' and 'leisure' were not words that Land Rover purists liked being associated with their very serious vehicle.

Spen King was no fan of market researchers; he thought them 'very likely to look sideways and backwards and to prove incapable of looking forwards'. But on this occasion he seized on Bannock's memo. He thought the Land Rover was antiquated and primitive. Previous attempts to domesticate it had foundered because of cost and lack of power. But looking at Bannock's proposal, King knew that Rover already had in its armoury all the key ingredients to meet the analyst's criteria: the V8 engine had the power and David Bache could deliver the style, all for a modest development outlay.

King's method was not to win the argument on paper or in meetings but simply to go ahead and build a prototype and see if it worked – a decidedly old-school approach. Wherever possible, just as with the Land Rover, existing parts were deployed. The firm's adopted V8 had already transformed both of their current road cars into fast motorway cruisers. Fitted to an adapted Land Rover chassis, with its four driven wheels anchored by more forgiving, long-travel coil springs, it could navigate a dry river bed and cruise the fast lane at 100mph.

No other vehicle in the world could do all that, and it was immediately approved for production. King and Gordon Bashford roughed out a body for the prototype to use. When it moved to the next stage, David Bache produced a more car-like shape. But no one liked it; the sculpted curves took it away from its more rustic roots. So Bache's team took the body that had already been fashioned for King and Bashford's development mule and simply tidied it up.

At its launch in 1970, the Range Rover was an instant hit, praised for its unique combination of speed and off-road agility plus its spacious estate-car cabin.

As with Issigonis's Mini and Malcolm Sayer's E-Type, function ruled the form. King said that of all the time they spent developing the Range Rover, only 1 per cent of that went on the shape, yet to this day, it remains the first and only car to be exhibited in the Louvre as an exemplary work of industrial design.

Just as with the Land Rover before it, no one was more dismayed by its success than Rover's managers. 'I thought it would be successful, but not that successful,' King said later. 'People loved it. It was never intended to be a luxury car, it was a work vehicle for builders and farmers, but it was dragged up by customer demand.'

They had done it again, a vehicle quickly cobbled together from existing parts and the inspiration of a few trusted engineers with no interference. It was the last mass-production car ever to be conceived in such a way, yet its unique combination of qualities would ultimately reshape the car market worldwide.

Robust and agile, it could cope with anything – even the scorched earth on which Britain's motor industry was about to self-destruct.

EPILOGUE:

BLOWING THE DOORS OFF

The perfect storm that obliterated Britain's motor industry in the 1970s was a collision of forces that bore down on it from a variety of directions. With hindsight, it's easy to see the warning signals, some of which had been flashing for decades, which makes it all the harder to understand how wilfully they were ignored.

When William Lyons launched his 100mph saloon, the Jaguar Mark VII, at Earl's Court in 1950, he chartered special trains to transport his entire workforce to go to the show so they could enjoy the event and the attention the fruits of their labour was getting. It was a grand day out for all, except that on the way back a train carriage was vandalised by a group of 'tinnies', the sheet-metal workers. Lyons was dismayed, as he always was by any workers' unrest, which – as he saw it – could only damage their fortunes just as much as his.

But it was not until the mid-1960s that disputes and stoppages started to really bite into profits, just as bosses were also facing fiercer competition and mounting complaints about product quality. Having heeded the post-war government's call to 'export or die', by 1950 the industry had grown into the world's biggest exporter of cars. For the rest of that decade it had found a healthy growth in demand at home as disposable income reached new pockets and output grew. But as exports levelled off in the 1960s, revived European producers started to enjoy similar growth. They found export opportunities right on the doorstep, thanks to tariff-free conditions of the Common Market. In 1959, 25 per cent of French car exports were to countries in Europe, compared to a paltry 6 per cent of Britain's.

French president General de Gaulle's veto of British membership of the Common Market in 1963 and again in 1967 effectively locked Britain out of unfettered access to its nearest and most compatible export market at a time when the American and Commonwealth markets for their cars were shrinking. Although some Europeans were prepared to pay the extra duty on a Mini or a Jaguar, mainstream models couldn't get a look-in.

The men at the top of Britain's car companies in the '50s and '60s were either tired or retiring. Their experience had been forged by adversity, surviving the Depression, the Blitz and rationing. Leonard Lord, William Lyons, the Wilks and Rootes brothers were independent-minded creatures used to juggling investment, engineering and sales to keep going and liked running their own show. They had fended off calls for consolidation, but when it came in the late '60s, wished on them by a Labour government panicked at the prospect of job losses, there was no new generation primed to take the industry through what would be a brutal series of forced mergers.

In 1945, Labour trade minister Stafford Cripps's call for rationalisation was booed by the then captains of the motor industry. Twenty years on, few disagreed with Prime Minister Harold Wilson that it had to be done – and fast. After the Rootes family's abrupt sale to American Chrysler in 1967, Wilson and his industry minister Tony Benn instigated a crash consolidation of the remaining British-owned companies into the British Leyland Motor Corporation. When it was formed in

1968 it was the world's fifth-largest motor manufacturer, a fact that prolonged hubris and postponed much-needed rationalisation.

At a stroke, Austin, Morris, Jaguar, Rover, Triumph, MG, Wolseley, Riley, Daimler and several others, plus most of Britain's truck makers, in all forty manufacturing companies, were thrown together. With over eighty factories, each with different customs and practices, some making very similar products, it would have taken superhumanly tough and uncompromising management to streamline it all. Donald Stokes, the former Leyland truck and bus salesman catapulted into the top job, was hopelessly out of his depth. Within a few years the whole edifice collapsed into nationalisation. Not too big to fail, but too big to succeed.

Among the first casualties of the British Leyland merger were some of its greatest heroes. With no patron any more, Alec Issigonis was first sidelined and then pensioned off, a No. 10 Meccano set presented to him as his leaving present. John Cooper and Donald Healey suffered a more perfunctory fate, their names erased from the company line-up as cars bearing their names were axed so the company no longer had to pay them any more royalties.

Sir William Lyons, almost as old as the century, having lost the son he had hoped would succeed him, stayed resolutely at Jaguar's helm. Jaguar's profits had remained healthy and kept its foothold in the American market. But even Lyons recognised that consolidation was inevitable.

After British Leyland was formed, he made sure he secured a seat on the British Leyland board, from where he was able to see off any promising new model that threatened Jaguar's position. Among the casualties was a futuristic mid-engined sports car thought up by Rover's Spen King and Gordon Bashford, using that handy V8. Faster than an E-Type yet £500 cheaper to build, Lyons had it killed. King fought a rearguard action, releasing the prototype to both *Motor* and *Autocar* magazines to test in the hope that their ecstatic write-ups would win the day. But without a board member fighting its corner, the car was doomed. The pliable Stokes buckled under Lyons's will. No British Leyland product could rain on Jaguar's parade.

The talented triumvirate behind the Range Rover – King, Bashford and Bache – all found themselves being sucked higher up the British Leyland hierarchy, presiding over new models that were each differently compromised. Their daily lives became less about design and more about cost-cutting and infighting within the bloated management hierarchy.

Not all British Leyland's multiple wounds were self-inflicted. Few could have foreseen the spectacular rise of the Japanese car makers or the oil crisis of 1973 which decimated sales, particularly of the larger, more profitable Jaguars and Rovers. After nationalisation and his own retirement, Sir Donald, later Lord Stokes, widely regarded as having steered the leviathan straight into the rocks, was philosophical. He said what he was trying to achieve, bringing together the disparate elements of British Leyland, should have started in the 1920s, not the 1960s and 1970s.

For Colin Chapman, none of this mattered. He was on a different trajectory. His Lotus Esprit, Britain's first mid-engined sports car, replaced 007's Aston-Martin in *The Spy Who Loved Me,* and in Formula 1 he went from strength to strength.

Boosted by the arrival of sponsorship in 1968, Formula 1 developed into a far better financed, more technological business – with Chapman in pole position. He had cemented the virtuous circle that brought together British driving talent, British design genius and one of the biggest beasts of the global auto industry – Ford.

Chapman had it all. He combined something of Issigonis's engineering vision with Lyons's style and ambition and John Cooper's can-do pragmatism. Always a smart dresser, he was also a grafter who broke rules and rewrote them to get to the absolute top of international motor sport. He was also the last Formula 1 team owner capable of working on a car in the pit lane.

His time with Jim Clark was Chapman's personal best. They complemented each other perfectly – the steady but gifted driver and the brilliant but impetuous team boss. With Clark gone, Chapman drove himself harder, his impatience for more success and his desire to be seen as a major industrial player pushing him towards ever-bigger risks.

Of all the industry bosses, it was Lyons Chapman admired the most. Only slightly older than the Jaguar founder's son John, Chapman would have been the right generation to take over. The two even tentatively discussed a partnership. But where Chapman lived to race, as Enzo Ferrari did, the more prudent Lyons was focused on creating the best and most beautiful road cars.

And Chapman was much more of a gambler. Greed and ambition ultimately got the better of him when he came into contact with the flamboyant former General Motors executive John Z. DeLorean. DeLorean had persuaded the British government to bankroll the construction of a plant in Belfast for his ill-fated stainless-steel sports car. Chapman initially came in to help DeLorean engineer his dramatic gull-winged car, but the pair were named as co-conspirators in a plot to siphon off millions of pounds of investors' money into a Swiss-based company set up by Chapman and his accountant Fred Bushell.

Chapman had a rare talent for getting into – and out of – trouble. Only a fatal heart attack in December 1982 saved him from jail. After a lengthy investigation by the Serious Fraud Office, it was his faithful accountant who was sent down. Sentencing Fred Bushell in Belfast Crown Court on 19 June 1992 for his part in the fraud, Lord Justice Murray said that, had he lived, Chapman would have 'merited a sentence of ten years for [his] part in the conspiracy'.

Despite the tarnished reputation, Chapman, helped by Cooper, left a formidable legacy: not just a company – Lotus still exists – but a whole industry. Today, with a £9 billion turnover, employing 45,000 people, Britain's motor-sports industry supplies most of the world's racing cars. Ironically, even the Mercedes-Benz team, the subject of Cameron Earl's secret 1948 government report on the Nazis' racing supremacy, is now based not in Stuttgart but Brackley. Renault is in Enstone; Red Bull in Milton Keynes; McLaren in Woking; Williams in Wantage; Haas in Banbury. Driver-turned-commentator David Coulthard describes it as 'the centre of the universe of motorsport'; the *Wall Street Journal* dubbed it Gasoline Valley.

It is a strange irony of Britain's automotive story that during the closing decades of the twentieth century, as the prolonged demise of one arm of Britain's indigenous motor industry was being played out through news headlines, another was quietly rising to world domination with barely a mention.

Yet, rather like the Terminator, incinerated, its limbs shot off, remnants of Britain's road-car industry clawed their way forward. Salvage parties picking over the industrial wastes of the Midlands found some badges still glimmering with past glory.

William Lyons lived until 1985, just long enough to see Jaguar liberated from British Leyland and floated off into private hands. A few years later, Jaguars were back at Le Mans for two more victories. Ford and General Motors fought a bidding war for the marque. Ford won, paying $2.38 billion in 1989, way over the odds.

Walter Hayes, godfather of the Lotus Cortina and the world-conquering DFV Formula 1 engine, finding his boss Henry Ford II still in need of retail therapy, persuaded him to add Aston Martin to his empire. Hayes even beat a path to David Brown's retirement penthouse in Monte Carlo to persuade him to let Aston Martin borrow his initials again. And John Cooper was amused to find BMW knocking on his door asking for his name as well, to grace the resurgent Mini.

But taming these recalcitrant Brits was a challenge. Between 1994 and 2000, BMW almost choked trying to swallow the denationalised carcass of what was British Leyland and spat most of it out again, all except Mini. Not long after, having spent a fortune on them, harder heads at Ford offloaded their British brands in a fire sale.

For those prepared to play a longer game, the rewards have been huge. Rolls-Royce and Bentley have both been reincarnated by Germans BMW and VW respectively. Jaguar and Land Rover, twinned under the Indian conglomerate Tata, are enjoying success undreamed of by their creators. Aston Martin, alone again, is preparing to go public, and Lotus, regenerated since Chapman more times than Doctor Who, is now in Chinese hands.

Memories of industrial strife and quality deficiencies have faded; the old badges have polished up well. What makes them so attractive after all these years is a priceless equity accrued though original, mould-breaking design and creative passion.

In the late 1960s, when British cars had been at the peak of stardom, a very British film paid tribute. Troy Kennedy Martin had a particular gift for capturing British character in his writing for TV and screen. *Z Cars* and *Softly, Softly* broke new ground in their grasp of the British soul, but his masterpiece would be a feature film, *The Italian Job*, in which a gang of British villains steal gold bullion in Turin using a trio of Minis as getaway cars.

But when the film went into pre-production, the cash-strapped British Motor Corporation, preoccupied with mergers, grudgingly offered only six Minis – at trade price – and demanded the full sticker price for the additional thirty cars (such was the casualty rate from those spectacular chase sequences).

There was a much better offer on the table. Not only would the cannier Italian Fiat chief Gianni Agnelli give the filmmakers the run of their company town of Turin, he also made them an offer the producer thought he couldn't refuse – a limitless supply of Fiat cars for free. Kennedy Martin put his foot down and insisted on Minis. They embodied the character of the film, as he explained: 'The idea of the script was a gentle send-up of British chauvinism and the Common Market, with all these criminals coming together and the solid British set against the cunning Europeans. The Minis came through the film as a powerful symbol of what we can do in Britain; they were the most remarkable elements of the story.'

Luckily for the film, and for all of us, the producer backed down. This British classic, too British, it turned out, to work very well in the US, also featured Aston Martins and E-Types. The film is a self-deprecating celebration of British hubris, can-do and self-belief. Charlie Croker, played by Michael Caine, is even reminiscent of another suave young chancer, Colin Chapman, with ideas above his station, unhindered by his common roots, getting all he wants with his irrepressible charm.

Alec Issigonis's Mini outlasted its designer. When he died in 1988, having lived alone in the bungalow in Edgbaston since the death of his mother, his creation would soldier on almost unchanged into the twenty-first century. Although at the time his achievements had been somewhat eclipsed by what befell his former employers after his departure, his memorial service in Birmingham Cathedral, a packed event, was a reminder of his influence.

Addressing the congregation, his old friend Lord Snowdon had this to say: 'Nowadays cars are designed by teams of people rather than by an individual and I doubt that there will ever be another single designer who will contribute as much as Alec did. He unquestionably advanced and altered the thinking of not only all other British manufacturers but also multi-national manufacturers the world over. His influence was colossal.'

Kjell Qvale, who died aged ninety-four in 2013, outlived them all, but he never lost his passion for the British marques that made his fortune. As he never tired of telling the story of that morning on a New Orleans street corner: 'Once you get hooked, like I did with an MG TC in 1946, there was no way out.'

ACKNOWLEDGEMENTS

This is my first crack at a non-fiction book and my first attempt to write at length about a lifetime infatuation. So my thanks go first to my late father, Lawrence Seymour Grimsdale, who had no idea of the consequences when he handed me my first Dinky Toy in 1957, and tolerated my passion even though he often feared it would lead to no good. He was the same generation as several of the characters in this book, who lived through two world wars and the Depression, who tolerated austerity, despised profligacy, and would never be subjugated. Their efforts and sacrifices created the conditions for the previously undreamt-of advances so widely enjoyed by their descendants in post-war Britain.

Jason Hartcup, who since our teens has shared in many of my automotive deeds and misdeeds. It was his demand for a book about cars that jump-started this endeavour.

Fellow enthusiasts Martin Rudland and Philip Skinner, who I met at Ecclesall Infants School in Sheffield in 1960, have both supplied sound advice and helped with sources.

Thanks go to Michael Quinn, grandson of Sir William Lyons, who very kindly let me read his grandfather's unpublished – and fascinating – memoir. The staff at the British Motor Museum and the BMIHT Archive at Gaydon have been always helpful and supportive on my many visits. Anyone who has enjoyed this book

and has not seen their magnificent exhibition should visit immediately; almost all the cars discussed here are in their collection.
The British Library has been an invaluable resource, as has the
reference library at the RAC in Pall Mall, whose staff were utterly
helpful – even though I am not (yet) a member.

In America, David N. Lucsko, associate professor and chair,
Department of History, Auburn University, and Jeremy Kinney,
curator in the Aeronautics Department, National Air and Space
Museum, guided me on my investigation of the British sports car's
impact on post-war America. I recommend Jeremy's excellent
paper, 'Racing on Runways: The Strategic Air Command and
Sports Car Racing in the 1950s'.

I also received invaluable help from Michael Skapinker of the
Financial Times, Simon Gunn (Professor of Urban History at
the University of Leicester), filmmaker Patrick Uden, Richard
Bremner of *Autocar,* David Kiss, Tim White, Nicholas Faith and
Patrick and David Tatham.

Further back, writer and racer Tony Dron, former editor of
Thoroughbred and Sports Car, published my first efforts on this
subject, followed by Richard Sutton at *Classic and Sports Cars*,
and Jay Nagley of Redspy.

My thanks also go to Peter Pagnamenta and Peter Ceresole,
who gave me the task of researching the car industry episode of
the 1984 BBC Two series *All Our Working Lives*, which gave me
a crash course in how cars are actually made and how the business
worked, and started me off collecting material for what ultimately became this book. I'm also grateful to Angela Holdworth,
on whose series *Now the War is Over* I learned about Stafford
Cripps and 'export or die' and met some of the team behind the
Land Rover.

And I'm indebted to Michael Jackson, who, as director of pro-
grammes at Channel 4, let me devote two entire evenings of the
schedule to Stirling Moss and the Mini.

At Simon & Schuster, I am mightily grateful to my publisher Iain MacGregor for showing such a keen interest in the book's subject and for his incisive comments on the text. And to his team, Melissa Bond, who was responsible for editing the text, Kaiya Shang, who helped with the picture research, and Craig Fraser for the design.

I thank my exceptional agent, Mark Lucas of LAW, for seeing the potential in what I initially feared would look like a vanity project.

My children Lydia and Lawrence Calman-Grimsdale lent moral support at all hours; Lawrence helped me decipher the mysteries of the 'polar moment of inertia'. And finally my wife, Stephanie Calman, who painstakingly read and reread and wants it known for the record that she loves cars even more now.

NOTES

Chapter 1: The Fire-Watchers

'As I stepped out ...' W. Lyons speech at the Motor Trades Luncheon Club, 25 June, 1947, cited in Philip Porter and Paul Skilleter, *Sir William Lyons: The Official Biography* (Haynes, 2001), p. 83.

'never get anywhere ...' in Porter and Skilleter, *Sir William Lyons*, p. 16.

'I became absorbed ...' in Sir William Lyons's unpublished memoir, 1976.

'The chassis from ...' Ibid.

'The effect was ruinous ...' Ibid.

'I pointed out ...' in Walter Hassan, *Climax in Coventry: My Life of Fine Engines and Fast Cars* (Motor Racing Publications, 1975), p. 61.

Chapter 2: Export or Die

'We have been ...' in John Bullock, *The Rootes Brothers* (Patrick Stephens, 1993), p. 142.

Chapter 3: Suburban Tearaway

'whenever there was a crash ...' in Doug Nye, *World Champions: Cooper Cars* (Osprey, 1987), p. 13.

'It really was quite something ...' Ibid., p. 12.

Chapter 4: Brief Encounter

'It wasn't that ...' in John Cooper with John Bentley, *Grand Prix Carpetbagger* (Foulis, 1977), p. 29.

Chapter 5: Two Sheets of Tin and a Bundle of Firewood

'The only words ...' in Kjell Qvale, *I Never Look Back* (Kjell Qvale, 2005), p. 7.

'All of a sudden ...' Ibid., p. 52.

'It had no bumpers ...' in Kevin Nelson, *Lunches With Mr Q* (Southampton Books, 2012), p. 24.

Chapter 7: Brick By Bloody Brick

'He awoke people ...' in Sir Miles Thomas, *Out on a Wing* (Michael Joseph, 1964) p. 172.
'Tommy, I'm going ...' Ibid., p. 181.

Chapter 8: Needs Must When the Devil Drives

'Severe restrictions on the use of paper ...' Jaguar sales catalogue, 1946.
'The lines of our cars ...' in Philip Turner, 'The Lyons Share – Philip Turner talks to retiring chief Sir William Lyons', *The Motor* (4 March 1972), p. 18.
'Lyons would say ...' in Philip Porter and Paul Skilleter, *Sir William Lyons: The Official Biography*, p. 108.

Chapter 9: Gone With the Wind

'a rich cream color ...' in F. Scott Fitzgerald, *The Great Gatsby* (Charles Scribner's Sons, 1925), p. 64.
'We landed at ...' in Sir William Lyons's unpublished memoir, 1976.
'I was quite astounded ...' Ibid.
'There never was such a business ...' *Automotive News* (26 June 1996).
'He was a very good salesman ...' in Sir William Lyons's unpublished memoir, 1976.
'I had to have it ...' in Clark Gable, 'My Favorite Sports Car', *Road & Track* (March 1950), p. 18.

Chapter 10: Lines in the Sand

'We reluctantly decided ...' in Harold Hastings, 'Beyond the Backroom Door', *The Motor* (10 August 1949), p. 46.

Chapter 11: This Chap Will Go Places

'There could be up to fifty ...' in Frankie Fraser with James Morton, *Mad Frank's London* (Virgin, 2001), p. 45.
'I was terribly shy ...' in Gerard 'Jabby' Crombac, *Colin Chapman, the Man and His Cars: The Authorised Biography* (Patrick Stephens, 1986), p. 28.

Chapter 12: Humiliation

'always liked to be well turned out ...' in Raymond Mays, *Split Seconds: My Racing Years* (G. T. Foulis, 1951), p. 14.

Chapter 13: Win on Sunday – Sell on Monday

'They laughed at my Cooper ...' in Stirling Moss and Doug Nye, *In the Track of Speed* (Putnam's, 1957), p. 15.

'What an ovation ...' Ibid., p. 16.

'None of them would trust me ...' in Philip Porter, *Stirling Moss, The Definitive Biography, Vol. 1* (Porter Press, 2016), p. 108.

'I was taking ...' Ibid., p. 109.

'Because it was wet ...' Ibid., p. 111.

'I am enclosing ...' Ibid., *Stirling Moss: The Authorised Biography* (Orion, 2005), p. 45.

Chapter 16: When Austin Met Healey

'If they didn't leak ...' in Peter Garnier with Brian Healey, *Donald Healey: My World of Cars* (Patrick Stephens, 1989), p. 16.

'The basic difference ...' Ibid., p. 79.

Chapter 17: The Blonde's Bombshell

'an artificial blonde among ...' in Lady Norah Docker, *Norah: The Autobiography of Lady Norah Docker* (W. H. Allen, 1969), p. 26.

'The dear boys ...' Ibid., p. 144.

'I was ashamed ...' Ibid., p. 107.

'We may even say ...' in Christopher Dresser, *The Principles of Decorative Design* (Cassell, 1873), p. 1.

'The best looking Yankee ...' in Graham Robson, *The Book of the Standard Motor Company* (Veloce, 2001), p. 122.

Chapter 18: No Style, Please, We're British

'The difference between working ...' in Matt White, 'Rover's Model Man', *Thoroughbred & Classic Cars* (March 1995), p. 52.

'My design for the P5 ...' Ibid., p. 53.

Chapter 20: The Moonlighters

'Colin still had his job ...' in Simon Taylor, 'Lunch With Mike Costin', *Motor Sport* (February 2012) p. 96.

Chapter 21: Catch This Dodger

'He was always a bit of a tearaway ...' in Chris Nixon, *Mon Ami Mate* (Transport Bookman, 2001), p. 5.

'We landed near Paris ...' Ibid., p. 229.

'The whole art of driving ...' in Rob Widdows, 'Moss and Fangio', *Motor Sport* (November 2007), p. 82.

'As I clambered out ...' in Stirling Moss and Doug Nye, *My Cars and My Career* (Haynes, 1987), p. 109.

Chapter 22: Cooking With Salt

'Damn it, why should . . .' in Mike Hawthorn, *Challenge Me the Race* (William Kimber, 1959), p. 150.
'still in one piece . . .' in Douglas Rutherford, *The Chequered Flag* (Collins, 1956), p. 138.
'Duncan talked to me like a father . . .' in Hawthorn, *Challenge Me the Race*, p. 152.

Chapter 23: Those Bloody Red Cars

'Eventually Peter went in . . .' in Nixon, *Mon Ami Mate*, p. 320.

Chapter 24: Duel on the Hog's Back

'My office was submerged . . .' in Hawthorn, *Challenge Me the Race*, p. 255.

Chapter 26: Sputnik

'In the old days . . .' in Wilfred G. Aston, *The Boys' Book of Motors* (E. & F. Spon, 1922), p. 7.
'You know many people assume . . .' in Gillian Bardsley: *Issigonis, The Official Biography* (Icon Books, 2005), p. 191.
'When Len Lord told me . . .' Ibid., p. 205.
'I found someone . . .' in Simon Garfield, *MINI: The True and Secret History of the Making of the Motor Car* (Faber, 2009), p. 103.

Chapter 27: Things to Do With a Fire Pump

'In his bedroom . . .' in George Melly, *Owning-Up* (Futura, 1985), p. 56.

Chapter 28: When the Ox Pushes the Cart

'After the race . . .' in Doug Nye, *World Champions: Cooper Cars* (Osprey, 1987), p. 152.
'When we came to make . . .' in Timothy Collings, *The Piranha Club* (Virgin, 2004), p. 83.

Chapter 30: Cometh the Ice Men

'Apart from two Mini-Coopers . . .' in Stuart Turner, *Twice Lucky: My Life in Motorsport* (Haynes, 1999), p. 56.
'It was highly unstable . . .' in Bill Price with Paddy Hopkirk, *The Paddy Hopkirk Story: A Dash of the Irish* (Haynes, 2005), p. 11.
'It was Bernard Cahier . . .' in John Davenport, 'Small Wonder', *Motor Sport* (February 2004), p. 30.
'Tony's final stroke . . .' Ibid., p. 35.

Chapter 31: Sex on Wheels

'Did you do this ...' in Philip Porter, *The Most Famous Car in the World* (Orion, 2000), p. 46.
'I simply drove it ...' Ibid., p. 89.

Chapter 32: For Sale: High-Class Motor Business

'James Bond flung ...' in Ian Fleming, *Goldfinger* (Vintage, 2012), p. 95.
'These included switches ...' Ibid., p. 97.
'When he came to Feltham ...' in John Wyer with Chris Nixon, *Racing with the David Brown Aston Martins, Vol. II* (Transport Bookman, 1980), p. 94.
'He was very much ...' Ibid., p. 38.
'He would indicate ...' in 'Working with John Wyer', Gordon Cruikshank, *Motor Sport*, October 2013, p. 127.
'At one continental race ...' Ibid.
'Aston Martin was a very nice hobby ...' in Nixon, *Racing with the David Brown Aston Martins, Vol. II*, p. 38.

Chapter 33: We've Been Expecting You

'The racing years ...' in Chris Nixon, *Racing with the David Brown Aston Martins, Vol. II* (Transport Bookman, 1980), p. 96.
'You might say ...' in John Wyer, *That Certain Sound* (Foulis, 1981), p. 93.
'I can only find ...' Ibid., p. 109.
'I went in ...' Ibid., p. 110.
'At first I couldn't believe ...' in Dave Worrall, *The Most Famous Car in the World: The Complete History of the James Bond Aston Martin DB5* (Solo, 1991).
'As soon as the film was shown ...' Ibid.

Chapter 34: The Shepherd

'I just happened to be there ...' in Jim Clark, *Jim Clark At The Wheel* (Arthur Barker, 1964), p. 18.
'I could see ...' in Simon Taylor, 'Lunch With Mike Costin', *Motor Sport* (February 2012), p. 96.
'I went round ...' in 'Jim Clark, 4 March 1936–7 April 1968', *Motor Sport* (April 1993).

Chapter 36: Gasoline Alley

'Colin Chapman comes ...' in Bill Libby, *Parnelli: A Story of Auto Racing* (Dutton, 1969), p. 56.

Chapter 37: The Jet Set

'a simple classical form ...' in James Taylor, *Rover P6 1963 to 1977* (MRP,

1993), p. 40.

'We can't get on ...' Filmed interview for BBC TV series *All Our Working Lives*, 1984.

'Everyone there was so bright ...' in Mike Taylor, 'Rover Years', *Thoroughbred & Classic Cars* (June 1986), p. 15.

Chapter 38: Grace, Space and Pace

'Sir William would throw ...' Interview with Fred Gardner, Automobile Association's *Drive* magazine (Autumn, 1968), p. 73.

'Unbelievable value ...' *Motor Road Test* no. 20 (23 May 1969).

'The wheels were enormous ...' in interview, Ian McCallum, *Autocar* (1999).

Chapter 39: World Domination

'I simply won't ...' quoted in 'Obituary, Keith Duckworth', *Daily Telegraph*, (22 December 2005).

Chapter 41: Home on the Range

'If we are ...' in Graham Bannock, *Range Rover: Creators of an Icon* (Brooklands Books, 2014), p. 97.

'very likely to look sideways ...' in Anthony Curtis, 'Spen King – BL's Guru', *Motor* (18 October 1980), p. 65.

'people loved it ...' in Simon Charlesworth, 'Range Rover: Father of the Breed', *Classic and Sports Car* (26 August 2014), p. 45.

Epilogue: Blowing the Doors Off

'Colin Chapman would have merited ...' in Regina v Bushell, Belfast Crown Court, 19 June 1992. From the transcript of Lord Justice Murray's Sentencing Remarks.

'The idea of the script ...' in Gillian Bardsley, *Issigonis: The Official Biography* (Icon Books, 2005) p. 258.

'Nowadays, cars are designed ...' Ibid., p. 433.

'Once you get hooked ...' Kjell Qvale, *I Never Look Back*, p. 23.

BIBLIOGRAPHY AND FURTHER READING

Collecting material for what became this book has been a lifetime's work. Still kept in the foolscap manila envelope in which they arrived is a letter dated 30 November 1961 from Rover's Gas Turbines Technical Sales Department, three large black-and-white photographs of their fabled jet cars and a feature from *Autocar*. This was my gateway to a car magazine addiction that took years to shake but also left me with a handy archive. Through my TV career, I have contrived to meet a number of people who were part of the story told here and my notes and transcripts of those interviews have been an invaluable resource as well as an inspiration.

However, I cannot pretend to be anything but a novice in the world of written automotive history, where others have been honing their skills over several decades. To approach their levels of scholarship would take another lifetime.

The list of bibliographic sources below is a treasure trove of entertaining and scholarly studies of Britain's motor makers, designers and drivers, all of which I can wholeheartedly recommend. But I would like to single out a few authors whose authority combined with a capacity to bring their subjects to vivid life are especially effective and also accessible to the general reader.

BMIHT archivist Gillian Bardsley's definitive biography of

Alec Issigonis is a masterpiece, a superb portrait which brings this exceptional and complicated man and his times into brilliant focus.

Karl Ludvigsen has been writing automotive history for well over half a century. His background as an engineer who has held senior positions in Ford, Fiat and General Motors gives him a unique insight. His study of what happened to Volkswagen after the Second World War, *The Battle for the Beetle,* is an exceptional work of social and industrial history.

Doug Nye is a revered motor-racing journalist and author of over seventy books. His works on BRM and Cooper are definitive, vividly capturing the people and places behind the marques as well as the technology.

The late Chris Nixon's double biography of Mike Hawthorn and Peter Collins, *Mon Ami Mate,* is an unparalleled piece of research that manages to be both moving and highly amusing. His study of Aston Martin's tumultuous battles with Ferrari, appropriately titled *Sportscar Heaven*, is a gripping and joyous read.

Philip Porter, author, publisher, balloonist, has also raced, restored and written extensively about Jaguars, with great verve and authority. In *The Most Famous Car in the World*, he lovingly interweaves the story of the E-Type with his salvation of one of the very first examples. His life of Sir William Lyons (co-authored with Paul Skilleter) and his majestic Stirling Moss biography are exceptionally well-researched and absorbing.

Richard Williams writes with equal authority on music and motor racing – and just about every other sport. His biography *Enzo Ferrari: A Life* is an unflinching portrait of a driven legend and *The Last Great Road Race,* his study of the 1957 Pescara Grand Prix, is a wonderful window into a pivotal time in the development of motor racing.

Addison, Paul, *Now the War is Over* (BBC, 1985).

Adeney, Martin, *The Motor Makers* (Collins, 1998).

Adeney, Martin, *Nuffield: A Biography* (Robert Hale, 1993).

Aston, Wilfred G., *The Boys' Book of Motors* (E. & F. Spon, 1922).

Bannock, Graham, *Range Rover: Creators of an Icon* (Brooklands Books, 2014).

Bardsley, Gillian, *Issigonis: The Official Biography* (Icon Books, 2005).

Bolster, John, *Specials* (G. T. Foulis, 1949).

Bullock, John, *The Rootes Brothers* (Patrick Stephens, 1993).

Campbell, Christy, *Mini: An Intimate Biography* (Virgin, 2009).

Clark, Jim, *Jim Clark At the Wheel* (Arthur Barker, 1964).

Clausager, Anders Ditlev, *Le Mans* (Arthur Barker, 1982).

Clausager, Anders Ditlev, Georgano, Nick, et al., *Britain's Motor Industry: The First Hundred Years* (G. T. Foulis, 1995).

Cleemput, Marcel R. van, *The Great Book of Corgi* (New Cavendish, 1989).

Collings, Timothy, *The Piranha Club* (Virgin, 2004).

Cooper, John with Bentley, John, *Grand Prix Carpetbagger* (G. T. Foulis, 1977).

Courtney, Geoff, *The Power Behind Aston Martin* (Oxford, 1978).

Cowin, Chris, *Export Drive: BMC & British Leyland Cars in Europe and the World* (CreateSpace, 2015).

Crombac, Gerard, *Colin Chapman, the Man and His Cars: The Authorised Biography* (Patrick Stephens, 1986).

Daniels, Jeff, *British Leyland: The Truth About the Cars* (Osprey, 1980).

Docker, Lady Norah, *Norah: The Autobiography of Lady Norah Docker* (W. H. Allen, 1969).

Dresser, Christopher, *The Principles of Decorative Design* (Cassell, 1873).

Dugdale, John, *Jaguar in America* (Jaguar Cars, 2001).

Earl, Cameron C., *Quick Silver: Development of German Grand Prix Cars, 1934–39* (Stationery Office Books, facsimile edition 1996).

Edwards, Robert, *Stirling Moss: The Authorised Biography* (Orion, 2005).

Fitzgerald, F. Scott, *The Great Gatsby* (Charles Scribner's Sons, 1925).

Fleming, Ian, *Goldfinger* (Jonathan Cape, 1959).

Fraser, Frankie with Morton, James, *Mad Frank's London* (Virgin, 2001).

Gauld, Graham, *Jim Clark Remembered* (Patrick Stephens, 1975).

Garfield, Simon, *MINI: The True and Secret History of the Making of the Motor Car* (Faber, 2009).

Garnier, Peter with Healey, Brian, *Donald Healey: My World of Cars* (Patrick Stephens, 1989).

Hamilton, Duncan, *Touch Wood* (John Blake Publishing Ltd, 2014).

Hassan, Walter, *Climax in Coventry: My Life of Fine Engines and Fast Cars* (MRP, 1975).

Hawthorn, Mike, *Challenge Me the Race* (William Kimber, 1959).

Henry, Alan, *Driving Forces* (Patrick Stephens, 1992).

King, Peter, *The Motor Men: Pioneers of the British Car Industry* (Quiller Press, 1989).

Lawrence, Mike, *Colin Chapman: Wayward Genius* (Brooklands Books, 2002).

Libby, Bill, *Parnelli: A Story of Auto Racing* (Dutton, 1969).

Ludvigsen, Karl, *The Battle for the Beetle* (Bentley, 2004).

Ludvigsen, Karl, *BRM V16* (Veloce, 2006).

Ludvigsen, Karl, *Colin Chapman: Inside the Innovator* (Haynes, 2010).

McComb, F. Wilson, *The Story of the MG Sports Car* (Dent, 1972).

Mays, Raymond, *Split Seconds: My Racing Years* (G. T. Foulis, 1951).

Melly, George, *Owning-Up* (Futura, 1985).

Moss, Stirling and Nye, Doug, *In the Track of Speed* (Putnam's, 1957).

Moss, Stirling and Nye, Doug, *My Cars and My Career* (Haynes, 1987).

Nahum, Andrew, *Issigonis and the Mini* (Icon, 2004).

Nixon, Chris, *Mon Ami Mate* (Transport Bookman, 2001).

Nixon, Chris (ed.), *Racing with the David Brown Aston Martins, Vol. II* (Transport Bookman, 1980).

Nixon, Chris, *Sportscar Heaven* (Transport Bookman, 2003).

Noble, Dudley and Junner, G. Mackenzie, *Vital to the Life of the Nation* (SMMT, 1946).

Nye, Doug, *BRM: Front Engined Cars, 1945–60 Vol. 1* (MRP, 2003).

Nye, Doug, *World Champions: Cooper Cars* (Osprey, 1983).

Owen, Geoffrey, *From Empire To Europe* (HarperCollins, 1999).

Pagnamenta, Peter and Overy, Richard, *All Our Working Lives* (BBC, 1982).

Palmer, Gerald, *Auto-Architect: The Autobiography of Gerald Palmer* (Magna Press, 1998).

Plowden, William, *The Motor Car and Politics 1896–1970* (Bodley Head, 1971).

Porter, Philip, *The Most Famous Car in the World* (Orion, 2000).

Porter, Philip, *Stirling Moss: The Definitive Biography, Vol. 1* (Porter Press, 2016).

Porter, Philip and Skilleter, Paul, *Sir William Lyons: The Official Biography* (Haynes, 2001).

Price, Bill with Hopkirk, Paddy, *The Paddy Hopkirk Story: A Dash of the Irish* (Haynes, 2005).

Qvale, Kjell, *I Never Look Back* (Kjell Qvale, 2005).

Robson, Graham, *The Book of the Standard Motor Company* (Veloce, 2001).

Robson, Graham, *The Rover Story* (Patrick Stephens, 1977).

Rutherford, Douglas, *The Chequered Flag* (Collins, 1956).

Sharratt, Barney, *Men and Motors of the Austin* (Haynes, 2000).

Slavin, K. & J. and Mackie, G., *Land Rover: The Unbeatable 4×4* (Gentry, 1981).

Stevenson, Heon, *Advertising British Cars of the 50s* (Magna, 1991).

Stevenson, Heon, *British Car Advertising in the 1960s* (McFarland, 2005).

Taylor, James, *Land Rover: 65 Years of the 4×4 Workhorse* (Crowood, 2013).

Taylor, James, *Rover P4: The Complete Story* (Crowood, 1988).

Taylor, James, *Rover P5 and P5B* (Crowood, 1997).

Taylor, James, *Rover P6: 1963 to 1977* (MRP, 1993).

Thomas, Sir Miles, *Out on a Wing: An Autobiography* (Michael Joseph, 1964).

Turner, Graham, *The Car Makers* (Eyre and Spottiswoode, 1963).

Turner, Graham, *The Leyland Papers* (Eyre and Spottiswoode, 1971).

Turner, Stuart, *Twice Lucky: My Life in Motorsport* (Haynes, 1999).

Whyte, Andrew, *Jaguar, The History of a Great British Car* (Patrick Stephens, 1980).

Williams, Richard, *Enzo Ferrari: A Life* (Yellow Jersey, 2002).

Williams, Richard, *The Last Great Road Race* (Weidenfeld & Nicolson, 2004).

Williamson, Geoffrey, *Wheels Within Wheels: The Story of the Starleys of Coventry* (Geoffrey Bles, 1966).

Worrall, Dave, *The Most Famous Car in the World: The Complete History of the James Bond Aston Martin DB5* (Solo, 1991).

Wyer, John, *That Certain Sound* (G. T. Foulis, 1981).

INDEX